IS ANYBODY THERE?

Memoir of a Functional Alcoholic

IS ANYBODY THERE?

Memoir of a Functional Alcoholic

George Albert DeFrehn, III

IS ANYBODY THERE?

ISBN: 978–1515279402

For more information visit: www.georgealbertdefrehn3rd.com

The author has tried to recreate events, locales and conversations from memory of them. In order to maintain their anonymity in some instances the names of individuals and places have been changed, as well as some identifying characteristics and details such as physical properties, occupations and places of residence.

Cover image: icsnaps/shutterstock.com
Cover and book design by DCS Designs

Printing History: First Printing 2015

PRINTED IN THE UNITED STATES OF AMERICA
10 9 8 7 6 5 4 3 2 1

DEDICATION

This book is dedicated to the still suffering active alcoholic who cannot imagine life without alcohol.

And although dedicated to all alcoholics, it is dedicated in particular to those, who because they have great jobs, college degrees, homes, cars, retirement accounts and plenty of money, cannot or will not admit they have this disease. They believe they are functional drinkers, functional alcoholics. Here's hoping they realize there is no such thing.

I would like to also dedicate this book to the three sponsors I have had in sobriety. If you ever read this, you know who you are. You helped in saving my life and continue to do so today. I love you guys.

If this book assists you on your own journey into sobriety, remember that all credit goes to your Higher Power, however you understand Him.

FOREWORD

I did not pretend to be an expert regarding the disease of alcoholism when I met George in 1991, as he applied for admission to a master's degree program. However, since I had advised students on a college campus for many years, I was under the impression that I could relatively easily discern when a person's life was in distress. I soon discovered that I could not claim that talent either.

George is a creative, clever and warm-hearted guy with a wickedly funny sense of humor. He has always been a man of deep and abiding faith, as well as a fantastic story-teller and terrific teacher. He is intellectually accomplished; a man with a love of history and music. George has a wonderful, loving wife and five great children. In short, he had it all; he had it made. Or so I thought.

In reality, George had been sick with alcoholism for years; a dead man walking. Although he was not the proverbial alky, homeless guy sleeping in the street, he was that guy's brother sharing their common disease of alcoholism. Maybe he was you. Maybe he was someone you love.

If you are a brave soul, one who is willing to look the devil of alcoholism in the eye, George's story is for you. His is a raw, honest account of his downward slide to hell and back. It is an account of the depth of destruction of alcoholism.

You will read the scope and breadth of addiction's imprisonment and its damage. In fact, those of us who struggle with less lethal addictions will recognize the characteristics of addiction in ourselves. Hopefully, one alcoholic, or addict will experience his or her epiphany and learn that hope is possible; there is a solution.

Take this courageous journey with George, who was a so-called functional alcoholic; one who never lost a job, never had a DUI, and never landed in jail due to alcohol consumption. Yet, he was the same one who was plagued by fears, loneliness, and alienation that all alcoholics experience. George relates his experience of purchasing a book during his travels in 1997; a book that he claims to have saved his life and helped him to step into the rooms of sobriety to discover the glimmer of light that pierced years of darkness.

May this book be an epiphany for you or someone you both worry about and love.

Karen J. Crowell
Assistant Dean
Rider University
July 15, 2015

PREFACE

In Act II of the patriotic Broadway play 1776 there is a scene where the Bostonian revolutionary, John Adams, is standing alone at the end of a hot, humid, miserable day in Independence Hall in the city of Philadelphia. He is in conflict with John Dickinson of Pennsylvania. Dickinson wants reconciliation with Britain. He has also been in a verbal blood bath with Edward Rutledge of South Carolina, debating whether this new nation in its Declaration of Independence should ban slavery from the colonies now and forever. Slavery, which in 87 years will tear this nation asunder in bloody Civil War, is now the issue that might prevent these 13 colonies from uniting against King George III and England.

Rutledge wields the power of King Cotton in the South. The southern colonies feel obligated to stand with him, although not all southerners favor slavery. This internal struggle of North vs. South, of northern industry vs. southern agriculture, of free labor vs. slave labor, of colonial Yankees vs. southern Rebels, continued to eat away and feast on the bellies of these Continental Congressional representatives sitting daily in the City of Brotherly Love.

We find Adams at wit's end. General George

Washington is waging a revolution against trained British Red Coats. He has an army of militia, basically tradesmen and farmers. His greatest triumph to date has been his retreat from Manhattan Island into New Jersey. All appears hopeless. On top of everything else, Adams is friendless. His candor and lack of political finesse make him an easy target of the entire Congress, especially those in the South.

So again, we find Mr. Adams alone. The music playing is melancholy. In a raspy, emotionally depleted, almost defeated tenor voice we hear the words, "Is anybody there…does anybody care…does anybody see what I see?"

I am an alcoholic. I remember one cold, frigid night sitting on a lifeless, iron-plated bench across the street from Mr. Adam's Old North Church in Boston. I was attending a sales meeting and was scheduled to do my part as stand-up comedian. I am a humorous fellow. It was January of 1992. My drinking career was very slowly crawling to a close. I still had a five-year run of drinking left, and I knew something was wrong. I just did not know what it was. I had downed a couple of Guinness Stouts and was filled with anxiety. Tears flowed freely from my eyes. I do not remember why but I felt completely empty, waging a war against an enemy whom I thought for 24 years was my friend. Like Washington, all I could do was retreat; and like Adams I felt alone and friendless.

As I looked up into the belfry of the Old North Church where Paul Revere saw two lit lanterns telling him the

British were coming by sea, I repeated those words of Adams said some 216 years prior, "Is anybody there…does anybody care…?" Then I wandered the Commons of Boston discovering the Black Rose, a pub near Faneuil Hall, sauntered in and did what I did best. I ordered a Guinness and another then another, then another, until the pain went away. "Does anybody see what I see?"

Now you may ask, what is this alcoholic dude writing about: slavery, bloody civil war, retreat, revolution, hopelessness, friendless, blood bath, and internal struggles? Depending on your point of view, all of this may mean absolutely nothing. Then again, if you're an alcoholic like me, it may mean everything. As an active alcoholic I became a slave. The civil war that raged within did more damage to me physically, spiritually, emotionally and mentally than if I had stood on Little Round Top and had been wounded at the Battle of Gettysburg. So if you have picked up this book for yourself or a loved one and because of alcohol you have felt alone, friendless, hopeless and in constant retreat at what life can throw your way, well, then maybe you are one of us. However, only you can come to that conclusion. Other people may have said it behind your back or possibly to your face, but only you can say, "Hi, I'm John, or Hi, I'm Mary and I'm an alcoholic."

This brief memoir is my journey from light to darkness and hell and back to light. It is my journey from alcoholism to sobriety. It is filled with both humorous and tragic elements. I have changed the names of all who are mentioned here in keeping with the spirit of anonymity found in the rooms of Alcoholics Anonymous (AA). If a specific individual is now deceased, I may use their given name or nickname; again, something that we also do in the rooms of sobriety.

Although I mention Alcoholics Anonymous and reference their literature, the opinions within are mine and mine alone. I do not have to promote AA, nor will I. It is through attraction rather than promotion that people "come into the rooms." This book will uphold these principles throughout.

When I sat down to write this book I had to look at my motivation. It ran the gamut of producing a New York Times bestseller to just getting it done and hoping for the best. Typical alky thinking—it's either all or nothing. After praying about it, which is what we are taught to do when making any decision, my goal is a humble one (although I am not humble), to reach at least one suffering alcoholic who is baffled by this disease and cannot imagine life without booze.

Also, on this journey I have encountered the term functional alcoholic. I walked into the rooms of sobriety with a college degree and owned many "things." I had not lost a job or ever had a DUI, never found myself living on the streets or monetarily bankrupt…so how could I be an alcoholic? I learned the answer to this question in the rooms of AA, but more importantly I learned I do not have to stop drinking alcohol forever; I just have to stop and not have a drink today!

"Is anybody there?"

CONTENTS

INTRODUCTION

Hear ye, Hear ye! Buyers beware…this is not a self-help book. You find those books in the psycho-babble section of your local book store or on Amazon.com. This is a book about drinking, my personal discovery of the disease of alcoholism, and my walk in sobriety. I will be using many of the sayings that have been handed down through the years from one recovering alcoholic to another along with the Twelve Steps of Recovery in Alcoholics Anonymous.

In each chapter I will tell you a facet of my story; my journey with alcohol; what it was like, what happened, and what it is like now.

Part I is titled INTO DARKNESS. In this section, you will read about both tragic and hopefully humorous events of my life before sobriety. Part II is titled INTO THE LIGHT. I refer here to the light of sobriety. Again, you will read about events of life from my first day sober until the present. I still may refer back to an event that occurred while I was actively drinking, but the message in each chapter will be about the gifts of recovery.

Warning…if you are turned off by the talk of God, I ask you only to be tolerant and have an open mind until you reach the end. Yes, God and a spiritual life are a very integral part of recovery, but they are not the only part. There are atheists and agnostics that have lived a life in recovery. Some even discover their own "higher power," some will even call this power God.

A brief note about me, the author; I was born and raised in the streets of the Olney section of North Philadelphia. My Father died when I was eight years of age. I became a street urchin. I learned life's lessons on those streets, yes, those lessons…sex, booze, drugs, rock 'n' roll and foul language…not proud of any of it, except the rock 'n' roll part. I still dig rock 'n' roll music!

Part of me today would rather forget about all of that; however, the other part of me wears it all like a badge of honor. To be able to say you were street smart was a great compliment where I came from. So up front, I ask forgiveness if I drop an occasional shit, damn or other four letter word into the story of my journey. This journey for me was both raw and emotional. I, maybe like you, sometimes find these words offensive. Yet, at other times I find them invaluable, especially when clarifying something or using it as part of a great punch line in a great joke. Enough said.

I know I am breaking my anonymity in writing this memoir and did not make this decision lightly. I have started and stopped this project for more than ten years. Here is why I undertook this challenge. In 1997 I was in the throes of this disease and could not stop drinking. On the way to our vacation home I purchased a book, and what the author described about herself and about alcoholism saved my life. I have no delusions of saving anyone. However, if I can shed more light on the disease of alcoholism, I believe for that I will be content. As an active alcoholic I rarely finished anything I started that was worthwhile. When it got tough, I drank and then I quit. I also rarely took ownership for my actions. My intention, therefore, is to complete this task and own it. My name attached to this book will let me know I have succeeded on both counts.

Lastly, in the book titled Alcoholics Anonymous, (also known as the "Big Book") it states that alcohol is "cunning, baffling and powerful."i This is serious business. On page 66 of the same book it exclaims, "…that for us to drink, is to die."ii And that does not just mean physical death, but a mental, emotional and spiritual death as well.

"Wow," you might find yourself saying, "if this is what sobriety sounds like, maybe I should keep drinking!" But, be of good cheer, we are not a gloomy lot! As a group we alcoholics, for the most part, love to laugh, cry and sometimes satirically sigh. And yes, there is a solution.

CHAPTER 1

AND THIS BUSINESSMAN SLOWLY GOT STONED

It was a miserable Monday afternoon during one of those muggy, overcast, humid, drizzling days in the summer of 1997 with the temperature hovering around 75 degrees Fahrenheit. My heart and soul were just as overcast. Heck, truth be told, they were as dark as the sky was when Katrina hit New Orleans. The date was August 25. I was working for a large medical manufacturing concern at the time, enjoying what I perceived to be the good life. I was a sales manager and had all the great perks that went with the job. I had worked the morning in our corporate offices in a suburb of Boston, then drove down to Worcester, Massachusetts to visit a client.

Now natives of Massachusetts pronounce Worcester as Wusta. Hey, they pronounce chowder as chowda. What a country! Subsequent to the client meeting, I ventured into an old Irish Pub (is there really any other kind?) for lunch near the Jesuit College of the Holy Cross. We drinkers have all been in pubs like this. Dim lighting, a whispered hush at the bar, sparkles of dust visibly floating in the air which is stale, smoke lingering from cigarettes not finished in ash trays, a juke box mournfully playing "Danny Boy" or "Four Green Fields." The food is barely describable, but we never actually came for the food.

I had no other meetings for the afternoon. The calendar

was clear. I had a flight out of Logan about 3:00 p.m. through Pittsburgh, then on to Atlanta. I had my afternoon and evening mapped out. Sit back, relax, eat and drink. I was on the road, away from home which was in Pennsylvania, so my company picked up the tab for three squares a day (and yes, drinks, too). I ordered a pint of Guinness Stout and a small tumbler of single malt scotch. No need to rush. Lots of good time to drink lots of good booze.

Needless to say, not in a million years could you have told me that this was the beginning of my last load; the last time I would be drunk; the last time I would black out in my hotel room.

Later, I will describe some of the details on my trip to Atlanta from Boston and into sobriety. For now suffice it to say, I arrived safely but not soberly. Bluntly stated, I was hammered. I got behind the wheel of a rental car while intoxicated, stopped at a gas station, purchased two quarts of Bud (in Georgia they sell gas and beer at stations…go figure!) and then drove to my upscale hotel on the outskirts of Atlanta.

I could very well have killed someone or myself, but none of that entered my inebriated state of mind. After dumping my luggage in the room, I made my way down to the hotel lounge where I proceeded, by all indications the next morning, to get obliterated on alcohol. The local piano man was playing. I have a decent voice and had been here before. He welcomed me with a rendition of "Piano Man" by Billy Joel. I pulled up my chair next to those ivory keys and sang tunes with him until the barkeep asked for "last call."

In my mind's eye these many years later, I remember early in the morning, most likely between 2:00 a.m. and 3:00 a.m., of August 26, leaving a voice mail for my sales rep telling him that I had just arrived in my hotel room and would not make that 8:00 a.m. client meeting he had scheduled in Marietta, Georgia.

A lie, but I needed some shut eye. I knew that I would have a severe case of the "Irish flu." I told him to pick me up at about 10:00 a.m. and would continue the day from there. What a gem of a manager I was, eh?

Thus, it was at the end of that working day on August 26 that I finally ascertained I had a serious problem. I was still "hung" when I entered the lobby of this five-star hotel in the suburbs of Atlanta, Georgia, around 6:00 p.m. Upon entering the lobby, I pulled out my plastic room key with the magnetic strip on the back, walked to the bank of elevators, and as the doors opened I took one step forward and stopped dead in my tracks. Immediately I realized I had no friggin' idea where my room was located! I then sheepishly walked back to the front desk, approached the hotel clerk and embarrassingly told her that I had a late night last night, a rough day at work, and could not remember what my room number was or on what floor it was located. She looked it up and kindly said, "No worries. It happens all the time." But I knew this to be another lie. It had never happened to me, and I knew why it had happened. I drank until I blacked out the night before. Only God knows how I got to my room that last night of drinking. It appears the old saying may be true that "God does take care of little children and drunks."

CHAPTER 2

I Never Had A...

To begin at the end seems most apropos for an alcoholic. We are wired differently. I am wired differently. It's part of the disease. The date was August 29, 1997. Three days earlier, as noted, I had come back to earth from my last bender. In April of that year, my wife and I had purchased a condominium at the Jersey shore as a vacation home. Life was grand! We left our home in Pennsylvania and headed east and south. We are beach people! We love it! We are addicted to it! Give me a good book, a beach chair or blanket, sun and sand for the next five hours...it does not get any better than that.

I love to read, a gift I inherited from my mom. Usually I am working on two or three books at a time. We noticed a strip mall with a book store as we approached town, so we stopped and in we ventured. My wife loves a compelling mystery or some epic romantic novel. Me, I love history. If no history is available, I immediately gaze over the New York Times Bestsellers. On this occasion, I happened upon a book titled ***Drinking: A Love Story*** by Caroline Knapp. The back cover described this to be the journey of a woman who was a journalist in New England, college educated who at one time in her early years "loved" alcohol and all that it did for her. Yet, as years passed by, this love turned sour. She freely confesses she had a "love affair" with alcohol; but as it is with most affairs, it betrayed her. It almost killed her. That caught my attention.

I purchased the book and it ended up not only changing my life but, without sounding too dramatic, it saved my life. Through the lenses of an alky named Caroline, whom I did not know, I discovered I was truly an alcoholic.

Yet, I still remember that next night, August 30, 1997, my first full day sober, thinking how could I be an alcoholic? Here I was sitting on the deck of our Jersey shore condominium a block from the beach. Sure, I loved drinking alcohol. And like Ms. Knapp I can say it was my first true love. After all, I discovered at an early age that it was the answer to all my problems. Until I truly experienced the effects of alcohol, I never felt part of anything. I never felt I belonged. I was a misfit among normals.

On top of that, I had a college degree and was half way through my Master's Degree. We owned a huge, four-bedroom home that sat on an acre of ground in the woods above a large meandering creek. I had a beautiful wife, five children and the coolest Labrador retriever named Goldie. Two cars sat in the driveway. How could an alcoholic acquire all of this?

Crap...I went to Church every Sunday, confession once a month, and taught religious education to kids in our parish for thirteen years.

I was well respected in our community. I did not drink every day. I never had a DUI. I never had spent a night in jail. I never had lost a job due to my drinking. I never had to be admitted to a rehab facility. I never had anyone tell me that I drank too much or that I was an alcoholic. I never had purposely hurt anyone while drinking. (Or so I thought!) I never had been thrown out of a restaurant while drinking. (Notice I did not say Pub or Bar.) So what the hell happened?!

I did not sleep on rusted, filthy, grimy, greasy manhole covers or under dilapidated, rat infested bridges. I worked for a Dow-thirty company. My nights on the road were spent in lavish four or five-star hotels, eating glorious meals of Beef Wellington Chateaubriand, accompanied with a top-shelf bottle of a vintage cabernet sauvignon, in cities like San Francisco, New Orleans, New York, Chicago and Boston. Yet I knew in my heart of hearts that I had a problem with booze. I had known it for the last couple of years.

But it wasn't all bad, was it? I had some really, really fun times drinking with family and friends. I mean what would the holidays be without alcohol…Christmas, Thanksgiving, New Years, the Fourth of July, Memorial Day, Labor Day, Ground Hogs Day and of course the drinking day of all days, St. Patty's Day?

Then there were trips to the movies or to Broadway. I mean who the hell saw the movie Animal House sober? Dinner and drinks before Phantom of the Opera or Les Miserable made the music more enjoyable, did it not? Then in business, the national sales meetings in LA or New Orleans or Atlanta, how could one not imbibe with the rest of my comrades while glorifying our sales achievements?

Yes, there were good times.

Yet, as the sands of time washed over my life, I found the fun going out of my drinking. I could not find the "warm glow" that alcohol had always provided. I had to drink more and more just to get a decent buzz on, and the buzz did not last. Toward the end, truth be known, there was not enough liquor around to get me drunk. On top of that, I felt a huge void in my life, and I had no idea how to fill it. I had never really felt this way before, yet I knew I never wanted to feel this way again. I just had no idea what to do. All of those "I never hads" that I kept on my scorecard of life meant jack shit. It was still August 30, 1997. I did not know much, but this I did know: I was an alcoholic and if I kept drinking I would surely die.

So, if you feel you or a loved one has a problem with alcohol grab a chair or a blanket, a beach if one is available (but anywhere will do), sit back and see if you can identify with the disease that I and many others have; and maybe you do too, namely alcoholism.

CHAPTER 3

The Waffle House

It is truly an amazing phenomenon this act of getting sober. When it came to drinking, I just thought that I drank like everyone else. Didn't everyone drink to get buzzed…to get drunk? Social drinkers were amateurs. Also, I readily confess that I loved drinking. Why would I not? It made me feel great and killed the pain in my head and sometimes even in my body. I drank when I felt sad, and I drank when I felt glad. I drank at the thrill of victory and the agony of defeat! It was medicinal for all occasions in life from the birth of children, to graduations, to weddings and to funerals and for anything in between. I truly believed that alcohol was God's greatest invention, until that fateful week at the end of August in 1997.

It is now the first week of September in 1997, I know I am an alcoholic, but what the heck do I do with that knowledge? I'm scheduled to work in South Carolina with my sales rep in the South, a guy named Willie. He is a good 'ol southern boy from the deep south. We meet at a Waffle House near Charlestown, South Carolina. Christmas! Everyone meets at Waffle Houses in the south. To many southerners it is the Le Bernardin of the South!

I arrive a few minutes early, and my stomach is doing flip-flops. The Waffle House is overflowing with sons and daughters of the Confederacy. It smells of coffee, bacon, grits, and sausage, burnt toast, biscuits, gravy and, of course, waffles. I've known Willie for a while, and I'm guessing what I'm about to tell him will floor the shit out of him. He arrives, we shake hands, and we order coffee. Before the pretty southern bell waitress can return, I spring the news on Willie.

"Got something to tell you, buddy. You're the first person I'm sharing this with. My wife doesn't even know."

Mid-slurp of his coffee, Willie stops aghast and asks, "What's wrong, dude? Did someone die?"

I pause, a little more nervous than I thought, and tell him, "Willie, I'm an alcoholic." There I got it out. Not knowing what to expect, this good 'ol boy southern friend of mine gets this shitty grin on this face and then starts to laugh!

I am dumbfounded. "What the fuck are you laughing at?" I say a little louder than I intended. Hell, I'm pissed now. Does he know what type of courage I needed to have to admit this?

Then he lovingly smiles, puts his hand on top of mine and says, "Shit George, I knew you were an alky the first time we sat down and had beers. I was just waiting until you finally found out for yourself. Now maybe I can get to know the real George!"

And then he laughs a deep southern laugh that starts in the toes of his feet and erupts from the top of his head. But it is not a hurtful, sarcastic laugh. It is a laugh of friendship. Then, I too, begin to giggle, then laugh and howl at the absurdity of it all. All those years I was trying to dupe people into believing I was just a guy who liked to drink and have fun. Hell, if Willie knew I was an alcoholic, I gotta believe there are others who know, too. Shit, this is a lot more complicated than I thought it would be.

We work together for a couple of days. Eating dinner each night in restaurants is becoming an out-of-body experience. In 24 years I have never ordered a meal while dining out without first ordering a glass of wine or a bottle of beer or shot of single-malt scotch. I mention this to Willie. Again he laughs and I await the punch line, still a little pissed off.

"George, you never just ordered ONE bottle of beer or ONE glass of wine or shot of scotch. You ordered two bottles of beer or a bottle of wine or Guinness Stout with a shot of scotch!" I was ready to argue the point with him, but how could I? He was telling the truth. Damn, did I really drink like that? Hell, I thought I drank normally—like everyone else! Now I know I did not. But still what do I do with this new epiphany? What else is going to be revealed as I begin this journey into sobriety?

The date is September 10, 1997. I have left South Carolina, worked a couple of days in the Atlanta area and am about to head home. Now in the past, Atlanta's airport had great—and I mean *great*—chili dogs. A couple of these babies and a few brews and the flight home to Pennsylvania was always pain free. But this is my twelfth day without a drink so chili dogs are out. I stop into one of the airport's book stores trying to pass time. I have to kill two hours before my flight back to Philly. I white knuckle it for an hour then find a place that sells vanilla milkshakes, the only other beverage I really enjoyed besides alcohol.

I arrive at the gate for my flight with 30 minutes to kill. I have finished reading the book by Caroline Knapp, ***Drinking: a Love Story***. She mentions Alcoholics Anonymous enough that I know soon I must get to a meeting. I know nothing about AA. Another epiphany occurs. I rush to a pay phone (yes they still existed in 1997) and call my old boss and buddy Jay who lives in Florida and has been sober a few years.

He picks up the phone on the first ring. "Yo, Jay," I say, "Guess what's new in my life."

He says, "No idea."

"Well, you're the second person I'm telling this to; I am an alcoholic."

Now Jay is a little more politically correct with me than was my buddy, Willie. "No shit, when did you discover this?"

"Twelve days ago, to be exact."

"No shit, 12 days…that's a long time without a drink."

I say, "No shit, tell me about it." After a couple of more "No shits" I finally ask Jay straight out, "you and I drank together and smoked doobies together, does this news of mine shock you?"

He honestly says, "Nope, but I've been praying you would get into the rooms of sobriety since I came in seven years ago."

"No shit?"

"No shit," says Jay.

Well I'll be a horse's ass. Even one of my best friends, who I drank with far into many a night, knew I was an alcoholic. But I did not. And he was praying for me! What is *that* about? It's almost time to board my plane, maybe 15 minutes to spare. I ask Jay about AA and how do I find a meeting to attend back home. He tells me to call information in Philly and ask for the number for Alcoholic Anonymous Intergroup. They have a list of meetings. I hung up; called Intergroup in Philadelphia, and that night I walked into my first AA meeting.

I was still wearing my business suit with French cufflinks, looking dapper as ever. I sat next to this "Harley Dude" with a leather jacket and all the regalia that goes with bikers. His name was John. I extended my hand and said, "I'm George, and I think I'm an alcoholic."

John said, "No shit. Sit down and listen."

CHAPTER 4

Before The First Drink

There is a story in the literature of Alcoholics Anonymous that suggests we alcoholics had alcoholic tendencies and thinking processes before we picked up that first drink. When I read that line, my first thoughts were, "bullshit." But then the author started to describe how he quit just about everything he ever started as a kid, things like little league baseball, pee-wee football and the high school football team. He described how he felt awkward around girls the older he got, didn't know what to say to them or act around them. Then there were the guys he hung with…he never really felt part of them either. I knew immediately that this was not "bullshit." This was real. This was me.

To clarify, my old man died when I was a young kid. I was lost. My mom, God rest her Irish soul, did what any mother would do for her young child who in the course of a 24-hour period became fatherless; she tried to find safe outlets for me so I wouldn't end up on the streets of Philly.

One of those outlets was the Cub Scouts. I mean, here is an organization that was really perfect for a fatherless child who needs direction. Well, I got through the first year of Cub Scouts. The second year was a graduation to something called Webelos. I went to the first meeting, which was held in my grammar school in Olney. Now, I was and still am a funny kid. Like most kids around ten years of age, bodily sounds are fun. It was the end of summer. There was no air conditioning in schools in the early 1960s, so all of us were sweating profusely. This was my Holden Caulfield moment. As you may know, if you cup your hand and place it under your arm pit and pump your arm up and down, it makes the greatest sounding fart in the world.

My goal upon entering the classroom with the other pin-heads who had gathered was to get tossed. I'm sure the men who were running things were great guys. You had to be to put up with a group of potential delinquent boys from North Philly. I tried heckling the first speaker, but that just got me a reprimand. When the second guy got up, I tried shooting spit balls and hitting the nerdiest kid a few rows over in the back of the head. I was right on target. Hell, he had a head the size of Jupiter. He turned around and yelled at me. Initially he got in trouble, but one of the scout masters knew I was behind the ruckus. Within a few minutes, I knew I had to resort to drastic measures. Sure enough the fart of all farts brought the house down in laughter. Even the one scout master tried to stifle a laugh, but the head guy had had enough of my act. He came down the aisle to where I was sitting, pointed me toward the door and said, "Please, I'm begging you to leave and don't come back."

Mission accomplished! I was elated as I ran down my neighborhood street. I burst through the front door of our tiny row home where my mom was sitting on our sofa reading a book. She was a little surprised to see me home so early and asked me why that was. I told her a half-truth; that I was asked to leave because I was *somewhat* disruptive. She knew this was a lie. She also knew I really did not want to be a scout, but she didn't have the wherewithal to fight me on the point. But what I remember most was the disappointed look in her eyes as she went back to her reading. I knew I had hurt the one person who loved me unconditionally in life. Sadly, it would not be the last time.

The nuns who taught us in that grammar school were tough old girls. They had to be. We had between 60 and 80 hormonal kids in a classroom. As I got a little older, I got into more trouble at school, but these good women knew I was fatherless and poor. They would keep me after school, call it detention for some bone-headed thing I did in the classroom, and I would end up helping them clean up the basement of the convent. Subsequent to this, they would then give me homemade cookies, milk, soda, and other treats and tell me I was a good kid. It got to the point where I would get in trouble on purpose just so I'd get detention! What normal kid does that?

Another travesty occurred when I entered the sixth grade. Sister William Loretta pulled me aside one day and said she thought the best thing for me was to become an altar boy.

Me...an altar boy? I told her right up front that she needed to rethink this one. But no, her mind was set; I would be an altar boy. She told me to go meet with Father

Dougherty after school to begin practices. Now Father Dougherty, Irish of course, was this tall, gangly, baritone sounding, raspy voiced man who chain smoked cigars. No shit, cigars! You could always smell him before you saw him.

Well we had a few practices, and they went ok. This was pre-Vatican II so all the Catholic Masses were said in Latin, which was completely Greek to me and many other Catholics of that era.

The thing I enjoyed most was ringing the bell. This was a hoot. Now it was rung at very solemn times of the Latin Mass. The first time occurred during the part called the Confiteor. Confiteor literally means "I confess" for you Latin aficionados. Half way through this prayer is the "Mea Culpa" where we sinners say, translated, "Through my fault, through my fault, through my most grievous fault." In Latin it is "Mea culpa, mea culpa, mea maxima culpa!" Well, at the first Mea Culpa, the altar boy rings the bell in reverence, three times for each mea culpa. Not me. I built it into a crescendo sounding like Tchaikovsky's 1812 Overture.

By the third "Mea Culpa," Father Dougherty had stopped the Mass and was just staring at me, mouth opened like a guppy looking into the eyes of a great white shark. My mom was in the front pew with my sister. Mom was in a state of complete shock. My sister was laughing hysterically. The rest of the congregation was stunned or in total awe. Dougherty was still staring, and I was still ringing the bells! I don't really remember the rest of that

Mass except they took the bells away from me.

Needless to say, I never served Mass again. I was dishonorably discharged from altar boys. Again, mission accomplished! Again, I saw that sad look of disappointment in my mom's eyes after Mass. Damn, maybe that author in Alcoholics Anonymous was right after all. Maybe, I was an alky from birth. Is that possible?

CHAPTER 5

A Little About Alcoholism

Before continuing this epic, a little must be said about the disease of alcoholism. Until the 20th Century it was not classified as a disease. Most alcoholics were thought to be of poor moral upbringing, lacking in character, amoral to the core, thoughtless, narcissistic, slovenly, ill kept, disgusting to be around, jobless, living in poverty over manhole covers while carrying the proverbial brown paper bag covering a cheap, very cheap bottle of wine or cheaper quart of beer.

Today, the famed Mayo Clinic on their website, defines it this way: "Alcoholism is a chronic and often progressive disease that includes problems controlling your drinking, being preoccupied with alcohol, continuing to use alcohol even when it causes problems, having to drink more to get the same effect (physical dependence), or having withdrawal symptoms when you rapidly decrease or stop drinking. If you have alcoholism, you can't dependably predict how much you'll drink, how long you'll drink, or what consequences will occur from your drinking."[iii]

The National Council on Alcoholism and Drug Dependence, Inc. (NCADD) states this on their web page regarding the question, *Is alcoholism genetic?*

> "Whether a person decides to use alcohol or drugs is a choice, influenced by their environment—peers, family, and availability. But, once a person uses alcohol or drugs, the risk of

developing alcoholism or drug dependence is largely influenced by genetics. Alcoholism and drug dependence are not moral issues, are not a matter of choice or a lack of willpower. Plain and simple, some people's bodies respond to the effects of alcohol and drugs differently.

Fact: The single most reliable indicator of risk for future alcohol and drug problems is **Family History.**

Research has shown irrefutably that family history of alcoholism or drug addiction is in part genetic and not just the result of the family environment. And millions of Americans are living proof, based on personal, firsthand experience that alcoholism and drug addiction run in families.

Plain and simple, alcoholism and drug dependence run in families."[iv]

The NCADD also states there are approximately 18,000,000 adults who are dependent on alcohol and abuse it in the good old USA. That comes to one in every 12 adults in our population. Now you may ask, how many of those are members of Alcoholics Anonymous? The answer may astound you; the General Services Office of Alcoholics Anonymous states that there are only about 2,000,000 members. Thus about 89 percent of the people who should be in AA getting sober are still "out there!"

CHAPTER 6

The Old Man

After he died in October of 1960, I had no feelings toward him at all. My last memories of him were not good to say the least. I feared him. He scared me. I knew I didn't like him. I always felt inferior around him. He was the old man. He was *my* old man. I was named after him and my grandfather. My name sucked, so I hated both of them for that. Imagine growing up with a name like Elsmore Ralph, III, or Clarence Bartholomew, Jr. Not my real name but you get the drift.

Years after I got into the rooms of sobriety, I asked my mom if she thought the old man was an alcoholic. She did not think so. She said after he came back from the War, "he liked his beers." Then I asked her if she remembered that night, about six months before he died, when he beat the shit out of me, and I pissed my pajamas after the beating. Oh yeah. She remembered. How could she forget? In my mind's eye, here is how I remember that night.

Both my sister and I had most likely been acting up and probably ticked the old man off. We were sent to bed early. The night was just like any other except that there was a show on television I wanted to see. I'm thinking it was either a rerun of the *Honeymooners* with Jackie Gleason and Art Carney or an episode of the *Leave it to Beaver Show.*

My favorite character in the *Honeymooners,* played by

Art Carney, was that of Ed Norton, the infamous sewer worker in New York City who labeled himself a "subterranean engineer." What a hoot he was. My old man, in turn, loved the domineering Jackie Gleason. Mom said the old man did not want to be disturbed when watching this show.

Those of you, who might remember, *Leave it to Beaver* was a sit-com seen through the eyes of a 10-year-old kid, nicknamed "Beaver." His real name was Theodore. He hated that, so I could really relate to this dude since I, too, hated my name. He had a brother named Wally. The Cleavers, their last name, were the all-American middle-class family. Actually, I think they were more upper-middle class based on the cool home in which they lived. One of the characters in the show was named Eddie Haskell. He was a pain in the ass type of kid that I could identify with. He was always trying to manipulate himself into the good graces of Mrs. Cleaver. He always fucked it up, but he kept on trying. Point being, I related to Eddie Haskell! I guess the show itself was irrelevant, what happened next was not.

Now, there was a partition between our living room and dining room. I snuck downstairs, thinking no big deal. If they catch me, back upstairs I go. Five minutes into the program I sneezed. This was not the brightest thing to do. The bomb then exploded. The old man came around the partition, picked me up and drop-kicked me across the dining room. I crashed against my mom's hutch, and then tried desperately to get to the stairs.

Didn't make it. The old man was an athlete and former Golden Gloves of America boxing finalist besides being a decorated Field Artillery Sergeant in the Army during World War II in the South Pacific—one tough son of a bitch. He pounced on me like a cheetah on a crippled rabbit. He grabbed me by the neck and literally kicked me up the stairs, dropping me, picking me up and kicking me again and again.

By the time we reached my bedroom I was in shock. I got to the bed, got under the covers and blacked out. Not sure what happened after that. Mom cleaned me up next morning. I did not go outside that next day nor do I ever remember speaking to him again until the day before he died. I feared him and hated him. And all I wanted to do was see Ed Norton, the subterranean engineer or my buddy, Eddie Haskell, get over on the parents of the "Beav." I paid the price for that mistake. I was eight years old.

Needless to say, I did not know that in six months' time he would be dead of a ruptured peptic ulcer. There were no "purple pills," no Nexium in those days. My sister and I pretty much saw him die before our eyes, spewing blood while paramedics had to put restraints on him as they fought to lay him on a gurney. Like I said, the old man was one tough son of a bitch.

Mom said he did have a "couple" of beers that night. But she was of that generation where to be stoic and keep peace in the family was the way it was. Me, I believe he was shitfaced. No man thinking rationally could have beaten me the way he beat me, at least no sober man could or would. Today, do I think he was an alcoholic? Honestly, I do not know, nor will I say. Only he could have answered that question. Sadly, he never got the chance.

As I got older, I finally was able to call him, "my" old man instead of "the" old man. Later, I was able to call him my father. Today, I call him my Dad. But that was a long, long journey.

Once again I brought up alcoholism in the family to my mother. I knew that the old man's old man had died when he was struck by a trolley car in Camden, New Jersey, a couple of years before I was born. It appears they were not very close. However, my old man was very close to his mom. I knew my paternal grandmother, Grand Mom, lived in Bucks County, Pennsylvania. I asked my mom was my grandfather working in Jersey when he was killed. No, she told me that he lived there. Huh?

"Yes," she said, "they had separated because he had a problem with the drink!" Say what! So, the old man's old man was an alky after all.

Later, I found out Mom's brother, my Uncle John, was also a full-fledged alcoholic. He had crashed a couple of PTC (Philadelphia Transportation Company) buses as a driver in the 1950s. Also had an Uncle Lou; he, too, was a drunk. He punched me out at a family reunion when I was about 6 years old. Don't really remember that one, but Mom told me the story. Then my old man beat the shit out of him in front of the whole family for hitting me. So, through all of this happy horseshit, I guess I can say that at least once the old man was on my side.

Now, does any of this mean that I became an alcoholic because of my old man, his old man, mean old Uncle Lou, or my sad Uncle John? You are not going to like this answer. Yes and No.

Yes, because the medical community today, as noted above, through research believes that alcohol and drug dependency runs in families; it is genetic.

No, because none of these four men, nor any other human being ever poured an ounce of alcohol down my throat. Never. I was responsible for every drink I ingested and every doobie that I smoked; every one. On top of that, my sister is not an alcoholic and until DNA can prove otherwise we came from the same set of egg and sperm donors: our Mom and the old man.

CHAPTER 7

The First Drink

If you are reading this masterpiece, either you know someone who has been troubled by their use of alcohol or you might be thinking like I did, "Something's wrong but I don't really know what it is."

If you fall into the former category, you may or may not remember your first drink. Not so if you fall into the latter group. I stated earlier that we alcoholics are wired differently. This is one of those differences. Every alcoholic in recovery that I have known for almost 20 years remembers their first drink or their first drunk or when they first started drinking. Normal drinkers do not and could not care less. Alcohol in their lives is not a priority. But for us who lived and loved to imbibe, and later found ourselves sitting in an AA meeting in the basement of some old, dark, dingy church, remember. Alcohol was always a priority, always. We remember.

It was the Summer of Love, as coined by the hippie movement in the Haight Ashbury section of San Francisco, the year 1968. It was the year I fell head over heels in love with alcohol. She was my first true love. She came in the guise of a whiskey sour fountain at my cousin's wedding in Washington D.C. It wasn't that she looked all that great, but damn she sure made me feel great. She told me I was handsome, funny, debonair, charismatic, dashing, bold, adventurous, a rock star, a leader of men and an amazing athlete.

Prior to drinking this wondrous elixir I was an awkward, skinny, boring, insecure, afraid, cowardly teenager with an inferiority complex. My self-esteem inhabited the gutter. I was a nothing and would never be anything.

Then…BAM!!! The warm rush that went through my upper body, down to my toes, and back up again to the brain stem was intense. If you are truly alcoholic, you know what I'm talking about. If you are not alcoholic, you're probably reading this and saying to yourself, "Say what?"

Again, we are wired differently. Alcohol flips a switch in us drunks that we cannot explain. We lose all inhibitions. We actually feel we belong. We are no longer alone, no longer afraid. When that switch first went "on," we knew we had arrived. We had discovered the answer to all our problems. We fell in love with alcohol and we thought alcohol loved us in return.

Obviously, that last statement proved false in the long run. Yes, we loved alcohol and could not imagine life without it. But alcohol has no ability to love in return. In a true love relationship there is always a give and take from both parties. Alcohol never gave, but it took a great deal from most of us while we actively pursued a drinking career. And, if you are still *out there,* not in recovery, it is still taking from you. You just don't know it yet.

Briefly, back to that Summer of Love 1968. Our

household was now down to three people, my loving Mom, my sister and me. We never had alcohol in our home. Mom was a teetotaler and Sis and I never had touched the stuff. Life was about to change for us; well for me anyway.

I had never been to a wedding. One of my friends, Smitty, told me the Church service was nice but it was the reception that made the event worthwhile. Days later I caught up with him, we compared notes and both agreed that the reception rocked, but it was the booze that really made it rock!

My cousin and his beautiful bride are cool people and fun to be with. At their reception they had both a band and a DJ. In 1968, the adults at the wedding were from the "Greatest Generation," Great Depression children, survivors of World War II. Their music and ours were like water and vinegar. The band played the Big Band sound, Sinatra, Glenn Miller, Dean Martin, Crosby, Hope, Como, Andy Williams and Danny Kaye.

The DJ played Motown, Beatles, Stones, Doors, Aretha, Marvin Gaye, the Temps, Supremes, and the Isley Brothers singing "Shout!"(Still played today at most weddings I've attended...like we said, Rock 'n' Roll is here to stay!)

While the band played a set of really boring music, I ventured back to the bar area. Innocently, all I wanted to drink was either a coke or glass of lemonade.

Then my eyes beheld for the first time something I'd not seen before. Directly in front of the actual bar was a fountain. A golden fluid was pouring out into a huge bowl-like device that seemed to recycle the liquid; amazing!

Curiously, I wandered over to the fountain, picked up a plastic cup, filled it to the rim and casually walked away. Now, although I had never had alcohol in my life to this point, I knew this was booze. I could smell it. I could sense it. Not wanting to get caught I quickly ingested it. Wow! It did taste a little like lemonade. As already noted it was a whiskey sour fountain. Within minutes the BAM occurred and I was hooked.

When the DJ came back on to play our music, I was one of the first ones on the dance floor. I spotted a gorgeous blonde, sauntered over with a swagger and asked her to dance. We never stopped dancing. Her name was Barbara. She was from D.C. That's all I ever knew. We fast danced, slow danced—leaving no room for the Holy Spirit—and finally kissed. Holy shit was that great! We snuck outside, found a bench and continued to kiss. At one point I thought she was trying to drive her tongue into my left lung! I was in shock but loved every bit of it. I thought of asking her to marry me, but I was still in high school, didn't have a job or a car so we just kept kissing.

Not really sure how that day ended. I did sneak over to the fountain with Barbara again once or twice. Soon the wedding was over. Mom and Sis were gathering their things together and told me to gather mine. I kissed Barbara goodbye, told her I'd stay in touch. Never saw her again.

Next day upon awakening, I briefly thought of Barbara,

but what I really thought about was the booze and the BAM! I chased that BAM for the next 29 years and although I got close a couple of times, I never attained that same feeling. Time is fleeting. That Summer of Love will always be with me in my mind's eye, but in a blink it was gone.

Years later, the old-timers in the rooms would continually make a statement that would baffle me. They would say, "It's the first drink that gets you drunk." My arrogant reaction was that these old dudes and dudettes must have had a pretty weak constitution when handling booze. Hell, after one drink I hadn't even gotten the BAM feeling. After some time I discovered what they meant. Once I had the first drink, the next five, ten or twenty sometimes were not enough. I drank until the pain went away; oblivion. It was that first drink that started the compulsion to pick up the next and the next and the next. Yep, alcoholism is indeed cunning, baffling and powerful. It was the first drink that got me drunk. And I thought I was smart.

CHAPTER 8

Liver Enzymes—Really?

If you are anything like me and are honest with yourself, you will agree with the following statement; "I thought I drank like everybody else." Hell, I knew this to be a true statement in 1969 and I still believed it through that life changing week in 1997.

I hung on a corner in Olney with guys who had nicknames like Weed, Moo, Chicky, Groove, Earl, Boone, Juzz, Mouse, Puerto Rican Deacon and Red Bird. I drank like them. They drank like me. However, there is one salient difference between all of us. I am the only one who is an alcoholic. Big difference, eh? So, hindsight tells me I did not drink like everyone else.

A few of us used to get served at a bar on Ogontz Avenue in the Oak Lane section of Philly. It was in an African American neighborhood. We went there because the white bars in Olney wouldn't serve us. Three of us usually made the trip, yours truly, Stretch and Joey Bag a Donuts.

It was 1969, Vietnam was happening. Three white guys walking into a bar in a black neighborhood was not cool. So, we decided no one would hurt us if we looked like we had been in the military. Got us some army fatigues at a local Army-Navy Store on Broad Street and "presto bingo" we just got home from Nam. Now Stretch was about six feet five inches tall; Joey was six-three; and I came in at six feet two. We all had beards and shaved, smoked cigarettes and with collars turned up we thought and believed we looked the part.

Now I am stopping the story here. Yes, we entered the bar and got served. But did we fool the black bartender? Not a bit. He just shook his head and laughed. Told us to take the beer and take our honkie asses back to the other side of the tracks. Here's the point, most—and I am saying most—people would never think to do something as stupid and as dangerous as that which I just described...for a beer.

Think about it, we knew some guys in the neighborhood who were 21 and could drink legally. A couple of them really did serve in Vietnam. They would have gladly taken our money, charged us interest and bought us beer. But no, we fabricated a story; a lie just to procure booze. Racial tensions in cities like Philadelphia, within a year of Dr. King's death, were high. Did we think about that? Obviously not. Our mission was to buy beer; to get a load on; to be cool; to get drunk. Thoughts about danger and life and death were trivial.

The cost of putting us in this precarious predicament was priceless. Actually, the army fatigues set us back more than the booze. Three quarts of Pabst Blue Ribbon beer...for you and me, a buck or as the kid in the commercial says, "For you, one dollar."

Normal drinkers don't do this, but as already ascertained, I was not a normal drinker.

Sadly, these characteristics of my drinking would only get worse and sometimes more dramatic, placing myself or those around me in grave peril. Sadly, years later, we were told that my buddy Stretch died of cirrhosis of the liver at age 49.

I bumped into Joey at a neighborhood reunion about ten years ago. He eventually enlisted and went to Nam. At this party he was ripped before he arrived. After about an hour, he saw that I was not drinking. He said to me, "Yo, why arenchu drinking, George? Are you one of 'those' now?" I knew he meant was I in AA?

"Yep, I am," said I.

Joey, slurring, then said to me, "I know I ain't no alcoholic."

Curious, I asked, "How do you know, Joey?"

He answered, "I get my liver enzymes checked every six months!"

Really? Now what fucking normal person gets their liver enzymes checked every six months? When I tell this story in the rooms of sobriety, chuckles ensue. Yet, I understood Joey the moment he said this. I never did that, but if I had thought of it when I was out there, I would have done it. I would do anything to reassure myself that I was not an alky; that I could control this; that I could drink like everyone else; that this love affair that I so desperately needed would never end.

Humbly, I pray for Joey whenever he crosses my mind, that he discovers the rooms of sobriety and lives. He showed me pictures of his beautiful wife and daughters and his eyes got misty. Joey is the low-key drunk. He drinks and gets more sentimental. He actually becomes quieter and more withdrawn as the night passes by. As we parted, he asked for my phone number saying that he would call me and maybe come to a meeting with me. I did not hold my breath. I knew he would never call, but I keep praying.

At the same reunion, one of the guys whose nickname is Levi was there and he is a different kind of active drinker. At the beginning of this evening, Levi showed up with a little buzz on. At other high school reunions through the years it was the same. He'd come in, start greeting everyone with a hug and then...off to the races. Unlike Joey, Levi was loud.

Possibly because this was my first neighborhood reunion sober, I was more cognizant of my environs and the people there. Two hours into the party Levi came over to me, stood there and in a disdainful voice said, "What the fuck is wrong with you? Heard you're not drinking. What did you get religion or something?" Now if I didn't know Levi I might have clocked him and put him down, easy enough to do when you're sober and he's drunk. Yet sober, Levi is a great guy; drunk—well, he is the human, "Dark Knight."

An hour after he asked me if I got religion he became incoherent. He started wandering from person to person asking each of us, "Did we really like him?" Before we could answer, he would give our answer for us, "Nah, you think I'm a fuck up, right? Wish I wasn't here." And off he would stumble.

That was not Levi talking. That was alcohol talking. It strips the alcoholic of all, even the good, in a person. I've known Levi since 1961. He was a funny kid, always with a smile on his face and would do anything for you, anything at all. I still have memories of riding in his VW Beetle in 1969 singing Johnny Cash's "A Boy named Sue," one of my fondest memories of him. It's because of Levi that I fell in love with that VW Beetle. Owned a few in my lifetime. Now, 30-plus years later, he is someone you'd rather avoid when he's drunk.

I was the first to depart from the reunion. Three hours of watching old friends climb the ladder of drunkenness was enough. And you know what? There was a pinch of envy lingering within my heart. I did not want to drink. But there was part of me that was pissed that somehow I could no longer join in the camaraderie of my peers, to lift a glass in a toast to life with old friends. Why couldn't I just have one glass of wine or Scotch? Then the answer hit me, I never just had one glass of wine or Scotch.

The family that hosted the reunion, the Dundees, was riddled with alcohol and alcoholic drinking. Mr. Dundee owned his own business and made beaucoup bucks.

He liked his booze as did his wife, but we never saw them as fall-down drunks; they were just happy. About a year ago, we heard through the old hood grapevine that Mrs. Dundee had died. She took a header down a flight of stairs. Hopefully, alcohol was not involved, but some heard it might have been. I pray it wasn't.

As my time in sobriety has moved forward, I have gotten more and more melancholy at neighborhood and high school reunions and I can't say I like melancholy. In the rooms, I've heard many times that while actively drinking, many of us alcoholics loved the chaos that surrounded us. Again, heads nod in affirmation.

I was still drinking at the 25th high school reunion. I arrived with only drinking a shot and beer at home, so I was sober, comparatively speaking. I still recall meeting old friends and acquaintances, men and women I had known for decades, people who I should have felt comfortable around, and not feeling comfortable. You see, I was just like Levi, I felt that I was the screw up and these people did not really like me.

Alcohol is such a liar, in fact, it is pathological. In the beginning of my drinking career, it told me I was great, that I was handsome and loving. At the end, it told me the exact opposite, that I was a lowlife, a hanger on, not worthy of your friendship, not worthy of anything or anybody. Stretch was still alive at this reunion. He showed up and all was ok for a couple of hours. We hung together and got tuned. Sometime around midnight as the crowd thinned, I looked for Stretch but he was gone. That's another thing about booze. In the chaos, you lose track of who you are and those around you. I never got to say goodbye.

At the 30th reunion I was told he was dead from cirrhosis. At that reunion I was now three years sober and my good friend was planted six feet under as a direct result from alcohol.

Alcohol was not just a liar, it was now a killer. Yes, I realize the reality. Alcohol in and of itself is not bad or evil, but in the hands of an alcoholic it like putting the muzzle of a loaded Glock 17 to one's forehead and pulling the trigger.

CHAPTER 9

The God Thing

I hate to use this metaphor about my Higher Power, but the 600 pound elephant sitting in the middle of the room and in this book is God. As stated earlier, I have seen atheists and agnostics stay sober. I have even seen them discover God. And I have witnessed everything in between.

Some people come into the rooms of sobriety and then relapse. Some say they "went out" because they didn't get the spiritual aspect of the program. Many recovering alcoholics and addicts say they never had a problem believing in God. They just didn't believe in a caring, loving kind of God. To many, God keeps your life scorecard on his heavenly desk, always judging you and, for the most part, judging you poorly. "He always seems to see me fucking up but appears asleep when I do something truly noble and wonderful for my fellow man."

Maybe if I tell you about my relationship with God you can identify. I was raised predominately by my mom who was this sweet and holy, four-foot-ten inch tall, compassionate, stern, stoic, tough-as-nails Irish Catholic. As a kid, Mass every Sunday. The only time we were allowed to skip Mass was if we had to call the priest and he was going to administer the Sacrament of Extreme Unction, the sacrament of the dying, to one of us! Thus, never! I had eight years of Catholic grammar school, four years of Catholic high school, and two years of college in a Catholic Seminary, studying to be a priest, and finished my degree with two more years at a Catholic university in Philly. Trust me, that is a lot of friggin' Catholic!

Now, I am not asking every reader to identify with that. Hell, we have Protestants, Jews, Buddhists, Hindus, Muslims, Mormons, Fundamentalists, Jehovah Witnesses, Atheists, Agnostics, and Evangelical Christians in sobriety. You name the religion and I guarantee there is at least one alcoholic in that denomination and most likely at least one of them in the rooms of AA.

What I am asking you to identify with is my knowledge of God. Notice I did not say my belief in God; my faith in God, just the knowledge. Even a good atheist will argue for hours about a Deity he or she does not believe in. Let's say you did not believe in the existence of the universes that exist beyond our Milky Way. Would you spend a lifetime defending your non-belief in something you have personally not seen, yet billions of people believe exists? Think about it.

I am asking you to identify and be tolerant and patient with me. I came into sobriety with tons of knowledge about God, sixteen years of Catholic education and two years studying to be a priest will give you that knowledge.

Hell, I knew tons of shit about God. He had resided in my head for over four decades when I made my first AA meeting. Yep, He was in my head.

A brief sidebar; if you are truly alcoholic and eventually

come in to the rooms of Alcoholic Anonymous, people are going to tell you that you have to get a sponsor. A sponsor is a mentor who will guide you through the Twelve Steps of the AA Program. The guy I asked to be my sponsor during that first month sober is a guy named Chuck. In a later chapter I'll talk about Chuck and sponsors. For our purposes here, Chuck tried to set me straight when it came to this God business. The Third Step says, "We made a decision to turn our will and our lives over to the care of God, as we understood Him."

I know you're thinking, big deal. I had the same exact thought.

You see, I told Chuck I had no problem with the God thing. He knew my background after the first time we talked at length. One day he told me to study the Third Step. Study it, are you kidding me? So to appease Chuck, at the next meeting, I told him I studied the step. I also told him that as the good Irish Catholic boy I was, I went to Mass daily…daily! Told him I went to confession once a month and prayed the Rosary daily. Told him I taught religious education to middle school kids for thirteen years. I got it, ok! I got this God thing!

I was awaiting Chuck's retort to all of this. I could tell he was a pretty smart guy, maybe not as smart as me, but pretty smart.

There was a moment of silence between us. He gets this shitty grin on his face, just like the one Willie did in the Waffle House, and asks me a question. And I got pissed again!

"George, do you know the difference between you and God?"

Now dogmatically, I know I knew more than Chuck on the subject, but rather than argue I say, "No, I don't."

Chuck then pauses ten seconds for effect and says, "God didn't wake up this morning thinking He was George."

Without being blasphemous, that just blew me the frig away. I stood there stunned. You cannot attain that kind of wisdom in a classroom. Chuck had a high school diploma, I was almost finished my Master's Degree. He knew he had me.

To top it off, he then asks me, "Did all those Masses, all those confessions, all those rosaries, and all those classes you taught in religious education and all that knowledge you had attained about God, did any of it ever keep you from picking up a drink and getting drunk?"

I stood in silence again. Again, he knew he had me.

Lastly, he questions me, "So, do you now realize and will you admit, not for me, but for yourself, that you really don't know the first thing about getting and staying sober? And can you confess that you may have God in your head, but He does not exist in your heart?"

The first question was easy to answer. Yes, I did not know squat about getting and staying sober. But if I answered the second question in the affirmative, I would be admitting that I really did not "know" God. I knew "about" Him, but that would not be good enough. Not if I wanted to stay sober.

Why this discussion about God, about a Higher Power, you may ask? First of all, we need to set things straight. You need not believe in anything in order to become a member of AA and enter the rooms of sobriety. That is one of the reasons I love Alcoholic Anonymous. You can believe that God is your pet turtle or nothing at all. The Third Tradition in AA simply states, "The only requirement for membership is a desire to stop drinking." That's it! If you came to meetings every day and did not pick up a drink one day at a time, your chances of staying sober increase exponentially.

However, since its founding in 1935 by Bill Wilson and Dr. Bob Smith, experience has shown that there is more to living a sober life than going to meetings and not drinking. Actually, in a piece of AA literature it succinctly states, to paraphrase, "Although you are sober, someday you will find yourself in a precarious situation and you will have no defense against the first (next) drink except for your Higher Power.

Not sure about you, but when I was out there throwing down one Guinness after another, I said a shitload of "foxhole prayers."

You know the kind. Listen to the whine in my voice; "Oh God, please get me out of this fucking jam (Do not recommend cursing in a prayer). If you do, I promise I will stop drinking and become a better husband...If you let me pass this breathalyzer, I promise to cut down and only drink at home on weekends...If my wife (husband/partner) forgives me this one last time, I promise to only drink when I am with them and then I will only drink beer!" (Many active alkies do not consider beer alcohol…Go figure). Foxhole prayers…and you know the old military saying, "There ain't any atheists in foxholes." Never been in a foxhole, but I understand the saying.

To bring this chapter full circle, the Second Step in AA states, "We came to believe that a Power greater than ourselves could restore us to sanity." Again, you sigh, "Big friggin' deal…whatever…what the heck does it mean?" Well, let us look at the statement and break it down. "We came to believe in a Power greater than ourselves…" That's part one. So the assumption is, once you come into the rooms and start living a sober life, in order to stay sober you are going to have to discover a Power greater than you.

Now, you may find this difficult if your ego was as big as mine when I got sober, but again, if you cannot call your Higher Power God, can you at least believe that the people in the rooms of AA who are sober, know more about staying sober than you?

The AA literature says "great." So make the rooms of Alcoholics Anonymous your Higher Power. Part two, depending on your own personal situation, states that this Power can restore you to sanity. Wow! Think about that for a moment. You at least will have to admit, that while you were "out there" your actions were insane. For many newcomers in sobriety this is either extremely easy or extremely difficult.

During those last few years, I knew I drank differently

than my wife and most of my friends. Concrete example, I loved going to Japanese Steakhouses and not just for the show and the food. I loved sake. I mean I worshiped and adored it. When the little Asian lady came around to take drink orders, my wife and friends might order sake or a glass of wine or a bottle of Japanese beer. I would immediately order two sakes. Why? Because I knew it would take the little Asian lady about twenty minutes before she made it back to our table. Then when she came back, I would order two more. Thus, before I ate a morsel of food, I had consumed four sakes.

That is not normal drinking. Meanwhile, everyone else was still nursing drink number one when the chef started his juggling act and cooking, and that is when I ordered drink number five! Insane drinking.

But that just touches the surface of my insanity. As my downward slide into alcoholism continued, this insanity became more apparent to those I loved and who loved me and it did not just center on alcohol.

My ability to make good sane decisions in everyday living became diminished. My ability to make sane business decisions also became disjointed. And what scared me even more, once I had a few months sober and I could no longer anesthetize myself with booze or dope, I truly felt insane and found myself acting out in ways I did not think possible. That's where Chuck and the other guys in the rooms of Alcoholic Anonymous came to the rescue.

Statement…yes, "God did not wake up this morning, thinking He was George." If you're still reading along, even if you are a professed atheist, you might be saying, "Thank God!!"

It is time to meet Gandhi.

CHAPTER 10

Gandhi

Now normal drinkers will not usually sit around discussing and remembering the first time they got hammered. It is not important. It is not on their radar screens. Most alcoholics who make it into recovery, however, do.

It was the end of May in 1969. This was a couple of months before I did the army fatigue trek to the Oak Lane section of Philly with Stretch and Joey to procure quarts of Pabst Blue Ribbon from the African American bartender who is probably still laughing.

I had never been drunk. I had not had a drink since my cousin's wedding in 1968 where I experienced my first buzz with Barbara *WhatsHerName*. Oh how love is fleeting, eh? Stretch and I played basketball in 1969, our junior year of high school. We played for rival schools in Philly, but we were buds on the playground battles of round ball. We hung out, we liked the same music, Beatles, Stones, Doors, the Who, Hendricks and Dylan, and we dated two girls in Olney who were sisters. So I guess it was only natural that my first real drunk was with my buddy Stretch.

What I did not know was that Stretch came from a family of real heavy drinkers. I had met his Mom and Dad and brothers and sister.

I thought they were pretty cool. Sure his parents were usually having drinks whenever I saw them, and sure they were a really loud family, but I knew nothing about heavy drinkers or alcoholism. Shit, I just about knew who the hell I was. All looked normal to me.

On a weekend night in May, Stretch calls me and tells me to stop over his house to hang out and listen to some music. For his birthday he'd gotten both Sergeant Pepper's and the Beatles' White Album. This was not an unusual request. Sure, no problem, I was on my way. Arriving at the door I knew immediately something was different. It was quiet. These people were never quiet.

I rang the bell, he answers and proceeds to tell me that his parents and siblings went to Asbury Park, Seaside Heights or Brigantine, somewhere down the Jersey shore overnight. They trusted him to stay home and watch over the house. They would be back the next night. We ventured into the kitchen and on the table are six quarts of Bud, courtesy of his older brother, Marty.

Now without thinking of any consequences of what we were about to do, we each opened a quart, lit a Marlboro Red, put on the White Album, poured the Bud into frosted mugs, inhaled the entire scene around us and drank deeply. Wow! This was fucking great. I remember finishing that first quart and BAM that feeling I had experienced in D.C. was back. If I had stopped there and enjoyed the buzz, really nothing of consequence would have happened. It was still early enough in the evening to go play some hoops, work up a sweat, chew some gum, suck on some mints, anything so Mom would not smell the beer. Of course, none of that happened.

By the time we each got to the third quart, we had on Sergeant Peppers and were listening to Lennon's great song, "A Day in the Life of a Boy."

I have a decent voice. When the lyrics got to the part where John sings, "...I found my way upstairs and had a smoke, somebody spoke and I went into a dream, Ah, ah, ah, ah, ah, ah, ahhhhhhhhhhhhhh, ah..." I was playing an air guitar along with George Harrison standing on a kitchen chair. Next thing I knew, I was puking all over Stretch's kitchen trying to get to the back door that led out into an alley. I never made it. Stretch, meanwhile, was laughing hysterically.

I must have blacked out. When I awoke it was just me and my buddy in the kitchen. He was actually cleaning up and almost done. Except for the smell, the place looked pretty good. Yet, I was truly embarrassed. This was my first time drinking and I blew it. But Stretch just smiled and said not to worry. This kind of thing happened in his house at least once a week with his brothers and Mom and Dad.

My shirt was ruined. I tossed it down the first sewer I passed on the way home. I was shitfaced and shirtless. On top of that, waiting at home was my four-foot-ten-inch, Irish Catholic, teetotaler Mom who, with one swipe, would knock me off my size twelves. And she did.

During the next 28 years, for the most part, this is how I drank: to get drunk. I did not always puke or black out, but many times I did. But the goal remained the same. Chase the buzz, experience the buzz, and go past the buzz into oblivion. Why drink if not to get drunk?

It is February of 1998. I am six months sober. I am at an AA meeting in the basement of a local hospital, in a room clothed in ugly, industrial-green paint that is situated directly across from the morgue. Quite appropriate, actually. Some Saturday mornings we would come into this room and out in the hallway would be some stiff who had bought the farm the night before. As we passed the stiff, some old guy would mumble, "But for the Grace of God there go I." What he meant by that I did not know.

At this meeting in February, a woman by the name of Susan raises her hand and asks the same question I had been pondering for months, "Can anyone here please define alcoholism for me, because I'm not really sure I am one of you." Susan was also a white-collar, educated woman living in an upscale area loaded with Volvos, Audis, Jaguars and the occasional Porsche.

There was a smattering of snickers in the crowd. The old timers had heard this question before. Well, we got our answer. One of those old timers, a crotchety, old, leathered-skin, and wrinkled, foul-mouthed alcoholic in recovery by the name of Jeff raised his hand and was called upon. He rose from his chair (this took forever!), gazed over the crowd and smugly stated, "Shit that's easy. I define it this way. When I drank, I drank too much, and when I tried to stop I couldn't!" There it was. There was my epiphany. I truly thought this guy was friggin' Gandhi!

You could pay several thousand dollars for a Master of Philosophy Degree from an Ivy League university and never hear such a clear, succinct and profound answer to a question. For six months I had been part of the internal debating society; am I an alcoholic or not? Do I really belong here? Will I ever be able to drink again or not?

This old fart, who had dropped out of high school in the early 1950s, joined the Marines and probably had the equivalent of an eighth-grade education, in fifteen words of which only one had more than one syllable, defined alcoholism and in turn defined me.

There was no escape now. All the doors, windows and alley ways that I thought I could use for an escape from the rooms of sobriety and my fellow alkies were closed off. I was, indeed, an alcoholic.

How did I know this? Easy. When I drank, I drank too much, and when I tried to stop, I couldn't.

By the way, that old coot is still alive and is now sober for about 35 years. Today I call him a friend. But shit, how did this happen and why? Why could I not drink like a normal person?

More would be revealed in subsequent years and many more meetings. For now, they just told me to "keep coming back."

Fortunately, I did. And yes, "Gandhi" appeared again at other meetings. And if I kept an open mind and listened, I actually heard what he had to say.

CHAPTER 11

Powerless & Stinkin' Thinkin'

I remember reading the words of the First Step in AA after the fog began to clear. It reads, "We admitted we were powerless over alcohol and that our lives had become unmanageable." Immediately, I admitted part one of this, but the jury was out on part two. I knew I was powerless over alcohol. Think about it, if you gave any human being a huge portion of Brussel sprouts and after ingesting the sprouts this human being gets violently ill. Do you think for a moment that he or she will ever eat that shit again?

Now, give an alcoholic an enormous amount to drink where they lose the ability to cognitively make good decisions, become vocally obnoxious and absurd, black out, vomit all over themselves and possibly others, crash their car, piss their pants and wake up with a headache that feels as if a fucking rhinoceros is planted on their cerebral cortex. Do you think for a moment that the alcoholic will pick up a drink again?

HELL YES! It's how we are wired. The normal drinker appears to have a mental wiring system that, like in the television series Lost in Space, yells to them, "Danger, Danger, Will Robinson do not drink anymore." While we alkies are wired to say, "Screw Will Robinson…give me another."

I somehow knew I could not control the obsession to

drink, which usually led to some serious stinkin' thinkin.' I touched on the insane drinking topic briefly in a previous chapter; how, when everyone else was still nursing drink number one at a Japanese steakhouse, I had just ordered drink number five. There is more.

In 1988, I was given the gift of cancer. Now right there you may be saying to yourself, that sure is stinkin' thinkin', but you would be wrong. I have been a cancer survivor for almost three decades. Through these years I have been able to support and empathize with many men and women who are stricken with cancer and are deathly afraid.

If you haven't had the disease, you really do not understand what the person who has contracted the illness is going through. I do. Been there done that. I desire someday to write a book about this very subject.

Back to 1988. I am still an active alcoholic but do not know it. My wife and I have been married only eight months, a second marriage for both of us. We happened to meet through our daughters during the summer of 1986. It is August 7, 1988 and I am playing softball with my drinking buddies from the local watering hole. I'm a decent athlete. I play third base. It was one of those extremely hot, humid, no-air-to-breathe days that sometimes infiltrate the atmosphere around Philadelphia and its suburbs. After two hours of flopping and diving for ground balls in the dust and dirt, game over, we stop for a couple of beers. My wife is with me so it really is only a couple and we head home. I jump in the shower, towel off and am looking in the mirror of our bathroom.

Holy shit! My left nut is the size of a grapefruit! There is no pain at all. I cannot put on a pair of underwear, the testicle is that swollen. I slip on loose fitting sweat pants. We traipse over to the Emergency Room at our local, country-bumpkin hospital. It is the weekend; there is only a Resident on staff. He examines me, tells me to go home and check with my family doc the next day. Right there I knew something was wrong.

I awake the morning of August 8, 1988 (8–8–88) hoping my left jewel is back to normal size and my luck has changed. It is not and it has not. It has gotten worse. We head to our family doctor's office without calling for an appointment. He takes one look at it and sends me to a urologist.

This doctor sees us immediately. He unpleasantly examines me. Still no pain. I ask is this just a hematoma from flopping around third base. He says no. He wants to do an ultrasound. Within an hour, we are sitting across from him and his face is grave. I already know the answer. I have testicular cancer. Shaken to my core, I ask him what the worst case scenario is. He says worst case: you might have six months to live.

Now my wife, like her mom, can be a very stoic person. Quickly and without a trace of emotion in her voice, she says, "Only the good die young, he isn't going anywhere." I know she said it to lighten the mood, and it did.

I can still remember the night before surgery. The family had gone to bed. All were walking on pins and needles afraid to speak with me or just not knowing what to say at all. My feelings had vacillated between getting through all of this and being ok with death and dying. The thoughts of dying and never seeing my wife or children again were crushing. I remember being in the kitchen of our townhome praying and crying. "Why me, Lord?" Of course, the prayers were about me, the great and glorious "I."

Did I pray for my wife or children? No. When I decided that the Lord was asleep and not going to answer me, I drank. Yep, the night before cancer surgery, I poured a tumbler of Tullamore Dew… another…and another. No one knew. It was dark and I was alone. Oblivion was next. Maybe I wouldn't wake up.

August 11, 1988 dawned with rain and fog in the forecast. I was to have an orchiectomy, surgery where my damaged jewel was to be removed; subsequently I was scheduled to receive 30 radiation (RAD) treatments from clavicle to groin. RAD technology was not as refined as it is today. Everything got radiated: my lungs, my stomach, my heart, all of it. The stomach was the most sensitive. After each treatment, I became violently ill for a few hours with acute vomiting. Although married to a great, supportive and loving woman and having five great kids, I felt alone. All was dark. Death was awaiting me. The headless horseman was coming, if not tomorrow, someday soon. I was afraid. I wanted a drink.

I am an alcoholic. I had just started a new job when diagnosed with cancer. In AA you will hear the word "fear" tossed about like a volleyball at the beach. Every alcoholic I know in the rooms admits that fear governed their lives. Instantly, I became fearful that if I missed more than a week of work, I would be fired.

Can you guess my answer to this fear when radiation treatments began a week after surgery? I was back behind the wheel of my car, out on the road, selling. Now that is stinkin' thinkin'! But it got worse. After I puked up my guts, usually on the side of an exit ramp on the PA Turnpike until nothing but raw bile came out, I did what I always did to kill pain, I drank. Every day, I drank. That is nuts. That is stupid. That is insane. The normal drinker who does not obsess about booze would never do this.

I would wait until about 5 p.m. in the afternoon, never drinking during working hours, and then stop at my watering hole. The men and women who knew me were obviously concerned, but hey, they were in the bar drinking their problems away, too. This just added more drama to my life and theirs. I did not want my wife to know I was drinking, so I did not have a lot and limited it to two screwdrivers, vodka and orange juice. I was on my way home an hour later. All was right with the world. I might sneak a shot or two of Irish whiskey mid-evening when the bride was upstairs and I was down stairs watching a ball game. I would crawl into bed deathly ill, await the horseman and the next day begin the process all over again.

Albert Einstein defined insanity as, "Doing the same thing over and over again, expecting a different result." I believe the above scenario fulfills the criterion of this definition.

A humorous side-bar came out of this. On the day after surgery I was lying in my hospital bed. The bartender at our watering hole, a great guy named Gary, came to visit. He is not an alcoholic. I was still under the influence of the morphine dripping from an IV bag. Gary walked in and unashamedly I lifted up my hospital gown, in front of my wife and mother, and showed him my "one ball"…thus, I received the nickname OB. For about a year, when I would walk in for a Guinness after work, just like in the television series "Cheers," all at the bar would turn and in unison say, "Hey OB"! And a Guinness would appear at my bar stool. The hailing of OB eventually stopped, but when I tell my story in the rooms that fateful day, 8–8–88, is a huge part of that story…my story. Fortunately, I am still here to tell it.

I met a guy named Finn in the rooms of AA. He invited me to a meeting in Philly. City meetings were always more exciting and entertaining than in the affluent suburbs. This meeting was at a group called "Life and Death." I told Finn to say no more, that I would be there. When you walk into this meeting hall there is a banner in the front that says, to paraphrase, "If your friggin' way was so much better, then what you are doing here?" That got my attention right away.

The speaker was a guy named Upstate Stan. He grew up in North Jersey, but had that New York accent, where

New York came out as New Yawk, and George was Gawge. In his story he relates how he and his brother got involved with the mob—yeah, the real mob.

He was selling drugs, gun running, anything to make a buck. Unbeknown to Upstate, his brother was skimming off the top and the mob found out. One night, two guys appeared at Stan's home. Only he and his brother were home. The two mob guys had Upstate and his brother bound, gagged and blindfolded. He describes the night as chilly and overcast. No moon or stars, nothing to light the landscape. They then had Upstate and his brother kneel in their driveway and they executed his brother. Bang! Shot to the head. They cut the rope binding his hands and told Upstate to keep kneeling until he hears their car pull away, then count to 1,000. He does as instructed.

At 1,000, he removes the blindfold. Half of his brother's head is missing, his body still in a kneeling, slumped position.

Now you would think that after something like that you would never drink or drug again. Not so. Upstate stopped working for the mob, but he did not put down the booze for many more years. How could he? How would he kill the pain in his head? He only knew of one solution and that was alcohol.

After the meeting, Finn and I stopped at a diner in Northeast Philly for coffee. Finn was sober at this time for eight years, I had eight months.

He asked me what I thought. First I told him my initial reaction was that maybe I really wasn't an alcoholic.

Damn, I was never involved with the mob selling drugs, gun running and whatever else Upstate Stan was into to. Finn just stared at me.

I knew the answer he was searching for. It was the end of the story that I could relate to, to identify with.

Upstate knew only one way to deal with the pain in his head, in his soul, in his spirit…booze.

And I did the same…that there is some serious stinkin' thinkin' and proved beyond a shadow of doubt that I was powerless over alcohol.

CHAPTER 12

Feelings of Fear & Rejection

At about nine months sober, I called my sponsor Chuck up one night and told him I was depressed, angry, pissed at the world, filled with resentments toward family, friends and coworkers. He smugly said, "Guess you're ready to do your fourth step."

This AA step simply states that we alcoholics "must make a fearless and moral inventory of ourselves." WTF. At every turn in sobriety they were always asking me to do more work. I stopped drinking. I got a sponsor. I went to meetings every day! What more do these "fother muckers" want? You guessed it, the fourth step.

There are chapters and verses in AA literature that describes how to do a fourth step. Chuck told me to remember back as far as I could and write an autobiography. Keep it simple. At this stage I had been around on this earth 45 years. That's a lot of writing. He told me to concentrate on the people and things that made me feel bad, that later in life made me want to drink.

At the conclusion of this exercise, two themes emerged: first, from an early age I felt fearful, not sure exactly why, but it was there. Second, I never felt "part of" anything, felt rejected even by my own family as small as it was.

As I picked up pen and paper, the first person I feared was the old man. No shock there. He was a war hero. He was a supreme athlete. He was larger than life itself. In my early years, I did not show a lot of athletic prowess. I was a tall, skinny, awkward kid. Hell, I am freaking sure Wilt Chamberlain was, at one time, a tall, skinny, awkward kid!

A vivid memory stands out. I was probably about six years old and the old man took me to work with him. It was summer. He had his own contracting business; he was a builder. He was in a hurry to get to the next appointment and I told him I had to pee.

Now we all know that kids, boys especially, when they are out with their parents, always have to try out the restroom wherever they may be. They go in, don't do anything, look around, run water over their hands and come back out. Been doing this since Adam and Eve had Cain and Abel (minus the running water). I am sure I did this, too.

However, on this occasion, I was riding shotgun in his truck. We had been on the road for quite a while and I really, really had to pee. I was holding it in, cupping my hand over my crotch and squeezing hard. Hey, it's what all little boys do. Did not matter to the old man. I am sure him stopping and wasting time for me to visit the water closet was costing him money.

Finally, we came upon a roadside diner. In my mind's eye I can still see it. Round edges, looked like a trailer, and the sun was beating off the silver exterior. We walked in and I was immediately overpowered by the pungent smell of eggs, bacon, sausage, toast, home fries, coffee, ham, and cheese, all of it. He saw the restroom sign, told me I had two minutes to hurry, piss and get back out ASAP.

Have you ever really had to take a leak and get to the toilet or urinal and you just can't go. I mean the brain is saying to the plumbing; "go piss."

The urethra, in return, is flipping the bird to the brain stem saying, "Fuck you, I ain't ready." That's what happened. I had to go, but could not go. I did not know the Catholic Patron Saint for taking a piss, so I prayed to every saint I could name. Nothing. Nada. Zilch. Zip.

Finally, it came out in dribs and drabs, but I was still struggling. On top of everything else the internal alarm clock in my head knew two minutes had come and gone and the old man was by now lighting a cigarette, pacing back and forth and ready to erupt. I was not disappointed.

Just as my equipment started to work, he comes in furious, like a bat out of hell, red faced, eyes bulging, yelling and asks what the hell I've been doing and physically spins me. You guessed it, I pissed all over him. I mean I drenched the son of a bitch in urine, his pants, socks, shoes. I got it all. Anything below his waist was now yellow.

He must have looked like an enormous, drooping daisy from the forest in the Wizard of Oz. Now the urethra was telling the brain, "ok, stop already." Brain stem flips the bird and says, "Frig you." The work day was over.

It was accidental and inadvertent, yet he never asked me to go to work with him again, until the day before he died. The old man and fear went hand in hand.

I have already discussed how the Cub Scouts and Altar Boys rejected me, won't rehash that. Next came my eighth-grade graduation.

The year was 1966. My mother was barely scraping by earning a threadbare living. She could not take off from work. That left my sister, Uncle Jack and Aunt Linda. The night before, my mom told Sis to be at the Church for the Graduation Mass at 10:00 a.m. sharp. She said no problem, she'd be there. Uncle Jack and Aunt Linda, ditto.

Well, I'm dressed in a new navy blue sports jacket that probably cost Mom half a paycheck. We process into the Church. All my buddies see their moms and dads, brothers and sisters, aunts and uncles while Polaroid cameras are flashing wildly. It was pretty exciting. I did not see Sis right away or my aunt and uncle. It was a big school, huge church, lots of people.

The graduation Mass lasted about 90 minutes. During the ceremony, they called out our names and we walked up to the altar, and Bishop John gave us something that said we were now out of grammar-school prison. Free at last! After the final blessing, all my buds took off looking for family members.

I scanned the crowd. Ran to the back of the church, down the side aisles, and back up to the main altar. The overflow crowd was in the choir loft, so I scooted up there.

Nope, not there either. By this time the church was fairly empty. I ran up the center aisle one last time. Sister Dorothy Patricia, my homeroom nun, saw me and asked what was I doing?

I told her I was searching for Sis and my aunt and uncle. She said let's go look outside near the main exit, that they might be waiting for me there. There were a few stragglers with a couple of my classmates outside, but no one for me was there. Dotty Pat (that was her nickname) knew my background. She told me to come with her over to the convent, and she'd make some phone calls.

Nah. I was no longer her student. She saw the look of disappointment and sadness on my face. I said goodbye to her, thanked her and walked away alone. The first sewer I saw I stopped and deposited my graduation certificate. No one really gave a shit, so why should I? Just another rejection. I was getting used to it.

I do not ever remember my mom asking me or talking to me about my graduation from grammar school that night. Maybe she did. At this point in her life she was in survival mode, struggling to keep the three of us together so the State wouldn't ship us to foster homes. She told me of some of these fears later in life.

The gulf between my sister and I widened and deepened. As years passed by, we grew farther and farther apart. At one point, there was a period of 23 years when we had no communication at all.

I still think back to that shitty day when I graduated from grammar school in 1966. But you know who I really blamed, the old man. And all he really did was die six years earlier. There was nobody there, and nobody cared.

You may be asking, "What do these two events have to do with drinking and alcoholism?" I asked the same thing to Chuck. He explained that if you connected the dots to the fears you could remember and the rejections you could remember, you would see a pattern. As a young kid, I obviously did not drink to escape from fear and rejection. I simply "checked out" in those relationships with people whom I feared and those who rejected me. After 1969, I found a better solution, alcohol. Before alcohol, when I checked out, I still had to deal with some horrid feelings. Alcohol helped me not to feel. Not feeling was the answer to my fears, rejections and any other problems I had to face in life. Alcohol became my friend. If you do not believe alcohol is a disease, how sick is that statement?

Here are some fear statements: Holy Moly...holy shit...WTF...Crapola...Piss my pants...out of my f'in' mind... scared shitless...fear strikes out...ascared (not a typo...From Spanky and Our Gang...google it) "...the only thing to fear is fear itself." When I first read that quote from Franklin Delano Roosevelt I genuinely thought two things: "That is really deep" or "This guy must have been an opium addict or whatever drug was popular in the 1930s and 1940s.

Fear, where to start? Here are some sober thoughts on the subject. Let's look back at our lives, all of our lives, alcoholic and non-alcoholics, for just a couple of minutes.

We hang in our mother's womb for nine months. Life is cool, plenty to eat, it's warm here, I'm learning to swim and breathe underwater. The months roll by and now the living space is getting kind of crammed. On or around the nine-month mark, since we were conceived and our life began, the landlord finally declares, "It's time to vacate these premises," and out we come. And to think, we fear absolutely nothing for the first few years of our life…nothing. We are invincible.

Can any of us truly remember our first real fear? I'm not sure I can. I do remember the day when I experienced real pain for the first time. I had to be three or four years of age. The old man was cutting the grass with a gas-powered mower. I was tagging along; I'm sure being a pain in the ass. At one point he stopped the mower and had to go into our home for something.

He pointed at the little gas engine that sat on the side of the mower, "Do not touch that." Well that was like telling Custer, "Do not go down into that valley."

I was probably one of those kids who appear to be a few French fries short of a Happy Meal. As soon as he left me and entered the house, I wrapped my hand around that engine and holy shit was that stupid. Within seconds I was screaming. Both Mom and Dad came running out. I'm sure the old man wanted to pummel me, but Mom scooped me up and we shot into the house. I can't see my hand because my mom is holding it against her body. I don't even think she knew what to do. It's not like they give parents manuals when kids do mindless shit like this.

The last part of the episode I remember is the old man holding a huge tub of Vaseline petroleum jelly and telling me to put my hand in it. I did as I was told: but the pain was immense and I just kept wailing.

When I pulled my hand out, I had so much goo on it, it

was like I jacked off an elephant. The end. As you can see, I do not remember much, but the pain I remember. Never went near another lawn mower for twenty years. Still carry that fear.

Most kids grow up fearing the dark and tons of other stuff—heights, horror movies, the ocean, thunder and lightning, ghost and goblins and even Santa Claus. My mom once told me in my adult years that Sis loved Santa Claus when we were kids, whereas I looked upon him as one would look upon a leper. She said they never had one picture of me with the jolly old man in the big red suit. Is anyone shocked at this?

I believe the fears of life come upon us when we start forming relationships with other people. This is just my opinion. I'm not talking about interactions with Mom, Dad and the immediate family. I'm talking about those that start forming around third, fourth or fifth grade outside the home. And what is the fear? Again, just my opinion, but I think it is the fear of rejection. Ever notice how kids, even today, when they are with their peers that they just want to be accepted? That's it. Accept me for who I am.

If it was only that easy. We all know that bullies exist, and kids can be cruel. Any kid can be rejected because he is too slow, too heavy, too awkward and even too poor. Kids reject other kids based on the clothes they wear, the lunches they bring to school, the district in which they reside, the "uncoolness" of their parents, the color and length of their hair. The list is infinite.

Before we know it, we are finishing high school and we

have slid into our peer niche. Some of us hang with jocks, others with the cool kids, others with nerds, others with musicians, others with losers and others with the gremlins of the class. And in American society, whether it was in my day in 1968 or today in the 21st century, we all discover alcohol. The cool kids and some of the losers discover cigarettes first, but sooner or later all of these groups, whether in the loneliness of their own home or at the Prom Queen's post-prom party, discover booze.

Most folks like what it does, will get drunk, and do stupid things. But they can take or leave it. It has no hold on them.

However, there is a group that drinks and drinks and drinks. No matter the trouble they find themselves in, no matter how ill they become when overindulging, no matter the privileges they lose as a result of their drunkenness, no matter the difficulties they find themselves with the law, no matter the trips to the E.R. to get their stomachs pumped, no matter the blackouts when the dust settles once again and the coast is clear, this group of individuals drinks again.

They honestly believe they have uncovered the solution to all their fears. Here is the logic. Before I drank no one really liked me. Once I started drinking, everyone liked me. Before I drank I feared asking a girl out on a date. Once I started drinking, I had more than one girl to ask. Before I drank, I was shy and withdrawn, afraid to participate; with drink in hand the shackles of the shy personality fell away and I became the life of the party.

Thus, logically if I drink, life is good. If I do not drink, I am afraid of my own fucking shadow.

This is alcoholic logic, not normal logic. What is the fallacy? Pretty obvious, eh? In order to survive in this life and not be afraid, I must drink. Thus, when life throws me a curve and I become fearful, I need only drink and I'll be ok. Thus endeth the lesson.

CHAPTER 13

High Bottom-Low Bottom

A term tossed around in and out of the rooms of sobriety that is the oxymoron of oxymorons is *functional alcoholic.* I have used this term as part of the title of this epic masterpiece. I mentioned in an earlier chapter that I came into Alcoholics Anonymous wearing an eight-piece suit with French cufflinks and a college degree. Hopefully, you have noticed I made a list of all the "I never hads." I would suggest that you read through it again.

Now, the low bottom drunk is the stereotypical alky; most times homeless, living out of a car or truck using green trash bags as suitcases, having little or no money, living in shelters. Their marriages have been destroyed by abuse of alcohol and drugs. They may have filed for bankruptcy, and their home is in foreclosure.

Most high bottom drunks are like me; white-collar jobs, college educated, married, with kids, beautiful homes, luxury automobiles, exotic vacations, travels to Europe and beyond—in three words, the good life.

High-bottom drunks can also be blue-collar workers, owners of their own businesses, like my old man, or just regular blue-collar men and women who are electricians, plumbers, roofers, carpenters.

These folks also own nice homes, have two cars or more, are married and have children. Our high bottom drunk has a bank account, a 401K and pension, looks around at all that he or she possesses and thinks, "I cannot be an alcoholic, look at my portfolio." If this sounds familiar to you or your loved one keep reading.

I will deal with the high-bottom drunk first and use myself as the example. You know my background already. I at one time covered, as a sales territory, Manhattan and the boroughs for a period of about three years while working for a Dow-Thirty company. I would leave on a Tuesday morning from my home in the suburbs of Philadelphia; take the Amtrak Metro-liner to Penn Station in Manhattan, then cab it to a five-star hotel in Midtown.

My clients were hospital administrators, CEOs, CFOs, CIOs, physicians and clinical directors of high-end departments such as cardiology, oncology, orthopedics and operating rooms. I would work from dawn to dusk until about noon on Friday, then reverse course and head back to Philly. But it was from dusk to dawn that I did most of my damage drinking, thinking all along that I was ok, that I was functional.

When I tell my story in AA about this period of my life, it goes something like this. I arrived on Tuesday morning in New York City, dropped my bags at the hotel and began visiting clients. At 5 o'clock in the afternoon there was a Catholic Mass at St. Patrick's Cathedral in Midtown each and every day. I would attend this Mass every day.

If alone, subsequent to going to Mass and thinking myself pious and holy, I would proceed to either a pub or restaurant and blow my brains out on booze.

Now I did it with class. Steak and lobster, vintage merlots or cabernets, crème brulee, topped off with a shot or two of single-malt scotch. Then hop a cab to the Hard Rock or Harley Davidson Café, drink Guinness', sing-a-long with a band or dueling pianos and await last call.

By 2 o'clock in the morning, I was whacked; rarely remembered getting back to my hotel room, passed out with clothes still on. Wake up call at 6 a.m., shower, change into clothes not slept-in, put slept in clothes in dry cleaning, grabbed a cup of coffee and bagel on the street and headed to the 8 a.m. Mass at St. Patrick's Cathedral. Prior to Mass a group of priests would be hearing confessions, so I knelt down and confessed my sins.

After Mass, my work day began going back to hospitals, working hard from dawn to dusk, and then repeating the entire scenario once again.

The kicker was the second morning. I would kneel down to the priest in confession and say, "Bless me Father for I have sinned, it's been 24 hours since my last confession."

Once in a while the priest would become agitated and say, "What the heck could you do in 24 hours that warrants Confession?" Then I would tell of my drinking escapade, and he would agree that it was good I came in and admonished me not to do this again. I would say I'd do my best but knew this a lie. Shit, I just went to confession and was already committing a sin by friggin' lying to the priest while I was still on the bloody kneeler!

All of this, of course, was on the dime of the company

that employed me. I did keep it all within "budget" but I took that budget to the max. Then there were times when I would entertain clients, again, CEOs, surgeons and high-end administrators. Now we were eating at top-ten New York City restaurants, where at the end of the meal, the tip alone might be in excess of $250. During the dinner, I would only have a glass or two of wine. We would wind things up, I'd shake hands with these good folks, depart their company and cab it to a pub and proceed to catch up on time lost not drinking during dinner.

By last call, I was hailing a cab from somewhere in Manhattan, handed a piece of paper to the cabbie who was from India, Iraq, Afghanistan, Syria, Russia or Iran with the name of my hotel, praying he would get me there in one piece and not sell me to the fucking Taliban.

I worked hard from dawn to dusk. I drank hard from dusk to dawn. It was never the work that exhausted me, although when I got back home on Friday this is what my family believed.

What was exhausting was all the effort I put into planning, executing and glamorizing "the drink." And for what? All of it resulted in a daily case of the "Irish Flu," commonly known as the hangover. Truth be told, on the weekends I spent my time hydrating myself with H2O, taking a nap when I could, and getting ready for when I departed once again on Tuesday morning. If you have been following along, I believe this another good case for Einstein's definition of insanity.

Now the low-bottom drunk most likely has an entirely

different story, but the end game is exactly the same. I know from being in the rooms that they, too, drank to get drunk and experienced the same Irish Flu I did. In actuality the only salient difference between us is that by the Grace of God, I got sober before I lost everybody and everything that was important to me.

They, in turn, lost all. I heard a great story in AA of a guy named Buzz who through his drinking and drugging had lost everything. This dude had seven DUI's…seven! He spent time in prison. Homeless, one day he stumbled upon a junk yard. In the far end of the yard was a burnt out trailer with only half a roof. It was January. Most alcoholics, by the way, are really smart and creative people. So this drunk got cardboard boxes, green trash bags and duct tape and voila...he had a home. Unbeknown to the owner of the junk-yard, the alky lived and kept himself alive through the harsh winter. He would beg for booze or for money. He would beg for food. In early spring, he found his way into a shelter and eventually into sobriety.

When Buzz told this story, he blithely said that he remembered waking up each morning in the junk-yard trailer with half a roof, with temperatures in the 20s, wind chills in the single digits and thinking, "Man, I am doing ok. I got a home, a roof over my head and half a jug of port wine. Life is good." Then he looked out over the crowd in the meeting and said, "And I thought I was fucking normal." We all cracked up laughing. That's the thing about sobriety. If you hang around long enough, get sober enough, you will actually get to laugh again and even laugh at yourself. It does not happen overnight, but it does happen.

I am not finished talking about the functional alcoholic. More will come in subsequent chapters. I think the message I want to leave you is this and hopefully my story up until now lends credence to this statement: if you think you are okay because you are a functional drinker, I have some news for you that was bestowed upon me when I told someone in sobriety that at the end of my drinking days I was a functional alcoholic. This wizened, crotchety old alky in recovery grabbed my hand and said, "Buddy, there ain't no such thing!"

Then Gandhi shook his head, laughed softly and kindly said, "Keep coming back."

Does anybody see what I see?

CHAPTER 14

"Oh We Got Trouble"

One day in early sobriety, my old friend Gandhi once again raised his hand to share. We all loved it when he shared because he pulled no punches. Here is what he said, "When I got into trouble I wasn't always friggin' drinking, but when I was drinking I usually got into friggin' trouble." Now this was early in sobriety and I swear I had heard this before, but he was the first to say it at a meeting that I recollect. Then it hit me, this was similar to what Caroline Knapp said in her book, ***Drinking: A Love Story***.

Now Caroline was a little more eloquent, "Bad things didn't happen every time I drank, but every time something bad did happen, drinking was involved."v

That is the cool thing about AA. Caroline got sober in New England, Jeff (Gandhi) in Bucks County, Pennsylvania. I have now been to meetings all over this country and in the rooms the message is the same. This shit has been handed down now for 80 years!

So, if you are reading this book and trying to decide if you are an alcoholic or not, reread either Jeff's declaration about trouble and booze or Carolyn's about three or four times, reflect on your life and see if it fits. Now back to trouble.

Another buddy of mine, Mickey, shared some high

school drinking with me and the other guys on the corner. We met during the summer before our senior year of high school and are still friends today. We are kindred spirits. We are both humorous fellows. We are both very Irish. We both loved to drink. I still remember the first time we got drunk together. How could I ever forget? We hung in Olney. It was football season. It was October 1969. Houses were decorated for Halloween; ghosts and goblins inhabited the neighborhoods.

We had intentions of seeing archrivals in the Catholic League duke it out on the gridiron. Alcohol had other intentions. We were to meet our worst fear and meanest goblin.

This is a true story. Some of the details are a little fuzzy, but here is what I see in my mind's eye. Mickey and I were riding in a car being driven by one of our drinking buddies. There were six of us. We had downed quarts of beer prior to leaving for the game, getting that buzz on that we all so dearly loved. The night was chilly, a full moon hung in the autumn sky. Mick had to take a leak. Unlike women, we guys can take a leak just about anywhere. About a half mile from the stadium, Mickey said he had to go and go badly. We pulled off on to a side street in Philly. He found a huge oak tree on someone's lawn, unzipped and began. Within 30 seconds he was surrounded by Philly cops. Our car was surrounded by cops.

Needless to say, he was scared shitless as were the rest of us waiting in the car.

Why the cops? Why? Because of all the houses numb

nuts Mickey chose to take a leak on, this house belonged to the Chief of Police for the city of Philadelphia, Frank Rizzo. If you are from Philly and reading this and are 50 years or older, you are saying, "Holy Shit, Frank Rizzo!"

If you are not of that age, just google him. Rizzo was the toughest, meanest, cruelest, nastiest chief of police in America at the time. They once wrote a book about him titled ***The Cop Who Would be King***, and here is our buddy Mick urinating on his lawn. Well, the cops told us to get out of the car and we stood with Mickey. We were sure we were all getting cuffed and placed in a paddy wagon heading down to the Round House (police headquarters in Philly). Finger prints, police records, a night or two in jail before our parents bailed us out and then beat the shit out of us. We were hosed.

However, once these boys in blue saw we were just harmless, stupid high-school kids trying to be cool, they scolded and threatened us then told us to go back to our own neighborhoods and piss there. After several hundred, "Yes, officers, and thank you, officers," we did just that. I am positive the cops of that precinct in Philly manufactured that story into a legend just as did we—Mickey pissing on Frank Rizzo's lawn and still alive to talk about it. From a street corner in Olney, that is where booze took Mick and the rest of us, a long time ago in a galaxy far, far, away.

Now Mickey and I had more in common than we knew when we first met in the hood.

Unbeknown to each other, we each had decided to enter

the seminary to study for the Roman Catholic priesthood. Thus, our friendship, and at times our drinking careers, would continue just like our other corner brothers, some of whom were heading off to "normal" colleges.

The seminary was anything but normal. Let me restate that. Academically it was. The first four years were in the college division where you graduated with a B.A. in Philosophy. In the real world that might get you a cup of coffee and a piece of toast; a worthless piece of paper in our American culture. The next four years were spent in the theology division, where most were ordained to the priesthood with a Master's Degree of Divinity. I stayed in for a period of two years. When I tell my story in AA, I always say the reason I left had nothing to do with celibacy, but had everything to do with the fact that I believed and still do that there will never be an Irish American Pope.

Obviously, there were also no girls in a Roman Catholic seminary, although we had a group of Vietnamese nuns who lived on campus and did our laundry. I remember the head nun, Sister John of the Cross; she would shrink the crap out of our tee-shirts, and then come to us in the sweetest Asian voice and say, "Shirts fit no more. I send to Vietnam, yes?" Sure Sister, not a problem. Four weeks into the semester, most of us no longer had tee-shirts in our wardrobes. Like I said, not a normal college.

One night in early March of 1972, about 20 guys from our class ventured into Philly for a theatrical performance of "Helen of Troy." There was a chill in the air. A fresh coating of snow had fallen making the night look pristine and magical. Now we could give a rat's ass about Helen of Troy, but after the play we were allowed to go out for dinner and if of age, a drink or two with dinner. I led one group of five guys into Philly that night borrowing the Dean of Men's VW Beetle. The Dean was this good priest who I'm certain thought at times that he was the warden in a prison, albeit a Roman Catholic one. His nickname was Skippy. Why? Well, when he spoke, especially when he got excited, he sounded like he had a mouthful of Skippy peanut butter.

Another classmate led the rest of our class taking the train into Philly. I told my guys that after the play, we could quietly go to an Irish Pub in Center City called McGillians. Simple fare; cheesesteaks, fries, Irish stew and, of course, Guinness and other assorted alcoholic beverages all consumed at a moderate price. The other group ended up going to the Middle East Restaurant, not far from McGillians, where not only did they serve food and drinks but had live belly dancers swerving their hips and other essential female parts while you ate.

I remember telling our group that those guys were screwed if Skippy found out. It would be scandalous if a group of seminarians were to be seen gawking at belly dancers in downtown Philly. We on the other hand asked, "What could possibly go wrong at McGillians?" Lots of shit, that's what.

Ok, ground rules for being out on the town as a Roman Catholic seminarian: one, you had to go to a restaurant that served actual food. Stopping at a bar and eating peanuts or stale pretzels from a bowl did not constitute real food. Two, yes you could have a drink or two with your meal, but again, food had to be served with the drinks. Three, and probably the most important was that you had to be of age to drink. In Pennsylvania that meant you had to be 21 years of age or older.

I was the oldest of our group of five having just turned 20 on the last day of February. Thus, we had broken rule number three before the night began. I thought that we had the other two rules covered. No matter how you look at it, in baseball, if you get two hits in three at bats, you're batting .667! Heck, no one is perfect, right? Well this was not baseball, and we went zero for three.

We got to McGillians at 9:05 p.m. It smelt of Guinness, whiskey and cigarettes. An Irish band was playing ballads with lyrics about the Finnian's and the IRA. In one corner a few Irish lassies were doing a jig. 'Twas grand to see the opposite sex. Hey, we might have been celibate, but we were not dead. All of us were psyched! We had to be back in our dorm rooms by 11:30p.m. It was about a 30-minute drive from Center City Philly to the seminary. That gave us almost two hours to relax, eat, drink and enjoy a night of Irish music and dance. Pretty Irish lass came to take our order. Four cheesesteaks for the rest of us and a bowl of Irish stew for Mickey were what we wanted, two pitchers of beer and a couple pints of Guinness for me. She sadly shook her head and told us the kitchen closed at 9 o'clock sharp. She could bring us peanuts and stale pretzels. Are you kidding me?

We begged her to beg the chef to make an exception. Please tell him it's for a group of men studying for the priesthood. She shook her head and said, "No, he wouldn't even do it for the Pope."

"Why?" we asked.

"Because he's a 'fooking' Protestant," says she. Are you *fooking* kidding me?

Decision time. The mature thing to do was to get up and leave. We all looked around the table at one another. Mickey placed a five dollar bill in front of him. I did the same. The other three followed. As Ben Franklin once said, "If we are going to hang, we might as well hang together," or some such bullshit like that. Not too fooking bright or mature, eh?

We did get back to the seminary by 11:30 p.m. all pretty wasted. One of us, a great guy we named Tinker, did the unthinkable. Upon arriving back at the seminary we tried to sneak in a side door. This door led to a room called the refectory, Catholic terminology for cafeteria. As we approached the door, Tinker barfed. I mean he did the most prolific projectile vomit any of us had ever seen. He must have puked for ten minutes. That pristine snow now looked like two large piss holes in the snow. The rest of us just looked at one another and started laughing. We finally got Tinker into the showers, hosed him off and put him to bed. I signed us all in at 11:28 p.m. All was good…or so I thought.

Two days later, Skippy came to my dorm room.

He wanted to know if there was anything bothering me. Hell, no, I was feeling good. Then he lowered the boom. He discovered that a sewer pipe had not broken outside of the refectory and that the stench came from the foul vomit of a human being.

Tinker, who was a great guy, got the guilts and spilled the beans. However, he did not mention any of our names. He didn't have to. I had signed the five of us back in upon our return. I was the leader. I would pay the consequence. I played for our college basketball team and was suspended for the next two games we were to play.

The other four of my comrades got nothing...nada...zero...zilch...zip. In the words of Skippy, I had led them into sin! As I walked away from Skippy, I turned and asked him, "What about the guys who went to the Middle East Restaurant and gaped at belly dancers?" He told me although disappointed in their choice, they did indeed eat real food and none of them puked all over the seminary grounds. I guess their sin was venial, while mine was of the mortal category.

Tinker, Mickey and I eventually left the seminary. We stayed friends for many years. Tinker died in the late 1990's as a direct result of depression and possibly alcohol. He was a lawyer and was one of the kindest guys you could meet. At the end of his life, he did not believe he had that many friends who really cared about him. He felt alone. He felt rejected. At his funeral Mass, it was standing room only, at least five to six hundred people. He was indeed loved.

I was sober about a year at this time. After we put Tinker in the ground, friends were reminiscing back at his home. How could this good hearted, caring, loving, generous guy not believe or know he was loved? Not many in attendance could understand, but I could and did. Alcohol had done the same to me. We were unlovable. We could stand in a ballroom of 400 people and be alone. Sound familiar?

Another episode of trouble following me occurred in the Bayou State. The year was 1985. It was late March. The last vestiges of winter still remained above the Mason-Dixon Line. My first marriage had failed. I was single. I was alone. We were living on the Gulf Coast of Florida at the time. My ex-wife and kids had headed back to Pennsylvania. In recovery we talk about the time we believe we crossed the line from heavy drinking to alcoholism. This was my time. Those feelings of rejection and fear encompassed all I did.

I had a sales trip planned to Lafayette, Louisiana, ending in Baltimore on the same night. Lots of frequent flier mileage on this one. I had been to New Orleans several times and liked it, thus, liked the great state of Louisiana. Even though the climate up north was still cold, in this part of the south it was not. This was one of those sultry, humid days on the bayou; mosquitoes appeared as toy helicopters. As I neared the hospital where I was to work in Lafayette, I pulled my rental car into a gas station to fill up and get directions to my final destination.

Suddenly, a huge, burly, overweight dude walked out in overalls, chewing tobacco and approached my car. He starts waving his hands, which resemble paws on a grizzly, like he's waving cars entering the last lap of the Daytona 500. Thinking he wanted to ask me a question, I opened the car door, poked my head up and this monster of a man starts yelling shit at me I could not understand. I did hear a "fother mucker" in the middle of it with "Yankee" attached.

Now I may be a Yankee and not a good old southern boy, but I ain't stupid and I ain't slow. That was my cue. Got my body back in, shut the door threw on the auto-locks and pulled the hell out of there burning rubber. I felt as if I were in a Dukes of Hazzard episode without Daisy Duke anywhere nearby to rescue me. When I got to the hospital and explained what happened to the nurses I was working with, they just started to laugh out loud. Told me the guy at the gas station was speaking Cajun. His name is Lee. Yep, just like in Robert E. Lee and he does hate Yankees. They were surprised that he didn't have his shotgun out as he approached my car. I failed to see the humor.

I finished my work in Lafayette, stopped in Baton Rouge to see another client and afterwards headed to the airport in New Orleans. I had a couple of hours to kill, so I loaded up on some chicken gumbo and chased it down with a few Coronas and a shot or three of tequila. I then upgraded to first class and settled in on my next stop, Baltimore, Maryland. I was still trying to shake the experience I had with that confederate bastard Lee, minus his shotgun, when the stewardess asked me the most vital question of all, "Did I want a drink?" Duh?

Yet, due to the fact that Robert E. Lee almost made me crap my pants, I remember not wanting to drink as much. Not sure why; maybe it was just the sheer fear of losing my life at a gas station on a bayou in Lafayette. It is approximately a two and half-hour flight from New Orleans to BWI, the airport just outside of Baltimore's city limits. I did have a couple of pony bottles of red wine and then fell asleep. Thirty minutes prior to landing, the stewardess awakens me. I immediately feel ill. I mean deathly ill; stomach cramps, chills, nausea. Either I had bad gumbo or bad tequila. Got to the first class restroom, where I begin dating one of the "ria" sisters; Dia.

The aircraft lands and I wearily walk to baggage claim and then to the rental-car counter sick as a dog. Usually, I'm a pretty good raconteur with anyone I meet. On this night, I just wanted the car keys. The shuttle bus takes me to my car. I get off the bus, slip and almost break my ass. An ice storm has hit Baltimore. I am no longer on the bayou. You would think someone at the rental counter would have said something.

Long story, short…within minutes on the Baltimore-Washington Parkway I lost control of the car completely, and slid on the ice. I can still see the guard rail as I plow head on into it probably going about 35 miles an hour. This is 1985; no airbags. I do a header into the steering column which knocks me out for a minute or two. I hear banging on the passenger side window. A guy is asking me am I all right? Initially, I cannot hear a thing, then the fog clears and I nod yes, I'm ok. He asks if I want a ride somewhere since the front my car is severely damaged. Like any good alcoholic, I tell him, no, I'm ok but thanks. He shakes his head and walks away. By some miracle, the car starts; I put it in reverse, straighten it out and head north toward my hotel.

I still think I'm ok. Steam is coming from the damaged radiator where the front end is completely pushed in. With the car finally parked, I walk into the lobby of the hotel and the night clerk screamed. No shit, she screamed. My first reaction is to hit the floor thinking there is some sociopath behind me ready to attack. When I do the swan dive to the floor, she immediately stops screaming. She is now as stunned as I.

What happened? I was bleeding profusely from a gash in my forehead that eventually required stitches. There was blood everywhere.

My suit and shirt were ruined. I looked like one of Santa's elves on Christmas Eve. Color me red! The clerk now calmly wants to know what she can do. Get me a new body? She has a first aid kit. She says she'll call 911 and I nix that plan. I take some gauze and some bandages, get my room key and off I go to clean up. I spent the subsequent day in that hotel room in Baltimore after cancelling my sales appointment for that morning and slept for ten hours. The following day I called my boss and told him what had happened. In a very round-a-bout way he asked if I had been drinking when the car did the header into the guard rail. I lied and said no. After all, it was the ice that caused the accident not my drinking. That is how an alcoholic justifies their drinking. That is how I did it.

So, why tell these stories that appear totally unrelated, starring me, Mickey, Skippy and Lee? Trouble and booze. Booze and trouble. This is the odd couple that somehow cannot rid itself of its unwanted partner. For us who drank to excess, did we want the trouble that followed us, hell no? But could we put the equation together; booze + trouble = consequences? Hell no.

Trouble would continue to follow me throughout my drinking. Most of it I would categorize as troubles with a small "t." Some however were huge, with a capital "T" that rhymes with "B" and that stands for booze. But regardless of the size, I failed to grasp the concept that maybe alcohol was the one ingredient that was contained in all the troubles that followed me when I drank. Go figure.

CHAPTER 15

The Lie: "Even Bad Sex Is Good Sex"

This is a line I am sure you may have heard before. I was not sure what to name this chapter. Just naming it SEX, seemed pretty lame, but really it is a three letter word that could fill not only an entire library but the entire Internet. Come to think of it, it probably has done both of those already. Let's see all those raised hands of everyone who truthfully remembers drunken, debauchery, stoned sex? I thought so; not many at all.

Let us get one thing straight right up front. If you are reading this chapter hoping for some new insight into sex, the sex life, the sex life of human beings or how to have really, really, really good kinky, whips-and-chains sex; go to the next chapter. I, also, have no intention of attempting to be offensive to anyone; however, if harsh language bothers you, again, proceed to the next chapter for this one does have some limited cursing within it.

Lastly, I have no intention of discussing the deep psychology of Freud's Oedipus complex. I had enough problems having regular sex with other women than the thought of dwelling on my mom as a possible sex partner. That is just creepy to me. Ok, let us move on.

Honest to goodness alcoholics and drug addicts, when they are sober for a while, will tell you they know shit about sex. For me, it was just something that followed a good load if I was lucky enough to be with a woman who was similarly ripped on booze. We did not make love; we fucked, plain and simple.

Notice that words such as "love," "relationship," "accountability," "respect," "responsibility," "caring," and "intimacy" are missing. Those are the things that alcohol dismisses. There is no intimacy in drunken sex. Substitute the other words for intimacy and all rings true.

Did you ever notice that until Eve screwed up in the Garden of Eden, there is no mention of alcohol in the Bible? Sex is. The Lord instructs both Adam and Eve, "...to go forth and multiply." However, He does not say, "Down a half liter of Jack, then go forth and screw your brains out while in a blackout and deal with the consequences of pregnancy afterwards."

If you are a woman right now, you are starting to get pissed. But it is true; look it up. Ok, I'm just busting them for you, even if you really don't have them. We guys do and trust me, they get busted on a daily basis. See, even when we are kidding around about this topic, sex is filled with such dread. Not necessarily when we are having it with someone we love, but talking about it, discussing it, going to counseling about it, loving it, hating it and most of all fearing it. Even the pronoun I'm using to substitute for sex, "it," kind of speaks volumes.

As I stated much earlier, I learned about sex in the hood, on the streets of Olney. Notice I did not say I had sex on the streets of Olney.

Actually having sex happened down the Jersey shore, in

a college dorm (maybe) and later in many, many, numerous hotel rooms. But from the get go, alcohol was involved.

Remember, alcohol told me that I was handsome, charismatic, daring, funny, and insightful plus all the other bullshit that went with it. Think about it, everyone in my family, all of my friends and associates, my peers at school or at work, the pastor of my parish, my teachers from first through twelfth grades, my professors in college and graduate school; all of these people may have told me, that I was a good guy, a good person, a funny guy who made them laugh, that I was courteous and kind. Yet, the only "thing" I believed in was alcohol.

What does that say about me, that I would believe a non-entity, like booze, about my own self-worth over the people who loved and cared for me? Pretty sick, eh? Can you identify with any of this? Read on.

Sex and booze...booze and sex. For me, what comes immediately to mind is the one movie I could not see without being both stoned and drunk back in 1978, "Animal House." I had to see it wasted. Who wouldn't want to be part of Delta House?

In hindsight, now decades later, I think there are many who might decline the invitation, but not me, not in 1978. Don't get me wrong, even nerds like Flounder and Pinto wanted no parts of Delta House as the movie began. Heck, they were hoping to be accepted by any fraternity other than Delta.

However, once they were voted in, they loved it and

there was no turning back. Reflecting on this, I deem there is a little bit of Delta House in all of us; the Toga Party in each of us; singing "Shout" and doing the worm; making out with a beautiful person while getting totally shitfaced.

In AA meetings we call it romancing the drink. The problem with romancing the drink is that little or no thought from the drunken person goes into the consequences that follow the toga party. We do not see ourselves in front of Dean Wormer while he gives Bluto his new GPA after final exams, "Mr. Blutarski, zero point zero."

Then there is the moral implication of it all. Remember the scene where Larry, a.k.a. Pinto, wanted to screw the girl who had passed out in his bed. A devil and an angel appeared. Not meaning to be crude here, but the devil states the dark side in many of us, "F**k her, f**k her brains out."

The angel uses his real name and says, "Now, Lawrence, if you lay one hand on that poor sweet, helpless girl, you'll despise yourself forever."

He chooses the angel over the devil, good over evil. But as I remember it, he really wasn't that wasted yet. She was. She had passed out.

That's what I'm trying to say. I, as an alcoholic (albeit in recovery), can and will justify and rationalize my actions, especially when it comes to sex.

If Pinto had taken advantage of the girl, would any alcoholic have thought any less of him? The self-righteous, pharisaic side of me might say, "Well of course. She was out cold. He was wide awake." But what if he was really whacked, stoned, and we discovered that his family really never loved him or that his last girlfriend had cheated on him?

See, this is how alcoholics think. We are wired wrong. I am wired wrong. We could rationalize screwing the passed out girl because life hadn't been fair to us. Pretty sick, eh? And the worse part of it, we probably, along with the girl, would remember nothing of what happened; well maybe, maybe not. We'll come back to that.

Finally, we all know there is little or no moral salvation in "Animal House." Otter pretty much sums up the immoral certitude of this flick to Flounder, when his brother's car is totaled after a night out with girls from a local college and a visit to a black bar to see "Otis Day and the Knights"

"Flounder, you fucked up; you trusted us." In this movie, the "us" implied Otter, Bluto, D-Day, Boon, Pinto, Stork and the rest of the drunks in Delta. You cannot really trust a drunk, even a well-meaning drunk. Booze clouds the issue, any issue. Read the book of Genesis in the Bible and see what booze did to Noah.

I want to go back to a statement made above, that probably both the girl and Lawrence would remember nothing in the morning, if in fact they had drunken sex. In between marriages, I was single for about two years. It was during these years that I believed I crossed the line from heavy drinking to alcoholism. Each night I went out, I had two goals in mind—not proud of either—to get drunk and to get laid.

Sadly, I achieved both a great deal. And you know what; I awoke many a morning not remembering a whole lot, but was filled with feelings of shame, guilt and remorse. These are the big three you hear in AA meetings; shame, guilt and remorse. Why? I believe it is because booze can kill both the pain going on in my head and in my body for a period of time, but it cannot and will not kill my conscience.

Upon awakening, even coming out of a blackout, I know I did wrong. My moral compass does not sleep, does not get drunk, and does not black out. That friggin' angel is standing on my right shoulder saying, "Lawrence, now if you lay a hand on that poor, helpless girl…"

Booze and sex. Sex and booze; a true story. Upon entering the seminary, I was all of 18 years of age. The Roman Catholic Priesthood is a celibate life. It is true you do not take your vows of obedience and chastity, and thus celibacy, until ordination. However, on the last Sunday in October, all "new men" are presented with their Roman cassock and collar. Put those babies on and you know that no woman is getting inside that shit! Or so you hope.

A man has eight years to discern if the priesthood is for him and likewise the diocese does the same, making sure the man is fit for priesthood. The unwritten law is no fraternizing with the enemy—namely, women.

Now that does not mean that you cannot or should not have friends who are women. I had plenty in my two years that I attended seminary. Yet, there is a huge difference in having a woman as a friend and making out in a college dorm, waking up in an elevator with a girl draped over my body, not knowing if we had done the deed or not. That is what booze did. That is what booze and sex do.

The evening in question started out safe and simple. A couple of my buddies invited me to a local college dorm party in Philly. It was the Thanksgiving holiday season and we were allowed home for the first time since we entered the seminary in early September.

The leaves on the trees that lined City Line Avenue in Philly had turned and had lost most of their color; a hint of winter was in the air. I was looking forward to home, Mom and Sis, turkey, football and a visit with my boys from the corner.

We got home on Wednesday, the day before Thanksgiving, and had to be back in our dorms by 6 pm on Sunday night. Freedom!

I did not realize how much I missed my old corner buds. 'Twas good to see them. What I did not realize, when I arrived on this local college campus, was that this dorm party was probably the fifth or sixth one they had since the semester began. I in turn had never been to one. The closest we had to a party in the seminary occurred when one of the guys in the dorms burnt his balls on the radiator in the men's rooms when we hung his cassock out the window. It was December, near Christmas, when we did this. He limped into the dining hall that night, 200 guys in Roman black began solemnly to sing, "Chestnuts

Roasting on an Open Fire." True story.

In my mind's eye I remember seeing my boys as they introduced me to their friends, both men and women. They busted my chops upon the introduction telling them I was studying for the priesthood and someday wanted to be the first Irish American Pope.

Laughter ensued but I did not feel part of it. I felt alone in an instant. Who the hell in a real college dorm, at a keg party, wants to hang out with a pretend priest? No one; at least that is what I thought.

But the old equalizer was there; alcohol, my best friend. Driving over to this college, I knew I had to act a bit different than my "normal" brethren. They were attending a normal college, whatever that was. I, in turn, knew I represented more than just me. I was a representative of the Catholic Church whether I wanted to be or not. It was just a fact and I knew it.

The mature thing to do would have been to have a beer or two, make the rounds, say my goodbyes and head home to Mom and Sis and left-over turkey dinner.

If you have figured this one out, then you just might be a drunk like me, because alcoholics never have one or two beers. We drink until our goal is accomplished. The goal this night was to "extinguish the feelings of not feeling part of the celebration and to not feel alone and isolated."

To not feel, that was the goal. One of the guys we called Puck, like me, loved the Beatles. He put the album Abbey Road on this humongous stereo system. Truth be known, on this night, beer and Beatles would have been enough.

Drunk and singing "Here Comes the Sun," I'm in another stratosphere. Problem this night, I do have a good voice and sing a mean "Little Darlin'," the first lyrics of this great tune.

A young woman named Donna ventures over to where I am hanging on a wall just listening and singing to Lennon & McCartney. We chat. She asks me about the seminary and the priesthood and why would a good looking guy like me want to be a priest.

Not sure what I said and it doesn't matter. Whatever it was, she bought it. We started talking more, drinking and laughing more and enjoying one another's company. And then, BAM! There it was. The glow appeared. That switch in my head flipped. I was not just some dunce attending a non-normal college studying to be a priest. I was Gregory Peck in the motion picture *The Keys of the Kingdom*; I was Charlton Heston as Judah Ben Hur in the movie *Ben Hur*; and I was Charlton Heston as fucking Moses in the *Ten Commandments*! I was handsome, dynamic, charismatic and lovable.

Last thing I remember was listening with Donna to the end of Abbey Road when McCartney sings, "...and in the end, the love you take is equal to the love you make." We locked lips, sucking face attempting to drive our tongues into each other's respective lungs. She tasted great. I'm hoping I did too. Scene goes black. It is morning. We are in the elevator; she is draped across my body. We come to and untangle ourselves, put our clothes back on and into place, laugh a little, embarrassed a lot and head our separate ways. Never saw her again. I am alone...again.

I remember feeling so guilty that day and the next and the next, filled with shame and remorse. Got back to the seminary on Sunday night and immediately called my spiritual director, a priest, so he could hear my confession. I told him everything I could remember. We talked it out.

This good and holy priest forgave my sins in persona Christi, blessed me and gave me absolution. At the same time he was sad and disappointed in me. The look he had on his face when I got up to leave was the same look my mom had on hers those many years ago when I got thrown out of Cub Scouts. It was a look I would sadly see on his face again. And yes, those same feelings of shame, guilt and remorse were there clinging to me like lint.

I would like to be able to say that at least, while I was in the seminary, that that was the one and only time I succumbed to booze and sex. If I did say that, I would have to call the priest again and go to confession for it would be a lie...a huge lie.

It was not until I met my present and beautiful wife that I was actually able to have sex with a woman and not be drinking or be drunk. That is a true statement. I was still an active alcoholic at the time. We met in early 1986 and were married in 1987. I got sober in 1997. Ten years of drinking to go, but with her I never "needed" booze to make love...and that, I think, is the difference. I finally fell in "love" with someone who loved and still loves me. She will tell you about my "unlovable" feelings, meaning I feel unlovable. She is not an alcoholic, thus, the truth of this is beyond her understanding and that is okay. I have many brothers and sisters in sobriety that do understand me and that is enough.

In closing this chapter, I pray I have made my point.

In writing this book, this is definitely the most difficult subject to discuss. As smoothly as booze and sex appear to go together, the opposite is really true. Booze and sex are lethal for the alcoholic, functional or not. Together they will kill love. They will kill relationships. They will kill all that matters in life. They are lies.

Love on the other hand is truth. As Paul of Tarsus said a couple centuries ago to paraphrase, "The greatest of all gifts is love." I have never once heard anyone say, "I love making sex." To hear someone enunciate the phrase "to make love" says a lot.

With love there is "relationship," "accountability," "respect," "responsibility," "caring," and "intimacy."

Notice the words booze and sex are not listed here. Those two things are what love dismisses.

Jesus of Nazareth said, "You must love your neighbor as yourself." He is telling us that we must first love ourselves. Now that, to an alcoholic, makes no sense at all.

So, you got it, right?

Ok, these are the cliff notes; Animal House, Bluto, Dean Wormer, Otter, Flounder, D-Day, the Stork, Boon, Pinto, Adam, Eve, Noah, Donna, Puck, Lennon & McCartney, Abbey Road, Rocky Raccoon, Charlton Heston, Gregory Peck, Ben Hur, Moses, Paul of Tarsus, Jesus of Nazareth, booze, sex and love.

This topic will raise its head again in subsequent chapters. But for now, let us go forth and…Oh yeah, and just for the record, bad sex is bad sex.

CHAPTER 16

Funerals, Death and Booze

Subsequent to the topic of sex, death is possibly the next issue that alcoholics deal with most poorly, at least I did. I am not attempting to be redundant here, nor wanting to keep piling it on my old man, but his funeral was the first I remember and to this day it remains cemented in my memory. And to show you that I have come a long way, for this part of the epic, I will call him Dad.

He died on October 15, 1960, two months short of his 43rd birthday. He literally was here one day and gone the next. As told earlier, he died of a ruptured peptic ulcer, bleeding out, when surgeons could not stop his internal bleeding. Until she died in July of 2012, I know and believe my mom never fully recovered from that devastating night. Regardless of Dad's faults, he was her best friend and lover and all indications it was a "ditto" for him.

I know I've told you some bad stuff about my father, but you need to know some of the good, also. This is so unlike an active alcoholic. If I were still "out there" drinking, you would never know the good side of my Dad. Alcoholics place blame, well, speaking for myself, I blamed him for all that went awry in my life and in my stinkin' thinkin' he deserved it all. As with all things in life, reality has a way of bringing the needle on the blame scale back to center.

Here is what I know from my mom and remember about my Dad. He met Mom in the latter part of 1940 while he was on leave from the United States Army. For both of them, according to Mom, it was love at first sight. He actually told her that he would go AWOL, not go back to the Army, to be with her. Knowing that he would face the stockade and time in the brig, I think we can call that true love. Mom was the sensible one. She told him his first obligation was to the Army. This is prior to Pearl Harbor. He had been drafted and had to serve at least two years, unless we entered into war. We know how that turned out, eh?

They grew up near each other in the Kensington and Allegheny Avenues area of Philadelphia. In Philly lingo, they were K & A kids. Tough Irish environs back in their day. Their paths never crossed for one very major reason; Mom was an Irish Catholic and Dad was a Methodist.

Today, it is hard to believe that not so long ago race was not the only thing that separated people. Religion had its place in the internal battle between ethnic peoples.

My dad was both French and Irish. My mom was Irish and English. We all know the following; the Irish hate the English, the English hate the Irish, and everyone hates the bloody French. So the fact that my parents even met is saying a great deal. The fact that they eventually married on December 18, 1941, was indeed the miracle of miracles. At one time they called it a "mixed marriage" when a Catholic married a Protestant. Initially, when Dad proposed to Mom, she said "No."

When she told me this I was astounded. She told me she loved my Dad more than any other person she had ever encountered in life. But her faith, which was unshakable, meant more. He told her he would do anything, even become a Catholic. She did not think that fair to him. His faith was important to him, also.

After consulting with a pious and humble priest, it was agreed they could get married in the Catholic Church, in a ceremony in the rectory. My Dad had to agree that any children that blessed this marriage would be raised as Roman Catholic. He did not hesitate. When she told me of this, I thought that here were two people that fate or love had brought together; but in 1940, a mere 75 years ago, of all things, their religion could have kept them apart. As I noted in a previous chapter, love does trump all.

However, my Dad's family, especially his sister Cindy, wanted no part of my mom and according to family members I've encountered over many, many years, the only reason was the fact that Mom was an Irish mick; a papist; a Roman Catholic. Dad was one of four children. One had died in the 1930s, leaving him with a brother and sister. My Dad's parents and his brother attended the wedding. Cindy did not. It got worse.

My Dad shipped out in early 1942 to the South Pacific. Mom would not see him until after V-J Day which occurred in August 1945.

Cindy began writing letters to Dad telling him that my mom was a whore. That she was sleeping around with other men in the neighborhood, when in fact, she was working two jobs, and had gotten an apartment hoping for his imminent return if the war ended early.

She saved almost all she earned for a down payment on a home when he returned from war. My Dad's mother found out what Cindy was doing and put an end to it, but the damage to brother, sister, and sister-in-law relationship was severe. Mom said Dad never really forgave his sister and yet, Mom did (here is where my Dad and I would finally agree on something).

As also stated in a previous chapter, my Dad was a heroic guy. By the end of World War II, he had earned three Bronze Stars, two of which we believe were for valor. He had been promoted to Staff Sergeant for valor in the field of battle. He was a field artillery sergeant. His regiment accompanied the Marines on to all those foreign islands we read about in history class: the Solomon's, Bougainville, Guadalcanal, Iwo Jima, and toward the end, the recapture of the Philippines.

Sadly, while in the jungles of the South Pacific, he contracted malaria. While he eventually recovered enough to go back to his troops and into battle, the symptoms of malaria—the sweats, fever, blackouts and the nightmares—never left him. His death certificate stated that he died of a ruptured peptic ulcer. In truth he died of post-traumatic stress disorder (PTSD). The GI's of that era were never treated for this as they are today.

Dad was a good provider for us. He had his own business as a building contractor. He took some risks in business that did not pan out, others did. We were living in a new home when he died in 1960. Other things I discovered about my Dad: he was a really funny guy, he was musically talented and played the guitar and sang, he was a tremendous athlete, and he loved to laugh.

Sounds like someone with whom I might want to be friends. At my Dad's mother's funeral a couple of old dudes came running over to me as we stood outside the church. I knew none of these men. Most were vets, friends of Dad who also had a great deal of respect for my grandmother. I was 21 years of age when my grandmother passed. They took one look at me and said, "You are George's son, look and built just like him."

They shared some stories. One in particular I still remember. They told me that when my Dad was in a bar having a beer with friends after work, if a woman happened to be within earshot of some drunk swearing and using foul language, my Dad would proceed to clean the floor with the dumb shit or literally send the drunk to his next dental appointment. He would not tolerate cursing around a woman. Chivalry was part of his makeup. I could admire that, not the beating up part, but the chivalry part.

Going back to us kids, he made sure that my sister and I went to Mass every Sunday in our Catholic parish. He was there for every sacrament we received. The last sacrament I received was the sacrament of Confirmation on October 14, 1960. After the Mass, he asked if I wanted to go to work with him. If you remember, that had not happened since I pissed all over him two years prior. For whatever reason, although still fearing him from the beating he administered to me six months prior, I said yes.

I can still visualize him that day in the back of the church. I still remember driving in his truck, riding shotgun, like I had done before. Although it was mid-October the weather was fair. We stopped for lunch. I can still see him vomiting his lunch up on the side of the road; he was obviously not feeling well. I had never really seen him so vulnerable.

I recall going over to him as he was bent over, rubbing his back and telling him that he'd be ok. He looked up at me and nodded. That is the last I truly remember of my Dad alive, the last time I looked into his eyes. Several hours later he died at 4 a.m. on October 15, 1960 in the same hospital where I was born.

I recall the wake the night prior to the funeral. I can see me looking down into the casket at my dead father. I honestly do not remember crying, then or until a couple of years later. Not sure why. Men with whom he had shared the field of battle told me that night that Dad was a hero. That he had saved lives in those jungles in the South Pacific a mere 16 years before. Two other men shook my hand and said they would both be dead if not for my Dad; one was an army grunt like Dad, the other a Marine.

The day of the funeral remains fixated in memory. Torrential rain enveloped the city of Philadelphia. It was as if tears were being shed for Dad from above; they were never ending.

My Uncle Jack and Aunt Linda (Mom's sister) had taken care of Sis and me for the last couple of days. Now we were reunited with Mom. She could not stop the tears. They were endless. I can still hear her deep, heartfelt sobs, even now 55 years later. We drove in a limo behind the hearse. He was to be interred at Beverly National Cemetery in New Jersey with full military honors; 21 gun salute and the playing of "Taps."

As they lowered him into the ground, I can still picture clearly my mom, literally, attempting to jump onto the coffin and being restrained by her brothers. Her heart was being ripped from her chest. Was there ever such a broken heart? I have never witnessed one since that fateful day. They handed Mom my Dad's flag as "Taps" began. She held that flag to her face, inhaling the last bit of God's creation that had touched my Dad, or at least had touched his coffin.

Two years later, in December 1962, I was selling programs at the Army-Navy football game in Philadelphia at Municipal Stadium. The father of a buddy of mine ran the stadium. He got both of us jobs selling programs. President John F. Kennedy was in attendance that day. Someone had pointed him out to me. Said he fought in World War II in the South Pacific on something called a PT boat. Less than a year later, he would be assassinated in Dallas, Texas. Mom and I watched that funeral along with the rest of a mournful nation. I had not cried since my Dad was planted in Beverly two years before.

The scene in Arlington on television was touching and

vaguely familiar. It was an overcast and rainy day. I still remember seeing the rider-less horse following the caisson that carried our dead president's body. Somberly walking with Mrs. Kennedy were her two brothers-in-law, Bobby and Ted. Toward the end of the service they showed the military honor guard, the 21 gun salute and then I heard the playing of "Taps." It was then that I finally cried for my Dad. To this day, I am still moved to tears whenever I hear it played, remembering the man—the hero, the provider, the father and loving husband. Yes, he was flawed, but he was my Dad. I think all I really wanted from him was his love and approval. Outside of one calamitous incident that I can remember, in his own way, he gave that to me. Even alcohol could not take that away.

The next funeral I recall attending was that of one of the guys from our corner in Olney. We called him Fred, a nickname. It was somewhere around 1980 when Fred died of cancer. I was 28 years old. He had only been married a short time. It was summer. I had been barbequing in our backyard, slamming down some beers, dreading going to the wake. When I felt somewhat numb, but decent enough to drive, I headed down to Philly by myself. I had not seen most of the guys for a few years. Shit, ten years before we were brothers down at the Jersey shore toasting the world with booze, singing tunes from Woodstock and feeling invincible. Fred was with us ten years ago, as invincible as the rest. Today he was dead.

When I arrived at the wake, some of the guys greeted me with warmth, others just waved as if we were distant cousins from another planet. I still remember as I went up to the casket, paid my respects to Fred, shook his wife's hand and said how sorry I was, someone near the waiting line asked did they think that I had been drinking. I heard it and dismissed it. Fuck them.

They could handle death in their way, I would handle it mine. The one corner brother who gave me an old bear hug was Mickey. He was married, too, having left the seminary in 1976. He arrived at Fred's wake by himself, also. After paying our respects to family and friends, Mickey and I departed. Where did we go? Harry's Saloon, a corner neighborhood taproom, where we proceeded to slam down beer and shots, saluted Fred, and attempted to remember happier days.

The rest is a blur. Alcohol killed the feelings of death and dying that had penetrated my being and for this I was grateful. Driving home numb, I failed to remember happier days. I was surrounded by death and hated it. I could still hear them playing "Taps" at my Dad's funeral.

Later in 1980, in December to be exact, another death shook me to my core, along with the rest of us Baby Boomers and former hippie-type people. One of the Fab Four, my favorite Beatle John Lennon was shot to death by a deranged Mark David Chapman. I had been working in Washington, DC on December 8th, a Monday.

I had stopped at my local watering hole at the time in DC, a place called the Apple Tree. The famous and sometimes infamous Howard Cosell was announcing the Monday Night Football game between the Patriots and the

Miami Dolphins. He was the first to break the story. Shock waves tore through the Apple Tree. It was the first time in memory that everyone shouted to turn off the game and get some news on the television.

I was sitting next to a woman at the bar smoking a Marlboro Red. She began crying, and I consoled her. I bought her a drink and another for me and proceeded to do this for the next two hours. She loved Lennon as much as I did.

I could tell she wasn't bullshitting because she talked of the split with Paul, the marriage to Yoko Ono, and the music of John and the Plastic Ono Band. The bartender had Walter Cronkite on the television. Volume was maxed out. We could hear it all. The scene was in front of Lennon's apartment complex, the Dakota.

Hundreds of people were milling about with candles lit, singing Lennon's anthem, "Give Peace a Chance."

There was no playing of the "Taps" this time around, but I cried when I heard "Give Peace a Chance." In my drunken state, which had turned to emotional rage, I was asking God, "How the hell can you let some peace loving man like John Lennon die at the hands of a deranged maniac while Muammar Gaddafi, the nut job of them all, was senselessly killing people by the thousands in Libya?" Never got an answer on that one.

I left the bar in the early morning hours of December 9th from the Apple Tree with that woman. We were both drunk, but over the last hour I had started downing some coffee, knowing I had an early start the next day.

She asked me to follow her home for safety. Being chivalrous, I agreed. I remember standing in front of a huge, old Tudor that night. She invited me in. To my shock, there was no furniture in the entire house. Now I was drunk, but not that drunk.

I asked her where the bathroom was located.

I locked the door, turned on the faucet and threw ice cold water on my face numerous times shaking the cobwebs out. This was a setup; she was the bait and I was the prey.

Fortunately, I am six feet-two inches tall and at that time weighed a solid 190 pounds. I burst through the bathroom door to the complete and utter shock of this broad and now some guy who was with her. Street smarts kick in. I went directly for him and punched him in the throat as hard as I could. Clean hit. He went down. Pushed her aside and I was out the front door, down the steps and heading east toward the Capitol Building where I had parked my car. No recollection of anything else.

I awoke and put the morning news on hoping that the night before was nothing but a nightmare, a very bad dream. It was all true. John Lennon at age 40 was dead. I cancelled my sales appointments for the day. I had to mourn and grieve and drink. I did all three. I possessed every Beatles album and that of the Plastic Ono Band. A case of Guinness did the trick.

I called Stretch midday on the 9th of December but did not get an answer. I could only assume he would be doing as I was, killing the pain of Lennon's death. The call of alcohol was strong. It was my healer. I was alone. So I drank.

Now you might ask, what about the woman and the guy and the punch in the throat? I can only say now, being an alcoholic in recovery that the risk to life and limb which was obviously present on that night in that home, meant absolutely nothing. In an inebriated state, I absolutely was not thinking that anything bad could happen. I was just walking a woman home who shared an evening over drinks, mourning the death of John.

The reality of it could have been very bad if it had played out as this woman and her comrade had planned.

Once again this caring God, whom I was cursing a few hours before, pulled me from alcohol's throws to safety; little children and drunks. He loves us.

CHAPTER 17

Epiphany

I mentioned in the beginning of this epic that I decisively ascertained I was an alcoholic upon purchasing the book, ***Drinking: A Love Story*** by Caroline Knapp after taking the same quiz that she did. I am about to present that epiphany.

If you have been reading and are still wondering if you are an alcoholic or not, please pay attention. You may or may not get another shot at this; meaning a sober life.

Ok, here are the 26 questions with my answers put forth by the National Council on Alcoholism and Drug Dependency (the NCADD).vi It was quite apropos that I had poured a glass of wine as I sat down to take this quiz. Read each carefully and if you truly and emphatically want to know the truth, YOU MUST ANSWER THESE TRUTHFULLY. Go figure!

1. Do you drink heavily when you are disappointed, under pressure or have had a quarrel with someone? YES

2. Can you handle more alcohol now than when you first started to drink? YES

3. Have you ever been unable to remember part of the previous evening, even though your friends say you didn't pass out? YES

4. When drinking with other people, do you try to have a few extra drinks when others won't know about it? YES

5. Do you sometimes feel uncomfortable if alcohol is not available? YES

6. Are you more in a hurry to get your first drink of the day than you used to be? YES

7. Do you sometimes feel a little guilty about your drinking? YES

8. Has a family member or close friend expressed concern or complained about your drinking? NO

9. Have you been having more memory "blackouts" recently? YES

10. Do you often want to continue drinking after your friends say they've had enough? YES

11. Do you usually have a reason for the occasions when you drink heavily? YES

12. When you're sober, do you sometimes regret things you did or said while drinking? YES

13. Have you tried switching brands or drinks, or following different plans to control your drinking? YES

14. Have you sometimes failed to keep promises you made to yourself about controlling or cutting down on your drinking? YES

15. Have you ever had a DWI (driving while intoxicated) or DUI (driving under the influence)? NO

16. Do you try to avoid family or close friends while you are drinking? NO

17. Are you having more financial, work, school, and/or family problems as a result of your drinking? NO

18. Has your physician ever advised you to cut down on your drinking? NO

19. Do you eat very little or irregularly during the periods when you are drinking? YES

20. Do you sometimes have the "shakes" in the morning and find that it helps to have a "little" drink, tranquilizer or medication of some kind? NO

21. Have you recently noticed that you can't drink as much as you used to? YES

22. Do you sometimes stay drunk for several days at a time? NO

23. After periods of drinking do you sometimes see or hear things that aren't there? NO

24. Have you ever gone to anyone for help about your drinking? NO

25. Do you ever feel depressed or anxious before, during or after periods of heavy drinking? YES

26. Have any of your blood relatives ever had a problem with alcohol? YES

You, yourself, can take this quiz online at the NCADD website. I scored a "17" out of a possible 26.

My first reaction was, *"Well, I'm really not that fucked up."* A typical alcoholic response, by the way. Here is what the NCADD has to say about my score.

Understanding Your Score:

A "no" is scored 0, and a "yes" is scored 1. The score above reflects the total number of questions that were answered "yes." A score of 2 or more indicates that you may be at greater risk for alcoholism.

If you answered "yes" to between 2 and 8 questions, you should consider arranging a personal meeting with a professional who has experience in the evaluation of alcohol problems. You should consider contacting the NCADD affiliate office nearest to you. A representative will be happy to assist you in the scheduling of a professional evaluation.

If you answered "yes" to more than 8 questions, you may have a serious level of alcohol-related problems requiring immediate attention and possible treatment. You should seek professional guidance. You should consider contacting the NCADD affiliate office nearest to you. A representative will be happy to assist you in the scheduling of a professional evaluation.

I italicized with bold print the part that my eyes zeroed in when I visited their website.

I was sitting on our small deck at our condo at the Jersey Shore while reading this. It was now roughly 7 p.m. I had poured myself a glass of cabernet sauvignon prior to sitting down. Although it was August, there was a slight chill in the salty ocean breeze. I had been enthralled by this woman's story. I recall nodding my head at certain points, as if I were saying, "Right, I can understand that." Or "Shit, that is how I drank!" And then in Chapter 8, the quiz, appeared.

I named this chapter "Epiphany" because at last I became aware. Dictionary.com defines epiphany as: a sudden, intuitive perception of or insight into the reality or essential meaning of something usually initiated by some simple, homely, or commonplace occurrence or experience.vii The commonplace occurrence was this simple quiz. I was alone at the time. My wife had gone to the food store. This was actually one time in my life I wanted to be alone.

I could not read another word. I was in shock. I had no saliva in my mouth. I started pacing around our condo not knowing what to do with this new-found knowledge, this epiphany that might have consequences beyond my understanding. "How the hell could I be an alcoholic?" I repeated this line over and over and over again.

With the temperature hovering around the upper 50s, I grabbed a beach towel, my rosary beads, a wind breaker and baseball hat and jogged down to the beach. Left behind was my final glass of wine, untouched.

In my mind's eye (and ear) I can see the ocean. It was one of those weird evenings when the ocean temperature appeared actually higher than the air temperature. I dropped down onto the beach towel. I tried to think and could not. I tried to pray, same result. Closing my eyes, I attempted to rid my mind of all the junk that was now permeating it through and through. Trying to calm myself, I discovered I could focus on one thing. Thank the Lord for the gift of hearing. I zeroed in on the sound of the pounding surf as it noisily attacked the sandy beach and then retreated back in silence. What do I do now?

It appears this chapter is appropriate for citing some alarming statistics regarding the disease and abuse of alcohol. The National Institute of Health (NIH) cites: Nearly 88,000 people (approximately 62,000 men and 26,000 women) die from alcohol related causes annually, making it the third leading preventable cause of death in the United States. In 2012, alcohol-impaired-driving fatalities accounted for 10,322 deaths (31 percent of overall driving fatalities).viii The economic burden directly related to the ingestion of alcohol is stunning. In 2006, alcohol misuse problems cost the United States $223.5 billion. Almost three-quarters of the total cost of alcohol misuse is related to binge drinking.ix

The study's findings were limited because it examined data from only 17 states and because blood alcohol measurements were available for only 70 percent of those who committed suicide in those states. Still, about one-third (33%) of those tested had some level of alcohol in their bloodstream at death the researchers found.

Here are more startling facts from the NCADD: 5.3 million adults – 36% of those under correctional supervision at the time – were drinking at the time of their conviction offense

Excessive drinking leads to criminal behavior:

The US Department of Justice (DOJ) estimated that a majority (>50%) of criminal offenders were under the influence of alcohol alone when they committed their crimes.

Federal research shows that for the 40% of convicted murderers being held in either jail or State prison, alcohol use was a factor in the homicide.

Alcohol is a factor in 40% of all violent crimes today: about 3 million violent crimes occur each year in which victims perceive the offender to have been drinking. Crimes include: rape, sexual assault, and robbery, aggravated and simple assault. About two-thirds of violent crimes are characterized as simple assaults.

Based on victim reports, alcohol use by the offender was a factor in:

37% of rapes and sexual assaults

15% of robberies

27% of aggravated assaults, and

25% of simple assaultsx

Lastly: Among all cirrhosis deaths in 2009, 48.2 percent were alcohol related. The proportion of alcohol-related cirrhosis was highest (70.6 percent) among decedents ages 35–44. In 2009, alcohol-related liver disease was the primary cause of almost 1 in 3 liver transplants in the United States. Alcohol has also been identified as a risk factor for the following types of cancer: mouth, esophagus, pharynx, larynx, liver, and breast.xi

In her book, Caroline Knapp says some pretty profound things in the chapter titled, "Addiction." Let me share them. "Normal drinkers seem to have a kind of built-in alarm system that tells them at a certain point to stop drinking. They ingest alcohol; it passes through the stomach walls and small intestine and into the bloodstream, then moves through cell membranes and mixes in the entire water content of the body: brain, liver, heart, pancreas, lungs, kidneys and every other organ and tissue system are affected. Alcohol basically depresses the central nervous system…at first alcohol increases blood flow, accelerates the heart rate, and stimulates brain cells, all of which make the drinker feel giddy, talkative and energetic. At higher doses the depressive effects are felt: the drinker gets uncoordinated; vision may be impaired; reflexes are delayed; speech gets slurred. The normal drinker usually calls it quits well before that point: that elusive internal alarm goes off and says, "No more."xii

I, and millions like me, do not possess that internal alarm. As I mentioned in an earlier chapter, we alcoholics do not hear the warning, "Danger, danger, Will Robinson…"

And pray tell, what do we call this malfunction? Alcoholism, plain and simple. Got it?

CHAPTER 18

I Am Unlovable

Throughout my many years attending AA meetings another theme permeates the rooms of sobriety. In order to keep it simple, I will simply tell you that through 29 years of drinking and, as you have seen well before that, I never *felt* loved. Why? Because I *felt* unlovable. I have highlighted the word felt, because in the rooms we learn that "feelings are not facts."

"Huh?" you might be asking. Bear with me on this.

Remember the story about my eighth grade graduation? Now seen through my eyes as a 13 year old and then as an active alcoholic, there is no way that my mom, Sis, Uncle Jack or Aunt Linda truly loved me or they would have been there. My Dad obviously did not love me because he died on me. That is how alcoholics think. That is how I think. Hopefully, in reading this, you know right darn well, as do I, that all of those people loved me. The degree of that love was probably different depending on their relationship with me at that time in 1966, but they still loved me. Feelings are not facts.

Alcoholism is about addiction. Whether you ingested alcohol or drugs in order to escape reality on a continual basis, I, and maybe you, were or are addicted. We have addictive personalities. I have met thousands of alcoholics in my sober lifetime and when you talk about having addictive personalities, 99.9% nod in affirmation. I loved alcohol and became obsessed about it. At one time, I was addicted to cigarettes; chain smoked those Marlboro Reds one after another. We alcoholics do nothing in moderation, good or bad. People who get sober and put down the drink usually discover their other addictions; could be food, sex, gambling, ice cream (my favorite addiction), garlic bread, broccoli, pizza, popcorn, the Internet or the cell phone. However, to keep on topic, most alkies are addicted to love, or more succinctly, addicted to the feeling of being loved.

I was at meeting where a woman named Dee raised her hand and told everyone in the room that she relapsed two weeks prior. She is divorced and has three children who live with her. She was so gut wrenching emotional we could all feel her pain. She had been sober for a year and a half and picked up. Why? In her words, "...because I needed to be loved. I became addicted to this man's need for me! By fulfilling his need sexually, I thought he loved me. He then broke off the relationship, if it ever was one, and I was left with nothing. Alone. I drove to a beer distributor knowing what I was doing was wrong and stupid. Three hours later I was passed out on the floor of my kitchen, lying in the middle of broken beer bottles, with my young daughter standing over me, crying hysterically, and thinking I had died."

Another guy named Norman has been in the rooms of sobriety as long as I have.

I saw him a year ago at a meeting and he was still

attempting to get six months sober. The most he ever had was a year. Norm had to have had a new girlfriend every three to six months; his addiction, the fear of being alone and desperately wanting to be loved by anyone. His sponsor would tell him that until he felt comfortable in his own skin and in the words of Jesus of Nazareth, "...love your neighbor as yourself," that he would continue to relapse and pick up the next drink. This quote of Jesus connotes that you first must love yourself. Active alcoholics do not love themselves. Currently, at this point in my sobriety, I can honestly say that "I like myself." On a really good day I can use the word love in that sentence. But it is a huge step for this alcoholic to even say that I like myself.

Here is another saying in the rooms that brings a chuckle and nods of affirmation, "While drinking, I was an egomaniac with an inferiority complex." I related to this immediately. How I would sit on a barstool and pontificate about all that was wrong with the world, our country, politics, religion, the school system, and health insurance, the NFL, Saturday Night Live, Comcast, Verizon and AT&T and conclude that they were all out to screw us! God, I was one knowledgeable son of a bitch...the great I am!

However, when I departed the barstool and was driving home, I could only think what a dick I was in most of the declarations I had just made.

That the people sitting with me really did not like me and truth be known they probably knew more about those subjects than I ever would. Plus, I knew when I got home that the wife, kids and even the dog would most likely shun me.

On top of that, I had a shitty day at work; the boss looked at me crooked and probably wishes he had never hired me. What a piece of shit I am.

THIS IS HOW AN ALCOHOLIC THINKS, at least *this* alcoholic.

This, in turn, is followed by another great AA cliché, "I ain't much, but I'm all I think about." First time I heard this I laughed out loud as did many others at the meeting. Active alcoholics are self-absorbed. I could not envision this until I had about six months of sober time. Shit, I worked like a dog to provide for my family; beautiful home, two cars, always paid the bills on time, took the family on great vacations, blah, blah and blah. Notice I never used the word love in that sentence. It was what I did and the things I provided that showed the world how great I was.

Meanwhile, all my wife and kids ever wanted from me was for me to love them completely. As an active alcoholic this was impossible. I was narcissistic. It was all about me. They should love me for the things I provided for them. How sick does that sound?

I will end this chapter with one of my favorite stories. I was attending a meeting, in the early days, on a Saturday morning in the ugly green room, where once in a while we would see a stiff who had died the night before resting outside the morgue.

It was a speaker meeting. In early sobriety, these are the best kind of meetings. You hear everyone else's bullshit story, the drunk-a-logs, the drama and what it is like now that they are sober. Well on this Saturday morning a woman named Elsa was the speaker. I did not know her. She wasn't all that pleasing to look at: old broad, thick glasses, shaking because she was nervous and did not like to speak in public. I had already prejudged her. There is nothing this old, blind broad could tell me that would make me feel any better today. Again, it was all about me!

Then, in the middle of her talk she said these words that have stuck to me to this day. With a voice that was trembling and filled with emotion a minute ago, in a loud, clear, succinct tone she said, "God doesn't make junk." Wham! Right across the bow! I don't think I heard anything for the rest of her story or for the sharing part of that meeting. I do remember going over to Elsa after the meeting and hugging her, thanking her for her message. Today she is my friend.

Now remember, the great "I am" was once studying for the priesthood and had aspirations to be Pope. As a young kid in Catholic grammar school, it was drilled into us by those good nuns that we were all made in the image and likeness of God. The great Thomas Jefferson infers this very thing in the Declaration of Independence, "...that all men are created equal." Created by God! So, if I truly believe that I was created in God's image and that all of us are equal in God's eyes, then logically it follows, "That I am lovable." Go figure!

I had spent so much of my life blaming others, being totally self-absorbed, worrying what others thought of me, attempting to be loved while feeling unlovable, that I had to ask myself could it really be this easy? Yes, I was indeed lovable. How do I know this? "God doesn't make junk."

Maybe, someone is really there.

CHAPTER 19

The Chameleon

This may be the most distressing to describe. In between marriages I became a chameleon. Now to call a chameleon a chameleon is not an insult. Call a human a chameleon…well I'm sure you get the drift, nothing but bad connotations. Usually, at an AA meeting, when this term is used, just about everyone knows what you mean. Let me get to it.

I was in New Orleans in 1985 at a medical convention. When the sun sets in the French Quarter, Bourbon Street turns into a magical kingdom.

The first things that attack your senses are the noise, music and the smell of booze. For an alcoholic, this is sheer nirvana. People are dancing in the streets. Some are hanging over balconies enticing the drinker to come upstairs for whatever they are selling upstairs.

A lone jazz musician might be camped under a lamp post playing the blues, serenading the crowd with his saxophone. On the next corner, an amateur magician is picking quarters out of little children's ears or a juggler is displaying his talents keeping five eggs in the air at once.

Opposite him might be a child no older than ten shining shoes for a couple of bucks. Many revelers are carrying their drink in hand (the Hurricane is the most famous of drinks, hopefully purchased at O'Brien's, where else?) and simply people watching. I discovered New Orleans to be the one city where being a chameleon was ok.

Now the dining experience in New Orleans is second only to that of San Francisco, in my humble opinion. Each time I visited the city I made sure I had a reservation, for at least one dinner, at the Louis XIV Restaurant in the Quarter. I understand it is now sadly closed. The French chef there created the most delicious Beef Wellington Chateaubriand ever served. It was a food group unto itself. I mention this, for this is how I began most evenings in the city, at a great restaurant.

The company was picking up the tab, so why eat at Mickey D's or Taco Bell? Usually, at dinner I would be with other sales reps reveling in the joy of the night to come.

Wine flowed freely, Guinness was available and the proverbial single malt scotch set it all on fire!

As the dessert order was being taken, I would usually leave cash with whomever was in charge of the bill and depart. In this city I wanted to drink alone. The bars off of Bourbon Street were usually quieter and a nicer clientele could be found. I went where I knew my peers in the company would not. They would stay on the Street, go into karaoke bars and sing the night away. Me, I preferred a good jazz or blues bar.

Into the pub I would venture, belly up to the bar and order a tumbler of scotch on the rocks in the best Irish accent you ever heard. The chameleon had appeared. On this night my name was Sean and I was from fookin'

Dooblin, blessed be Jesus! Bartenders and women cater more kindly to foreigners than to someone from Philly or New York. God forbid if I would ever let a woman know or be with the real me, for she would surely be disappointed. Remember the egomaniac with the inferiority complex? Thus, by night's end, I was sharing my travels with a pretty lass from Buffalo, New York, who was astounded that she was in the presence of this saintly Irish lad, Sean. Inevitably, we departed from the bar drunk and ventured to one of our hotel rooms. On this night, I am pretty sure we ended up in her room.

Hopefully, we made passionate love, but I doubt it for we both shared a doobie on top of the drinks we had and were quite stoned. The astounding thing was that for a period of four or five hours I spoke with a coherent Irish accent. Then morning came. I woke up first and began quietly gathering my things.

Coming out of a blackout is like the KO punch thrown from Muhammed Ali over George Foreman, you know you're alive, you're just not sure what planet you are on or what your name is. Then, in the darkness of the room, I hear a feminine voice say to me, "Hello, are you leaving?" And here is the kicker, in a cockney, British accent sounding like George Harrison from Liverpool, "That right, love. Sorry to 'ave awoken you. I just got out of the loo."

And she says, "I thought you were Sean, from Dublin." I reply, "Not sure who I am, but I'm off." And I was gone. Now, what normal friggin' person does that?

That is where alcohol took me.

Think about it. I had nothing to hide. I was single. I wasn't cheating on a spouse.

Yet, my self-esteem and self-worth were so low that I could not comprehend or believe for a minute that this woman or any other woman at that time would like me just for me.

Another time during this somewhat tragic and humorous time when I was single, I found myself working in Scituate, Massachusetts. Scituate actually sits on the water, on the east coast of the state. If you have seen the movie, "The Perfect Storm" that is about fishermen from Gloucester, Massachusetts, you can get a feel for Scituate. It had me at the sound of the gulls and the smell of the salt air.

I was a sales trainer at the time, educating a new sales rep on how our products worked. By 5:05 p.m. we were sitting in an establishment I believed was called the Grog Shop or something to that effect. It was a Pub where commercial fisherman frequented when they came ashore. It might have been blown out to sea by now, wasn't much to look at, but the lobster, clams and beer were fookin' good.

On this night it was packed. Two ships had come in so lots of fishermen and local women were stacked four deep around the bar. It was exciting. The tones of Boston/New England accents filled the air. "Give me some fuckin' chowda," someone would scream. "I want anodda beah" yelled someone three deep over my shoulder.

This was fun. The guy I was training, Billy, had a beer or two and left for home. I was laying over in a hotel within walking distance. I stayed. On this night, the chameleon, decided to be Gary Piccolo, a distant cousin of the famous Brian Piccolo, the star Wake Forest halfback who was drafted and played for the Chicago Bears and the subject of the great football movie, "Brian's Song."

Now if you are going to be related to someone famous, you better know something about that famous person. Immediately, one of these rough and tumble fisher-dudes asks me his million-dollar-am-I-bull-shitting him questions, "Where was Brian Piccolo from?" I grab for this guy's calloused and foul smelling, Charlie the Tuna right hand, shake it and say, "My cousin was born in Pittsfield, Massachusetts, on the other side of the state. Dad and Mom were named, Joe and Irene." This guy's eyes light up in instant recognition of the city and names.

I don't think I bought another drink for the rest of the night. When I was finished with one Guinness, another magically appeared. A few local women appeared interested in meeting me, but being a pretty smart street kid from Philly, I believed it best to stay on good behavior. If I hit on the wrong woman, I just might end up in the "ha-bah" (harbor) with a fish hook in my back.

Again, I ask you, would a normal person do anything like this? Fortunately, this phase of my drinking disappeared in 1986 when I met my present wife. As mentioned before, here is a woman who actually loves me just for being me. The chameleon was dead. Go figure.

CHAPTER 20

Signs & Red Flags

I need to restate something, especially for the reader who has this epic memoir in hand and thinks they are functional when drinking or drugging. Remember, no one and I mean no one ever told me I drank too much or that I was an alcoholic and needed to go to AA.

However, if I had read the signs and believed some of the red flags I observed, I might have saved myself a few years actively drinking and a lot of heartache. I mentioned earlier that by the early 1990s I started to feel something was wrong. Here is how it started.

It was summertime and once again my wife, I and our five kids were in Stone Harbor, New Jersey, for a week's vacation. We rented a nice cottage on the bay, so we could continue a tradition I started years before of catching crabs off the back pier of the cottage. Catch enough Jersey blue crabs, throw some veggies in a steamer, add some garlic bread and a couple of bottles of chilled chardonnay wine and you are on your way to Cape May and beyond.

As a kid I loved going to the shore and I wanted my kids to love it, too. After my dad died, my widowed Mom scraped, and I mean scraped, enough money for us to spend a week at the beach every summer. Funny thing, she hated the sand at the shore, detested it. So she would sit on the boardwalk, read a book while Sis and I and a friend or two would be on the beach somewhere within earshot and eyeshot of where she was sitting.

I think what still thrills me occurs when we come off the Garden State Parkway and enter the barrier island where we're vacationing, be it Ocean City, Avalon, Wildwood, Sea Isle, Stone Harbor or Cape May. The smell of salt air attacks the senses. I then invariably hear the lone cry of a sea gull and I know we are close. God it's exciting! I love it!

This cottage had an outdoor eating area in close proximity to the pier by the water where we set up our crab nets. The venue was majestic: sun was setting in the west over the bay, the cumulus clouds in the heavens were colored with a soft tinge of red and the sky was still a deep blue as the afternoon slipped toward dusk.

As the seven of us sat down for dinner, my eldest daughter asked, "Dad, why do you always have a bottle of wine in front of you at the dinner table?" She was 15. I was not expecting a question like this, obviously. So I mumbled something about not having to run back and forth into the house to refill a glass of wine. She seemed to buy it. I, on the other hand, did not. I know my daughter had no ulterior motive in the question. She's just inquisitive by nature. My wife was sitting there with her glass of wine, and I was sitting there with a bottle of wine. Call this the first shot across my bow.

I still remember not drinking much that night. We went to the beach next day, ready for five or six hours of glorious sun, heat and a frolic or two in the Atlantic Ocean with my kids. I became restless, which is not normal for me on a beach. After an hour or two, I told my wife I was going to head back to the cottage and walk into town.

The walk into town took me to the steps of St. Paul's Catholic Church. At first I hesitated; then I went inside, knelt down and tried to pray. My spiritual life at this time was pretty weak—honestly it sucked. I was doing the bare minimum, going to Mass on Sundays. I had not been to confession in a few years. My prayer life was nil. My faith was shallow. God was in my head, but not in my heart.

Here is another memory deeply engraved in my mind. I found a pew mid-church and sat on the end of the bench. I began praying. There was no one else in the church so I prayed out loud. Three words came out, "Help me Lord." I probably said this simple prayer 20 times.

Across the street from St. Paul's was an Irish Shop that sold items from the green sod of Erin. I knew they sold rosaries. So, I left the church, walked across the street, purchased a rosary and returned to church.

I had not prayed a rosary since my days in the seminary.

In returning to the same pew, one of those "God if you" prayers came to mind.

You know the kind, "God if you help me pass this exam, I'll promise to go to church every Sunday"; "God, if you allow us to win the lottery, we'll help the poor, crippled, widows and orphans." "God, if you get me out of these handcuffs, I promise I'll become a Jesuit priest." As I said, my faith and prayer life were pretty shallow, as

I'm sure you can ascertain by this type of prayer.

Regardless, I prayed, "God if you bring a priest over to church within the next 20 minutes, I will go to confession." Pretty cool, eh? It was mid-morning on a scalding, hot summer day in August. I'm sure the priest was sitting on the beach or by his air conditioner in the rectory. Also, giving God only 20 minutes I thought was pretty shrewd. He was up there running the universe with a lot of shit going on everywhere in the world; I'm sure this prayer went unheard. Well, as I counted down from 20 minutes to five minutes left, I knew a Las Vegas bookie would give me good odds on the priest being a no show.

Now I have been taught in AA to be rigorously honest. The truth, with two minutes to go, I began gathering my things from the pew along with the rosary. My head was down, and on God's Holy Bible, I heard the creak of a door and there standing in the shadow of a light was the friggin' priest. Are you kidding me?

He glides over to the tabernacle and takes out the Eucharist; for us Catholics, that is the Real Presence of the body and blood of Jesus Christ. He placed a host in a Pix, which is a small device that he uses to carry communion to sick people who are homebound or in the hospital. I knelt while he was doing this.

Keeping my head down, I am hoping to hear the creak of the door as he leaves the premises. A minute passes. I hear nothing. Then, I hear a slight cough and look up and he is standing right in front of me. He asks if I am all right. I nod yes. He smiles and turns to walk away, I cough, he turns and I say, "Father, I think you are supposed to hear my confession."

Are you kidding me? At this point I am sure the God of my understanding, was smiling the all knowing smile of a Dad who says to his kid, "I gottcha!" Shit, now I had to confess my sins. I did the best I could. I did tell him about my daughter's comment regarding drinking. He asked if I thought I had a problem with booze. I told him no, that I drank like everyone else. He told me to attempt to drink in moderation, especially around the children. He then gave me absolution and I was ready to leave.

He then asked a favor, would I pray for a woman named Pat who was dying of cancer. He was going to visit her in hospice. "Sure," I said. Then something came over me. I reached into my pocket and pulled out the rosaries I had just purchased and gave them to this humble priest, telling him to give them to Pat.

I felt a weight lifted from my shoulders. Not sure why. The rest of day was ok. I remember not drinking that day. Not sure why. The following day I decided to go to morning Mass. The priest saw me as the Mass was ending and gave me the "hi" sign to wait for him. He met me in the vestibule of the church and told me that Pat cried when he gave her the rosary. She knew she was dying and had once had great devotion to the Blessed Mother and lost it through years of illness and depression. He told me they prayed a rosary together, her first in over ten years.

I never saw this good priest again in my life, but I knew God had placed him there in that church at that moment.

On a side-bar, I love the story of the prodigal son. What I love most about it occurs when the father sees the son, far off, and runs out to greet him! I think on this day, God was running out to me, because I was far off in a distant county and he greeted me…with compassion and love.

Another event occurred in October of 1996 that should have also been a warning. Five years had passed since that day in Stone Harbor. I began going to daily Mass at a Franciscan monastery near home. I also had begun saying the rosary daily. I also kept drinking.

By now, however, I knew something was wrong. I felt depressed pretty much on a continual basis. On a positive note, my spiritual life had gotten better. I had a spiritual director guiding me.

I discovered a deep devotion to Mary, Our Mother.

At this time in history two events were clashing, one physical, the other metaphysical. The physical event was the war raging in Bosnia, part of the country of Yugoslavia that had broken away from the Serbs. The other was what I will term, other worldly. It had been reported that Mary, the Blessed Virgin Mother of God, was appearing to seven children in the town of Medjugorje in Bosnia-Herzegovina since 1981, similar to events that occurred in the 19th century to a peasant girl named Bernadette in the town of Lourdes in France and in the 20th century at Fatima in Portugal to three shepherd children.

I am not here to debate private spiritual revelation that may have occurred with these seven children or the Blessed Mother. Yes, all are important to me, but let's keep talking about reading the signs and messages I was receiving all along, especially toward the end of my drinking. Just to refresh your memory, we are now in October 1996 and I got sober in August of 1997.

There was a travel agency out of North Carolina that conducted pilgrimages to various holy sites throughout the world. For Muslims, they provide a pilgrimage to Mecca; for Jews to Jerusalem; and for Catholics, they had them to Rome, Lourdes, and Fatima and now to Medjugorje. I had been to Fatima and Lourdes in 1993. Rome was a bit pricey. Medjugorje fit my personal budget well. I could probably write a book just about pilgrimages and maybe someday I will. But today we keep our focus on booze and alcoholism.

I decide to take a pilgrimage to Medjugorje. I was both excited and petrified as the day drew near. I had never been to a third-world country, where poverty and a hard life reigned for the inhabitants.

Our tour group arrived in Bosnia on a Saturday. We had all met in Newark, New Jersey's international terminal and flew into Frankfurt, Germany, then to Croatia. We then embarked on a three-and-a-half-hour bus ride from an airport in central Croatia to our destination. By the time we boarded the bus, we had some knowledge of one another and by trip's end, indelible friendships would ensue. Three people in particular became my pilgrimage buddies. A young woman named Rosalia, who now resides in New England and a married couple from New York State, Tom and Jane. We prayed together, ate together, drank some wine together (in moderation…it was a pilgrimage and I was on good behavior) and a great bond of friendship was forged.

Spiritually on a pilgrimage, the pilgrim is likely to experience some hardship and the goal was to offer up any suffering or inconvenience to Our Lord. Our first hardship scared the shit out of all of us. The war in Bosnia was winding down but not over. About 90 minutes into our journey, we were all chatting, laughing, really getting to know one another. As the bus wound its way around mountains, we noticed burned out military vehicles, bombed out jeeps; the vestiges of war. It was pretty surreal.

All of a sudden, the bus came to a screeching halt. We looked out the windows of the bus and saw five or six men, dressed in military attire holding AK-47's in their arms. Whoa, Nellie! We are going to die.

The bus driver told us to be quiet. No problem there. Most of us had pulled out our rosaries and began to pray. One of the soldiers boarded our bus and demanded all of our passports. We were in no position to argue. It wasn't like we were in friggin' Hyde Park, New York.

We delivered our passports to the front; the soldier gathered them up and left the bus. Now we started to whisper to one another in earnest. As noted, I am a humorous fellow, so in order to relieve some tension I commented that since we all, someday, were going to die and if we had to die today, this was the best way to go while on pilgrimage honoring Our Lady and worshiping her Son. All Catholics know that martyrs go directly to heaven. Do not pass go, do not collect $200 does NOT apply to martyrs. It made sense to me. I wondered aloud how big my mansion in heaven would be. One wise guy who was getting to know me said, "Yours will be a small row home, just like your house in Olney!" As long as it's in heaven, I can dig that.

About 20 minutes later, the soldier returned with our passports, patted the driver on the back and said we could pass. Whew! And you know what the first thing I thought of was? Yep, you guessed it, a drink. Everyone else was praising God and I wanted a drink.

It was a pilgrimage of nine days. In those days there were no hotels, hostels or motels in this mountainous region. All pilgrims were housed in homes of the native people of Medjugorje, which was really cool. I, along with Rosalia and about ten others, were in one large home. Tom and Jane were in another at the other end of the village. Outside of our evening meal, the four of us hung together.

We had arrived on a Saturday. On Tuesday night, an American working for the Peace Corp in Budapest, Hungary, joined our group in our house. I can still see his face. His name was Tom. He was a charismatic Catholic. Simply stated, these were Roman Catholics who had a special affinity for the Holy Spirit, the Third Person of the Blessed Trinity. You see them at Mass praying with their arms opened, especially when the Lord's Prayer is recited. They also love to pray "over" people, an aspect of it that I am not particularly fond.

This gives me the "eebee-geebees." You can tell me you're going to pray for me and that is fine, but literally praying *over* me. Nah. So Budapest Tom, the charismatic Pape, prays over each of us after dinner on Tuesday night. I had to acquiesce. I didn't want to appear rude. After all, I was a pilgrim and was supposed to experience hardship.

On Wednesday the fun began. After breakfast Tom proceeds to tell each of those in our home a message he received from the Holy Spirit concerning us. Like, I said, I'm not comfortable with this shit, Holy Spirit or not. I duck out of the house and head into the village before he can give me my "message," and we begin our game of "man hunt."

I hooked up with Rosalia, Tom and Jane an hour or so later and we did our pilgrim thing. I saw Budapest Tom a couple of times before he saw me. I told my three companions about my feelings regarding Tom. They were cool with it, so I avoided him like the plague. Wednesday night he cornered me after dinner telling me he wanted to talk. Nope gotta go. Maybe tomorrow. He told all of us he had to leave for Budapest early Friday morning. Best news I heard in three days. I started humming the "Halleluiah Chorus."

Thursday came; I ate breakfast early and skedaddled off to the village. Twice I bumped into him. He wouldn't give up. He was a persistent bastard. Each time, I told him a lie about meeting a priest for confession or meeting with other pilgrims. At last, it was Thursday night. I skipped dinner telling anyone who asked that I was "fasting." You know, doing a holy, pious and noble act. What bullshit. But hey, I'm an alcoholic.

By 11 p.m. I had holed up in my bed. I had avoided Tom for almost three days and was utterly exhausted. I heard him stirring down the hall at about 2:00 a.m. Friday morning, packing up and eventually leaving. Praise the Holy Spirit on that. Hopefully at the airport, he would find some other moron to pray over and forget about me.

We all gathered again for breakfast, and I felt great relief as there was no Tom. As I was finishing up breakfast, a woman who had a room on our floor handed me a letter. It was addressed to me. Tom had slid it under her door by mistake. Crap, this dude would not leave me alone even in his absence. I took the letter and thanked the woman, went outside, sat under a tree and read it. I wish I had kept it all these years later. However, I can still almost quote it verbatim, as I do sometimes when I share my story in an AA meeting.

Tom wrote, "George, so sorry we could not hook up. I wanted to give you the message I received from the Holy Spirit when I prayed over you. I pray you know what it means. I saw you standing on the bow of a boat, on a vast body of water, being tossed around due to a terrific storm at sea. The look of fear in your eyes was astounding. The winds were hurricane force tossing the boat to and fro. I had never seen such fear on the face of another human. You were screaming something toward the heavens, I'm assuming at God. Then the waters calmed and a voice from the heavens spoke only one word, "Enough." I am positive the Holy Spirit will enlighten you on this word."

Enough. Excuse the French, but fuck me. I knew exactly what it meant; enough of the fear, enough of the resentment toward my old man, enough of the anxiety and worry I carried within me every day, enough of feelings about being alone, and most of all, enough booze. This I feared the most. I could not imagine a life without alcohol.

I told no one of this letter; not Tom, not Rosalia, and not Jane. When I first told my story six months sober at an AA meeting in Bucks County, Pennsylvania, it was to this group of drunks that I shared this letter. I was awaiting a big rejection on this one and the opposite happened. Every drunk in recovery in that room was nodding their head in affirmation. They knew what enough meant, just as did I. And then I fervently prayed, "Does anybody see what I see?"

CHAPTER 21

Controlling It

Regardless of your age and education, sooner or later you will hear the word oxymoron. It's like that word blasphemy. It just sounds cool. It's a great "try to impress them word" at a cocktail party. Here are some of my favorite oxymorons: rush hour, jumbo shrimp, act naturally, pretty ugly, exact estimate, civil war, clever fool, old news, original copy and virtual reality. Hopefully you get the drift. Here is the oxymoron for the alcoholic; controlled drinking.

If you are already in the rooms of sobriety, you are smiling. If you are reading this book and you're thinking you might be an alcoholic, think about this, can you or could you ever really control your drinking? And if you are reading this book because you believe a loved one is alcoholic, take note, there is no such thing as controlled drinking for us alkies.

Take a large dog for a walk, say a Labrador retriever, on a scorching, hot and humid day, then put a small bowl of water in front of it and see what happens. Then put a large pot of water in front of the dog and see what happens.

In the first case, after one huge slurp, the dog will look up at you and in essence say, "Are you friggin' kidding me?" In the second scenario, the dog will put his head inside the pot and drink and drink and drink, slurp and slurp and slurp. Most of the time there is still not enough water in the pot to quench its thirst. The Lab wants more. Now I am not comparing alcoholics to dogs, although I surely have been called worse!

In that quiz from the NCADD, question 14 reads accordingly, "Have you sometimes failed to keep promises you made to yourself about controlling or cutting down on your drinking? xiii

I did. I usually did it after an all-night party with family and friends. Usually did it after a very long night out while on the road for business. Usually did it after a funeral. Usually did it after a wedding. Usually did after a huge success in my life. Usually did it after a humongous defeat in my life. Usually. In between all these events, I still drank, but more moderately.

I was not a dawn-to-midnight drinker. Those who do this, usually, hold the title of low-bottom drunk. If you are having a glass of vodka with your Wheaties, you just might be an alcoholic. If you are hiding bottles of booze in the toilet tank of the second bathroom in your home, you too might be an alcoholic. To this type of alcoholic there is no, and I repeat no, controlled drinking. If you visit different liquor stores and beer distributors on a daily basis so that the guy at the counter won't really think you have a drinking problem, well, you guessed it.

Don't laugh. Like he or she really gave a shit anyway! This is where alcohol takes alcoholics to their lowest bottoms.

A guy named Rich spoke at a meeting a while back and

said that he was on a construction job and left a six pack of beer on the passenger seat of his pickup truck. It was late July with temperatures in the 90's. At lunch he played poker with his buddies and lost his shirt, meaning he lost his drinking money. When the whistle blew, depression overcame him. Where would he get a drink tonight with no money? He got into his truck and did not even look at the passenger seat, that is how despondent he was. Furious, he put the truck in reverse and gunned it. The six pack flew forward, crashing into the dashboard and one of the cans exploded. He slammed on the brakes. "The temperature in my truck had to be 130 degrees. To my utter amazement, I was not even pissed that one of the cans had exploded all over my truck, but I was fucking enthralled that I still had five good cans of hot beer to drink."

That brought down the house. And like the dog with the pot of water, he drank and slurped every one of those hot beers. Rich confessed he was the low-bottom variety of alcoholic.

The functional, even though there is no such thing, alcoholic is the high-bottom variety. That is what I am. Note, I did not say that is what I was, for even though I am 18 years sober, I am and always will be an alcoholic. Yes, I am an alcoholic in recovery, but will never be cured of the disease. I am one drink away from catastrophe; one drink away from another worse bottom; one drink away from a physical, emotional, spiritual or mental death.

It is this high-bottom drunk, like me, that has the

tougher time getting sober. Let's face it, if you're living in a junkyard, having vodka with your Wheaties or drinking beers that are 130 degrees in temperature, getting into the rooms of AA where you get a fresh cup of coffee at each meeting and maybe even a couple of donuts is looking pretty good. We functional alkies, well now that is a different story altogether.

In the book, Alcoholic Anonymous there is a paragraph that I must quote, "Here are some of the methods we have tried (in controlled drinking): drinking beer, limiting the number of drinks, never drinking alone, never drinking in the morning, drinking only at home, never having it the house, never drinking during business hours, drinking only at parties, switching from scotch to brandy, drinking only natural wines, agreeing to resign if ever drunk on the job, taking a trip, not taking a trip, swearing off forever (with and without an oath), taking more physical exercise, reading inspirational books, going to health farms and sanitariums, accepting voluntary commitment to asylums, we could increase the list ad infinitum."xiv

This was my second epiphany when I got into the rooms. If you remember, "Gandhi" gave me my first with, "When I drank, I drank too much and when I tried to stop, I couldn't." Now this.

You have got to remember that this book came out in 1939. How the hell did Bill Wilson, Dr. Bob Smith and the rest of those Depression Era drunks who published this know how I drank in 1969, 1975, 1980, 1985, 1990, 1996 and finally during that fateful week in 1997? Easy answer; they were drunks like me. Both had good careers and could function pretty well when not drinking. But, put booze in their hands and all bets were off.

In early 1978, I worked for an insurance company. One of the real old geezers in the claims department was retiring. He was a gentle soul, quiet, humble and one of the nicest guys there. We all really liked and admired him. I had only been with the firm for about six months, but everyone knew I was one humorous fellow. I always had them laughing in the cafeteria at lunch or early in the morning over coffee or at the local pub over a beer or two or three after work hours. Many of my peers truly liked me, some tolerated me and some just labeled me a class clown and, I'm sure, wished I would leave.

The evening of this gentleman's retirement dinner we had about 90 minutes to kill before festivities began. Not sure about you, but I can do a lot of damage in 90 minutes, six pack of beer minimum. A few of us decided to visit the local pub for a drink before dinner. We ate no food, just some drinks and the proverbial peanuts and stale pretzels that reside on the top of every bar known to mankind. I still remember believing that I was all right and controlled my intake of alcohol.

Post dinner, a few speakers got up and said wonderful things about this truly nice man. After that, dinner drinks were being served. I did have a few of these. I readily confess that I was buzzed. Then came the gifts from the company: a set of golf clubs, a grandfather clock and a vacation to some exotic island for him and his wife.

He had been with the company more than 40 years.

Here is where my first career began to end. As the applause stopped and before they introduced him to say some final words, as God is my judge, some douchebag sitting at my table let rip the grossest, raunchiest fart I have ever heard. I did not, as God is my judge, do this. But this dick turned around and looked at me as did every other person at the table. It reminded me of the time when I rang the bells for Father Dougherty when attempting to become an altar boy.

Looks of utter shock, amazement, amusement and disgust engulfed me. Regardless of my innocence, in the eyes of many I had ruined this gentleman's retirement gala.

Afterwards, I went up to him and told him that it was not me. He gently said not to worry, but I don't think he believed me. I told my boss what had happened, and it was like talking to Pontius Pilate. The only worse thing that could happen next was to hear some of my peers yelling, "Give us Barabbas!"

The next day, I began putting my resume together and within six months was no longer working in the insurance business. In hindsight, if I had been completely sober, I believe this could not have happened to me. But the combination of booze, my personality and humor and the wrong moment, and it was like Custer going into the Little Big Horn thinking things were just great.

My point here is that I did not have 20 drinks before all of this happened. I had zero drinks until we ventured into the pub. I controlled my intake at the pub. I let down my guard after dinner with a couple of cocktails and boom! I was not guilty for the fart, but guilty as charged for being drunk and being drunk allowed me to be the scapegoat. Another point needs to be made here. I think a non-alcoholic drinker, confronted with this situation would have put up more of a fight to salvage his or her reputation. My reaction: why bother? Why waste the energy to prove something I may never be able to prove and in the end still have people believe I did it.

Easier to just quit. Easier to just move on. Screw them; I can get a better job, and I eventually did. But I missed the point, eh? Hey, I'm an alcoholic, and in 1978 I did not know it.

I would like to end this chapter tying up loose ends about controlled drinking. Everything stated in the above quote from the Big Book is absolutely true. My drinking career began with just beer. I eventually gravitated to drinking wine. In the late 1980s and early 1990s I became a wine aficionado. My kids were giving me books concerning the best vineyards in California and Europe hoping I would get to visit them someday, thus, truly appreciating the nose, the taste and delicacy of each wine. Like I really gave a shit! I was drinking wine to get drunk, plain and simple.

Late in my drinking career I believe I was given the greatest warning of all. Through all the beers, Guinness' and wine that I drank, I had never acquired a taste for hard liquor, never. Then in 1994, again in New Orleans, this time at the famous Commander Palace Restaurant, one of my buddies named Peter ordered me a tumbler of single-malt scotch. Now I know as much about single-malt scotch or any other kind of scotch as I do about reading hieroglyphics, not a friggin' thing. How was I supposed to know you were to swirl it, sniff it and then slowly sip it? So, like any good alcoholic, I swallowed this $15 shot of scotch in one gulp. Peter looked at me quizzically. Do you know what you just threw down your throat in one gulp, his eyes said to me? Yep, my eyes said back in arrogance, and I turned to the barkeep and ordered another. Thus, my last bit of controlled drinking began. Four scotches could do the same damage as eight or ten beers and I'd gain less weight! Isn't alcohol great?

However, by 1997, no standalone drink of scotch or combination of a Guinness and shot of scotch could take me where I needed to go. Fact is there was not enough booze anywhere that could relieve the pain. I had finally been betrayed by my best friend and the love of my life.

On the other side of the coin, yes, I tried all sorts of drinking time frames, too.

I would only drink on weekends. I would only drink after work hours. I would only drink with my wife at dinner. I would only drink without my wife after dinner. I would only drink beer during the week.

Then it was, I'll just guzzle beer, well after all, beer wasn't really alcohol was it? I will only drink vintage European wines when ordering in a restaurant. I would only drink single-malt scotch on Friday and Saturday.

If you are reading this and are on the fence about whether you are an alcoholic or not, I will ask you one last question to end this chapter, "Would a normal, non-alcoholic human being, male or female, ever drink like this or think like this? I'm curious to hear your answer.

CHAPTER 22

Never Meant To Hurt Anyone

In the quiz taken earlier from the NCADD, question 12 reads, "When you're sober, do you sometimes regret things you did or said while drinking? Now the word sober here is being used very loosely. It does not refer to long-time sobriety. It implies that after a night getting blasted, the next day or the day after, if you haven't had a drink, do you regret anything you may have said to anyone before you get drunk again.

In another piece of AA literature there is a line that says something to the effect of, "We judged ourselves by our intentions, while the world was judging us by our actions." When I first read this I thought, oh shit, here we go again; another shot across the bow. Yet I cannot deny the validity of it.

I never intended to hurt anyone, ever. Actually, it says somewhere else in AA's literature that most alcoholics are very sensitive people. I am a sensitive guy. This does not infer weakness. It actually implies something positive. Sensitive people are usually aware of those around them. So what happens when you get a sensitive person and add alcohol to that equation? You get the answer to question 12. You regret a lot of things said and done, sometimes to the people you love and care about the most.

My best buddy, who I met in college, is named Reggie.

We are so different in so many ways, but similar, too. Reggie is Irish Catholic, one of eight kids, married to a terrific gal and friend, Abby. Without a drink in my hand, I would never do anything to hurt these good people, never.

One evening during the last year of my drinking in late 1996, they came over our house for dinner. You know that saying, don't discuss politics and religion, well we dovetailed right into a discussion about the Catholic Church. Now all four of us are practicing Catholics, meaning we go to Mass every Sunday and participate in our respective parishes. I could not even tell you what we were discussing. Reggie, Abby and my wife lean toward some liberal thinking, things that they believe should be part of the Church.

Their prerogatives—they, too, have First Amendment rights. I am more conservative. During dinner and through the discussion afterward, Reg and I were pounding down, you guessed it, some Guinness. Something was said by either him or Abby, and I took extreme offense to it. I considered it blasphemy. Isn't that a great word, blasphemy! I readily confess now that I was drunk. But that night, Reggie and I were equals: if I was drunk, he was drunk. Years later, I'm in AA and he is not. Go figure.

As this discussion got more and more heated, rather than change the subject or just end that tête-à-tête, I told them in no uncertain terms, and I quote, "Why don't you fuckin' people go and become fuckin' Protestants."

Pretty classy, eh? You know the acronym WWJD, what would Jesus do? I don't think JC would have told them to get fucked.

I left the kitchen and went to bed while our guests, my best friend and his wife, were in the kitchen with my wife. I am sure they were dumbfounded. Me, I was just plain dumb and drunk. I did call them the next day and apologized. Those old feelings of guilt, shame and remorse reared their ugly heads. But that night put a rift in our relationship that lasted quite a few years.

When I was about five years sober, the four of us were at a mutual friend's wedding. When the band took a break, I asked Abby if I could talk to her. We went out on a porch, sat down and I truly apologized for that awful night that almost cost me her and Reggie's friendship. Sober I would never have hurt them. Drunk I would hurt the Pope, the College of Cardinals and anyone else who didn't agree with me. That is what alcohol does. That is what it did to me.

Not sure you can identify with this, but here goes. Alcoholics love to call people up at two o'clock in the morning, talk to them for at least an hour, wake up hours later and have no recollection of these phone calls until a $465 phone bill appears in the mail. It's true.

Things were not going well in my first marriage. I was at a company function and got hammered. Sometime during this function, a couple of us went outside and toked on a doobie.

I was stoned on the drive home, and I remember seeing

a Philly Cop with his car lights all aglow. He had obviously pulled someone over. I wound down the windows in my car to get some fresh air and slowed down as I rolled past the cop. Don't really remember anything else, nothing.

The next day, right as the work day was coming to a close, I get a call from one of my old high school buddies whom I hadn't seen or heard from in six or seven years. His name is Joe, a great guy. He asked why I called him at such an ungodly hour—not just once but three times. Huh? I had no idea. I don't even know how I got his number.

He explained that at around 3:00 a.m. I got on the phone and started to tell him that I was sick of the way things were at home and tomorrow I was going to pack my bags, purchase an airline ticket and move to *fooking* Ireland. That was it. That was the whole plan and I called him three times to tell him that. I still remember thinking, "What the hell?" That cannot be the truth.

Yet, what motivation did Joe have in lying to me—none. When the bill came in, sure enough I had made three phone calls between 3:00 a.m. and 4:05 a.m. I was dumbfounded and embarrassed. I never did call Joe back. However, I recently found his home address through our high school reunion committee, wrote him a letter and asked his forgiveness. He wrote me back and all is well, but I lost 30 years of friendship due to booze. I plan to see him in person before the year is out and formally apologize. Joe was a great friend; alcohol proved not so good a friend after all.

I began this chapter with the statement, "We judged ourselves by our intentions, while the world was judging us by our actions."

When I graduated from college and began my business career, I had aspirations to one day run a company. To be the chief, the CEO, the guy who has that saying that came from Harry S. Truman, "the buck stops here," carved on a plaque hanging from a prominent place on a wall in the corner office. I was intelligent and people were attracted to me. I also had natural leadership qualities. And most of all, I was the greatest salesman I knew. (Can you see the humility bubbling through my personality?) I also intended to have as many children as God granted me and my wife and be the Dad the old man had never been. These were my intentions. And then life happened.

I could not find that company where all my great attributes would reach their potential. I was a great salesman; but there were others who were better; and I hated to confess that. The marriage that I thought was made in heaven wasn't, and after our third child I had a vasectomy. I think my first wife really liked me, but she did not really love me. I told her this on the day I finally left for good. She did not stop me. And then I drank.

I was not the Dad I intended to be. I had joint custody, but they lived with their Mom, and I got them every other weekend. I was no longer helping them with their homework or drying their tears when they were scared at night, not comforting them when their best friend betrayed them or when they broke up with a boyfriend or girlfriend. And I drank some more. And then John Adams appeared, "Is anybody there?" And the only person I saw was John Barleycorn.

CHAPTER 23

Five Minutes from Success

This is an expression heard at different times in the rooms of sobriety, usually at a speaker meeting. "I was five minutes away from success, did not know it and pissed it away." First time I heard it early on, my first inclination was to dismiss it. Like I said before, I'm wired differently. My glass was always half empty. I'm an alcoholic.

If you remember, I had to write my life story when Chuck asked me to do my fourth step in writing that fearless and moral inventory. Shit, drinking I was anything but fearless, and drunk I was anything but moral. Go figure. But in writing this, events in my life started to jump from the pages. Even going back to the Cub Scouts and altar boy stories, I discovered in sobriety that I had sabotaged both of these enterprises.

With a little bit of fortitude and discipline on my part I might have made a great scout. Not sure I would have hung in for all the Eagle Scout stuff, but I might have at least tried. If I had been blessed with even an ounce of humility, I might have made a fine altar boy serving Mass in the Church I loved, but again, I did not want to even try. Why was that? I can think of one word that tells all and that word is fear. More on that later.

My autobiography continued after these two episodes

into the seventh grade. My homeroom nun for this grade was the most beautiful and coolest nun I ever had. I pray she is still alive and maybe she'll see these words in this book and know how she affected me. Her name is Sister Joan Bernadette. Even with all the nun crap that they used to wear, you could see the beauty in this woman. Honestly, at 12 years of age, it felt weird having a crush on a nun.

Well, as usual, the school year started out rough for me. I continued to be the class clown, which I'm sure even Sister Joan appreciated some of the time. But I had a hankering to carry things to the extreme. This could lead to one ticked off, pissed off Sisters of St. Joseph nun.

For those of you who are not Catholic or were not taught by nuns, there are different Orders of nuns, just like there are priests. There are Franciscans, Dominicans, Sisters of Mercy, Sisters of the Immaculate Heart of Mary and the Sisters of St. Joseph (Josey's), to name of few. The Archdiocese of Philadelphia, for teaching purposes, had three dominant groups of sisters; the Mercy nuns, the Macs (Sisters of the Immaculate Heart of Mary) and the Josey's, who taught in our parish. The Mercy's and Macs had at least decent looking habits for the 1960s. The Josey's, on the other hand, looked like part of Himmler's Gestapo and SS squad members. Their uniform had lots of black, a huge white bib that would catch the slobber from the nun while she was verbally berating you, and a humongous set of Rosary beads that at times could turn into a lethal weapon. The only thing you could visibly see was the part of the face that went from the bottom of the chin to the top of the eyebrows. That was it. But even with that little bit showing, I could tell Sister Joan was a knockout.

Sister Joan, I am sure, having conversed with the nuns who had already taught me, knew my story. But rather than try the spiritual frontal attack that Sister William Loretta tried in the altar boy fiasco, Sister Joan went with a different, flanking route. She pulled me aside during the first week of classes and said, "I think someday I can see you in uniform. For this year, you will be on the safety patrol." What? Me wearing a badge and leading lines of little kids to the safety of their homes? I thought she was kidding and told her that. Then she told me the main perk. Not only do you wear a badge that lets the world know you are in charge, but you get to leave the last class of the day early in order to prepare for the last bell when all 2,000 pinheaded, hormonal, wound up like–a-top, Catholic boys and girls were led home, free from the penitentiary for another day. Yeah, man, I am 100 percent in on that gig.

For the first few weeks, I was doing ok. Then, Mother Superior—this nun who probably made Hitler or Joe Stalin seem like Mother Teresa of Calcutta—gave me ten days JUG for something I did not do. She would not even listen to an explanation. Again, being the class clown has its detriments. Oh yeah, in Catholic circles, detention was known as JUG or Justice Under God. Pretty cool, eh?

What this meant was that when I was finished with my patrol duties, I had to come back to school, sit in a classroom for an hour, writing something like, "I must not say the word fuck in front of boys and girls who say it more times than me," or some such bullshit, 500 times, and then take it home and show it to my mom who would then beat the crap out of me. Even Moms believed the nuns before they believed their own kids.

Next day, I led my group of third graders across the street, into oncoming traffic. Now I am a street kid. There really was no danger, but I made sure a couple of cars and a pickup truck starting leaning on their horns, making it sound like one of the ridiculous nuclear air raid drills we had back in the early sixties. Parents, kids, nuns, priests, the whole frigging neighborhood started running my way. When they saw there was really no danger, they all calmed down, except for Mother Stalin. She frothed at the mouth, took my badge and I was no longer a school cop. Good fuckin' riddance.

Now I know I've tried to make all of this sound humorous, but sadly, good Sister Joan was attempting to give me a position of responsibility and accountability. Maybe I might learn something really valuable about life as I approached my high school years. Nah, I pissed it away. Within five minutes, I was no longer a safety patrol member. With the Scouts, within five minutes I was no longer in Webelos, same as I did with altar boys.

This pre-alcoholic behavior continued in high school and then continued when as a junior I discovered the real-thing remedy, booze. The biggest thing I quit in high school was the varsity basketball team my senior year. I attended an all-boys, Catholic, suburban, wealthy, college-preparatory high school. As already stated I was poor, thus, I did not fit in. Sadly, this was an era when the word legacy did not just pertain to going to a college. Remember Flounder in Animal House? The only reason he got into Delta was because his brother Fred was an alumnus, a legacy.

Well, the same pertained to the sports teams at this high school. If you were the second or third generation of kid attending, and you were at least decent in a sport, you made the team. What this did was make the parents funding this expensive school happy and writing checks, but it usually made a sports team suck because it was filled with average athletes. This school is still in existence today and no longer follows this line of thinking in their sports endeavors.

I was a pretty decent basketball player in my day. In my junior year, I made the JV team (Junior Varsity); played and started several games. Senior Year arrived and on the first day of tryouts, there were probably 25 guys on the courts. I had spent the entire summer playing in two different leagues fine tuning my game. Within three weeks of everyday practices, the team would be narrowed down to about 12 guys. Each week passed and I made the cut. The final cut was coming. I knew it was between me and another kid who was wealthy and hated my guts. I did not have a prayer.

Finally, the coach called me in and before he spoke I asked him if I could speak first. I told him exactly how I felt about the whole, rotten way athletics was handled at the school—in my humble opinion. He listened, did not interrupt me. Then, I told him whether I had made the team or not, I quit. He was stunned. He saw the effort I had put forth for three solid weeks and saw my talent. Then he told me I had made the team! I quit. Thanked him and quit. Now what normal fucking kid does that? None that I know. By this time I had already discovered alcohol and knew that it would kill the pain of this sad development in my life.

While I continued with my narrative fourth step, the adult years of my life loomed ahead and I wasn't sure I wanted to continue. Look how screwed up I was as a kid, only God knows what is going to be revealed when I peel back the onion of my adult life.

Here was an immediate revelation. See if you can identify it with yourself or someone you may know. From the year I graduated college in 1975 until I joined one of the largest computing companies in the world in 1989, I worked for ten, count'em, ten different companies. Except for the first two, I held the position of salesman or sales manager, and I was really good at selling. I won awards, twice got promoted within the first year of employment, and still I quit and moved on. You need to know that when I quit and moved on, it was always for a better job, in a better company for more money, always. I joke when telling my story in AA that after 14 years of working in the sales profession and making good money, my pension was worth zip…zero dollars.

Most of these years were before 401K's but still, even

with a matching contribution from the company, I would have been worth about $37.00.

So why this propensity to quit even when things were going well? I reiterate what I stated at the beginning of this chapter, and it is one word, and that word is fear. Fear governed my life. It ruled over me with an iron fist. It paralyzed me. It crippled me emotionally and spiritually. It was there when my first marriage collapsed. It was there before I met my present wife when I was dating other women. It came out when I turned into Sean the chameleon. It really came out and haunted me in the business world.

As I kept rereading my autobiography, in my mind's eye, I could see every one of these jobs. Later, Chuck would keep telling me to connect the dots, in this instance, the dots of fear. And you know what, in many of the cases I was, indeed, five minutes away from success: and I pissed it away. Without boring you with all the minutiae, here is what usually occurred.

As you can surmise, sales is a numbers game. Quotas are given at the beginning of each fiscal year. If you make quota, you are a hero. If you don't, well, you better make it next year. For me, I normally made the sales number that first year. I was a hero. But the second year was always tougher. The quota was raised and doubt would creep in.

What if I did not make quota? What if I lost my job? Would the wife leave me because I was a failure? Would she take the kids and the house and the car, leaving me with my underwear, holding my dick in my hand? This is how alcoholics think. This is how I thought.

So, usually in the first quarter of the next fiscal year, the resume was on the street and I was searching for a new job. I would rationalize that I'd be joining a better company, with better opportunities for advancement and, of course, I would make more and more money.

Sadly, and I say sadly, because this is how it worked out. I look back over my shoulder and wonder what if in my early years I had just stayed with one of those companies? Or what if, in those early days when I made the move to a new company, that it blew up in my face?

That never happened. Today, I can only say that God had a plan for me and even though I tried to screw it up on numerous occasions, He made sure I always landed on my feet, even at the height of my alcoholism. God is good…little kids and drunks.

CHAPTER 24

I Really Am Sorry...Right

What is that old saying, "If I had a dime for every time you said ______, I'd be a millionaire." For us alcoholics and addicts, just place the words I'm sorry on the blank line and that person would be a bazillionaire ten times over. If you, the reader, have kids, doesn't it just piss you off to no end that your children think that they can light your sofa on fire, spill shit over your newly purchased or recently cleaned carpets in the family room, drop and break the picture frame that was handed down through four generations of your family, and then rear end an immovable 18-wheeler, crushing the front-end of your car and simply say, "I'm sorry" thinking that makes it AOK.

They cannot understand your anger. Then, after you're finally finished with your rant and at least got some of it off your chest and you ask the final parental pointed question, "Do you have anything else to say for yourself, Alice?" And she looks at you like you are fucking from outer space and says, "I already said I'm sorry." And you want to knock Alice to the moon! That is how I think the non-alcoholic person feels when dealing with an active alky. It is like dealing with a kid; a kid who has no bloody idea at the devastation that they caused.

In the rooms, many heads will nod in affirmation when the speaker or person sharing says, "I picked up my first drink when I was 16 years of age. When I put the drink down at age 45, I realized I was still 16 years of age. I had not grown, changed or matured at all." Some folks in recovery still hold on to some pride and won't admit this, but if they hang around long enough and keep coming back, they will. It's a fact.

Think about it. How do most people truly grow and change throughout their lives? How do most people attain wisdom? How do we gain the knowledge and fortitude to keep fighting the good fight of life when times get tough?

It's only my opinion, yet, now that I'm sober these many years; I gained this wisdom through my failures. I have learned 95 percent of all that I know about life and how to live it through my failures—oh, ok, through my fuckups. Maybe I have learned the other 5 percent through my successes, and that may be a stretch.

So how, may I ask you, can an alcoholic who has been slamming them down for 20, 25, or 30 years, know the first thing about dealing with the real pain of life, when all they really know is how to anesthetize that pain?

We had a guy in my home group in Central Bucks County, Leopold. His old man and old lady must have really hated his guts to have given him a name like that. Anyway, Leopold came into Alcoholic Anonymous at age 73. He started drinking at 14. I suck at math but that still comes out to 59 years of hard drinking. When he told his story, he related that he finally "gave up" the fight of wanting to drink until he died, when his adult daughter, age of 45, visited him at his retirement village. She had visited her Dad to have a nice dinner with him and some of his friends at the village. The other four elderly gentlemen were nicely dressed, courteous, kind, welcoming and sober. Leopold, on the other hand, was shitfaced.

At one point, he closed his eyes while chewing his food and did a swan dive into his Caesar salad and started snoring! When he told us this at our meeting everyone erupted in contagious laughter. And it wasn't that we were laughing at Leopold, it was more like we were laughing with him. Some of us had done just that or had come close more than once.

Well his daughter waited until the staff got Leopold back to his room, showered him down and started an IV of extra strength Maxwell House coffee. When he was finished one cup, his daughter instructed the staff member to pour him another. Leopold told us that his daughter had every intention of staying and saying what she had to say, and he better understand the consequences of her sermon.

He then related the following, "My daughter, who is a soft spoken, quiet, humble and lovely girl looked at me with daggers in her eyes when I was finally coherent. For the first time in my life, I knew I had crossed the line.

I mouthed the words, I'm sorry and she held her hand up. I awaited the onslaught. Yet, in her youthful wisdom, she looked directly into my eyes without blinking and simply said, 'Dad, I am ashamed to be your daughter. Get sober or die alone.'" She got up and left.

No one in that meeting was laughing now. We all knew that fear, the fear of dying alone. A few days later, Leopold walked in to AA and has been there ever since. And he agreed that on that night when he dove into his Caesar salad he was still 14 years old. He had never grown up. Was he sorry? Sure. But 59 years of "I'm sorry" gets pretty redundant. He said if his daughter had said anything else to him but what she said, he'd still be drinking. The fact that she was ashamed to be related to him and then told him to basically keep drinking and die alone, well that got his attention. It took a long time, but Leopold is sober today and has his daughter's love. I think that story is so cool. It also proves, regardless of your age, you can learn and the doors of sobriety are open for you, too.

I also remember in the early days of being sober someone sharing at a meeting that after a night out at a family function or at a party with friends, upon waking the next day really hung, they were sure they most likely offended someone, wanted to apologize but didn't know who the hell to call. Smiles on the faces of most people at the meeting.

When I heard this I identified with it immediately. Damn, these people in recovery are pretty smart. They seem to know me before I seem to know me. As I've already stated, I am a humorous fellow. In all humility, of which I possess none, I am really a funny guy when I get going.

The problem with my humor when I was drinking was

that I used it just as I used booze, to keep people at arm's length.

I would describe my style of humor as a cross section between Don Rickles, George Carlin and Robin Williams. (Can you see my lack of humility?) Rickles used to pick on people in his audience and just rip them to shreds. In the 1960s and 1970s that was ok. Today, Rickles would be banned from television for being politically incorrect. I used this tactic many times with people I knew, thinking it was ok. I found out it was not. Carlin was a great story teller, dry witted and great with one liners, like Name the Seven Dirtiest Words You Can't Say On Television. Google it.

And finally, to the late Robin Williams, with whom I readily compare myself; when he got on a roll, with whatever the subject at hand, you could not stop him. His adlibbing was unmatched.

Friends, Donna and Ward, had a New Year's Eve party in 1995. At this time they lived in a huge home which was a borderline mansion, at least to me, who grew up in a 1,000 square foot row home in Philly. My wife and I and three other couples rented a stretch limo for the night so no one would have to drive. Hey, it was New Year's Eve. For an alcoholic, a night like this, with the added incentive of not having to drive, was open season for some serious drinking. The home was tastefully decorated for the Christmas Holidays which for me just added to the romancing of the drink.

When we arrived, they had a piano player sitting at a

Baby Grand knocking out beautiful Christmas music. Candles were lit and purposefully placed around the home giving it a welcoming ambiance. The aroma of cinnamon, baked apples and strawberry attacked the sense of smell. Damn, what a perfect night for drinking in such a perfect environment. That sentence right there should tell both you and me that I am an alcoholic. I guarantee you my wife and the other six friends in that limo did not entertain that thought.

We indulged in some drinks in the limo. The other seven of my comrades for the night had one and maybe started a second drink in the hour drive from our homes to Donna and Ward's. If you remember our quiz earlier, question four reads: "When drinking with other people, do you try to have a few extra drinks when others won't know about it." I answered this with an emphatic "YES."

The reason is simple, I had to drink more to get where I wanted to go. On this night if I drank four Guinness' during the hour trek, hell, my bride probably would have said something and my other friends, well, they would look and tolerate it knowing I was really getting tuned. So to counteract this paranoia, I had a couple shooters of scotch before the limo arrived. Thus, I had a head start and a mini-buzz on, before the night began.

Did my wife know this or any of our friends? No. This is how alcoholics drink. This is how I drank.

These good and gracious hosts had an open bar with top shelf booze. Only the best for this functional alky. I apprehended a tumbler of Glenlivet on arrival and settled in for a long, warm, enjoyable evening.

Two events are worth mentioning that fit into this topic of saying "I'm sorry." During the first hour, as guests were arriving, my buddy Reggie and I ventured over to the Baby Grand and the piano player. Now both of us, along with our wives, years before, had gone to see Phantom of the Opera on Broadway and we loved the music. I asked the piano man if he wouldn't mind playing "The Music of the Night" and a couple of other tunes. As noted earlier, I have a decent voice and love to sing. Give me an audience and I really love to sing. At this moment in time the audience was small, Reggie and I and about six other people, one of which was a woman who, when she heard "The Music of the Night" went ballistic. This was her favorite song for forever!

The great music of Beethoven, Bach, Tchaikovsky or Mozart could not hold a candle to this one song. Now being the comedian I professed to be, I figured I'd adlib some of the words of "The Music" and get a chuckle from this small crowd. I did just that and did get a chuckle from five of the six other people gathered around the piano.

What I adlibbed is irrelevant, what happened, well let's just say it even shook me up. As I went into my first adlib while singing, this woman, who looked normal a moment ago, now had the countenance of someone like the fucking Unabomber or the Son of Sam. She stared at me unblinkingly for over a minute and for the first time in my life, and I'm not exaggerating, I was afraid. She looked like a sociopath, a serial killer. Holy Shit.

The small audience present also witnessed this and began drifting away from me, the piano man and the Baby Grand. Now Reggie and I are about the same height, six feet, two inches and weigh between 200 and 220 lbs. This woman was probably five feet tall and weighed all of a hundred and ten pounds. Yet, when the song ended we bolted, too, she was that scary.

The house, however, was huge and filled with so many people that I figured I could avoid the Unabomber with ease. Yet, every so often I would enter a room gaze in and there, still staring at me, was You Know Who. I guess she finally departed because at the end when everyone gathered in the kitchen she was gone.

Toward the end of the evening we entered the kitchen and it was here that the second "I'm sorry" event occurred. Again, specifics are unimportant. It is enough to say that I went into my Don Rickles mode and proceeded to rip everyone to shreds with my humor. When in this mode, Mother Teresa of Calcutta, St. Peter, the Pope and any other saintly being would not escape my humorous wrath. If I really ripped you, it meant you really knew me, and I loved you!

However, on this night I'm not so sure everyone felt that way. The ride home was subdued. It was early morning New Year's Day, but still you would think we'd at least be chatting about what a great time we had. Nada. I felt like a leper.

We got home safely but when I awoke New Year's Day I knew I must have screwed up. I just felt terrible, and not just physically. I remember sitting in front of our wood burning stove feeling numb and alone. My wife, a perceptive gal, asked what was wrong. I, in turn, asked her did I get carried away last night. She nodded yes. Shit, I needed to make some phone calls. However, like any real good alcoholic, I did not know who I truly offended.

I called Donna and Ward's home. Donna answered. This sweet woman asked was everything ok? I stumbled and mumbled and then came out with it, that I was sorry if I offended anyone last night with my humor. Now Donna and Ward love my humor, always have. She said she didn't think so. I told her about the Unabomber and she said not to worry. Her name was Sabrina and, yeah, she has issues and a personality disorder but overall a nice person. Normally, I would have asked for Sabrina's phone number, but I just asked Donna to tell her I was sorry if I hurt her feelings regarding "The Music of the Night." She said she would. Then I told her, if anyone calls and complains, to let me know, and I would personally call and apologize. That was the end of it. Never heard anything about that party again. I apologized to my wife who told me that there are times when I just go too far and cross the line between being funny and being mean.

In a hundred years I would never consciously hurt anyone. I really am a sensitive and caring person, yet put booze in the equation and all bets are off. I swore to myself that New Year's Day that I would never do that again and sure enough I broke that oath.

Why? Because when I drank I drank too much, and when I tried to stop, I couldn't. In 1995 I just did not know it, and meeting "Gandhi" was a still couple of years away.

INTO THE LIGHT

PREFACE-PART II

The journey into the rooms of sobriety or as I say here, the journey into light, to me, is still something of a miracle. In the preceding part, Into Darkness, I tried to show you where I came from, occurrences of which I had no control, the pain that resided in my head, and the solution I discovered for that pain, alcohol. Obviously not the best choice, but once made, the disease of alcoholism took over, literally. Hopefully, my discussion of the functional alcoholic made some sense to you, if you or a loved one fall into that category. After many years sober, and it is just my opinion, I have concluded there is no such thing as a functional alcoholic. For me it is another oxymoron.

I realize in Part I, I may have used some offensive language, sometimes in the extreme. When I made the commitment to write this book, I took a personal oath to be as honest as possible, remembering that a memoir is seen through lenses that visualize all in hindsight. Yet, my feelings are my feelings and as you read, feelings are not facts. Feelings are raw while facts are sterile. I guess if I grew up in a place like Martha's Vineyard, my language might be more apropos at times, yet I am sure there are drunks there who curse, and Olney is a far off distant planet from the Vineyard.

In Part II, my goal is to allow you to see life in sobriety, well at least my life. There will still be flashbacks into my world of active alcoholism, but only to show you how the light has conquered that darkness.

When I came into Alcoholics Anonymous I put down the drink and figured all would be well. A rude awakening occurred within days and weeks. In AA jargon, I put down the drink, but I still had all of my "isms." One of those isms was the "I am terminally unique-ism."

Basically, what the alcoholic is saying is, "If you had my wife or husband, you would drink, too." Or, "If you had my boss and my shit job, you would drink, too." Or, "If you had to live in the dump I live in and had the bum I have for a spouse, you would drink, too." I'm sure you get the drift.

However, as soon as you start going to meetings and especially the speaker meetings, where a drunk tells their story, you are utterly amazed that the person speaking is telling your story! My God they had a job like yours, a spouse like yours, kids like yours, parents who drank like yours, hit a bottom like yours and so on. I call these God-moments or Ah-ha moments. It's when I knew.

So, I am not terminally unique and if you are an alcoholic, neither are you. There is some comfort in that knowledge, at least for me. Thus, looking at my life in sobriety will not be a blueprint of how it occurs for everyone, nor should it. This is my story. You have your story.

I think you will discover my language improves as I

walk through this light of sobriety and that should make you smile a little. The upcoming chapter, They Were Waiting for Me, might be a little tough on the ears; but at this stage of the journey, my feelings were more than raw. I was hemorrhaging feelings and until I got into the rooms, I knew not how to coagulate them. I felt like a dead man walking.

I was spiritually bankrupt. I had a hole in my soul and booze could no longer fill it. If Alcoholics Anonymous did not work, there wasn't much of an alternative.

Thus, on the day I entered the rooms of sobriety, while I was still traveling from Atlanta to Philly to get to my first meeting, I still could not shake that image of John Adams standing alone in Independence Hall those many years ago, voicing those same haunting words,

"Is anybody there?
Does anybody care?
Does anybody see what I see?"

CHAPTER 25

They Were Waiting For Me

I will attempt not be repetitive here, but there may be some overlap. Hopefully, you remember the description of my epiphany, discovering I was truly an alcoholic, the episode at the Waffle House with Willie and the phone call to Jay from Atlanta's airport that got me to my first AA meeting. Well I need to expand on the phone call to AA in Philly; the date was September 10, 1997.

Jay told me to call the AA Intergroup in Philly, whatever the hell that was, which I did. They must have chosen the woman to answer the phone at Intergroup from angelicvoices.com because I can still hear it, kindness and compassion oozing through the phone. At her, "Hello," the great I am started fumbling and mumbling. I could not get the words out fast enough or coherent enough. I bet this woman could write the greatest book in the world about answering the phone and talking to men and women who just discovered they're alcoholics.

I did get my name right. She was very patient. Then she asked, "Are you looking for an AA meeting?" A raspy "Yes," escaped my lips.

"Ok," she asked, "What county do you live in?"

"Bucks, Lower Bucks County" said I.

She continues, "All right, we have meetings in..." While she is reciting the names of the towns in Lower

Bucks County, I am thinking what kind of alcoholics would attend these? I know shit about high-bottom and low-bottom drunks, never been to a meeting. But arrogantly I wanted to go to a meeting in a good, preferably affluent neighborhood. She finally mentions there is a meeting at 6 p.m. in Southampton. Southampton is an affluent neighborhood. I stop her mid-sentence and tell her, "I'll go to that meeting." She then gave me the phone number of the Southampton AA group. That is how sick I was, how arrogant I was. Well, God fixed my ass right away.

My plane landed at Philly International on time, which in and of itself was a friggin' miracle. It was about 4:00 p.m., the meeting started at 6:00 p.m., plenty of time to get there. My thoughts ranged from "this is the right thing to do" to "what the fuck am I doing?" I knew that if I made this phone call to get directions to this AA meeting, there would be no turning back.

Did I really want to give up alcohol forever? Never have a glass of wine with my wife again? Never bring in the New Year or salute St. Paddy with a glass of champagne or a Guinness? What about eggnog on Christmas Eve? What about a shot of Tullamore Dew celebrating the day of my birth?

Did I really want to order a bottle of Perrier at a business dinner when everyone else would be ordering top shelf booze? Did I not want to have a drink to toast my children at their respective weddings someday in the not-so-distant future?

How would I get through a funeral without having at least a shot of something before the wake? These were my thoughts. Hey, I am an alcoholic.

The day is sketched indelibly in my mind, temperature in the 90's, humidity a saturated 100 percent. The clothes on my back weighed a ton. Forlornly, with head down, I ambled to my car. I must have sat there for about 15 minutes having this internal debate. Right then and there I should have known that I had a serious problem with booze. Again, I ask the question, "What normal person would be asking any of these questions?"

I retrieved the phone number from my briefcase, looked at the phone and picked it up. It weighed a fucking ton. I put it down and picked it up again then I dialed. Now my alcoholic brain was saying, "Maybe the call will go into voice mail?" How fucked up is that? Can you imagine an organization that was in existence to help the next suffering alcoholic to not have a human being pick up the phone and answer it? What would the voice recording sound like? "Hello, you have reached Alcoholics Anonymous. We are sorry no one is here to answer your call. If you were only a beer drinker press 1; if a wine connoisseur, press 2; if a raging hard-liquor, fall-down-drunk, coming off a four-day bender, press 3."

Well, someone did answer the phone on the first ring. I still remember saying, "Hi, my name is George, is this the AA meeting in Southampton?" The guy on the other end said something short and curt like, "Yeah, it is," and then dead silence.

I'm assuming this dude wanted me to spill my guts right then and there; tell him my whole friggin' story. Well, screw him. I simply asked, "Can you give me directions to where you are located?"

"Sure," he said. This guy must have been educated in the school of "Hooked on Phonics." What's with the one word answers?

"Okay, can I have them," said I. And sure enough, in a very friendly tone, he gave me directions to the meeting.

In hindsight, I look back at this first encounter with Alcoholics Anonymous and still wonder how I ever really got into the rooms. I read the aforementioned scenario, and the one emotion that jumps from the pages is again, fear. I was afraid when I called Jay. I was afraid when I called the angel at Intergroup. I was afraid to live life without alcohol. I was afraid of the guy who picked up the phone at the meeting in Southampton. I was engulfed in fear, and I hated every fucking moment of it.

There was also a little paranoia thrown in for good measure. To me the dead silence on the phone was the AA dude waiting for my life's story. In reality he was just awaiting my next question about getting directions. My thought process in the beginning can only be described by one word, hope you are not offended, "Fucked."

After I got the directions, the guy on the other end of the phone says, "If you get lost, just call back, my name is Seamus, ask for me and I'll guide you in." Maybe that was actually my first God moment in sobriety, to have the guy answer the phone, an alcoholic, a drunk like me, having a great Irish name like, Seamus…pretty cool.

Now the moment of truth; I did not get lost and finally pulled into the parking lot with about twenty minutes to spare. God, I can still see all of this like it was yesterday. I first did a "drive-by" as if I were going to rob a friggin' bank like Al Capone. There were about five or six people standing outside smoking cigarettes and drinking what looked like coffee from Styrofoam cups.

I'm pretty sure this is the right place. Yet, just to make sure I do another drive-by. Now the guys with the Styrofoam cups see me coming back on this second drive-by, smile and one of them waves. I drive thirty yards passed them, park the car facing in the opposite direction, turn the ignition off and pray. I knew I was praying because I was saying things like, "Shit, God, what the fuck am I doing here?" Now that is a classy and pious prayer if I ever heard one.

But I kept it up. I am sure the good Lord was a little disappointed in my use of language but was at least happy that I was calling on him by name.

And…I just sat there.

I kept looking down at my watch every 30 seconds, counting down like a NASA engineer at Cape Canaveral, like that was going to make this any less painless. At about five minutes before 6:00 p.m. I extricated myself from the car. My shoes felt like they were nailed to the cement I was walking on. I got to the door, and a couple of guys were still there smoking cigs and drinking coffee.

This big fother mucker turned to me and said, "Hey,

I'm Ned, welcome." He had to be 6'4" and weighed a good 275 pounds. He was obviously not a "Lite Beer" drinker. I extended my hand; he crushed mine. I mumbled my name and entered Alcoholics Anonymous for the very first time in my life. Outwardly, I'm sure I looked calm, cool and collected. Internally, I wanted to shit my pants.

I quickly found an empty chair in the back of the room. This is a Catholic thing. I'm not shitting you. Go to any meeting of any organization. If you were to poll all the folks sitting in the back row away from the speaker, I guarantee that 90 percent of them were raised Catholic. Protestants and Jews go right to the front fearing they will miss something. Catholics go right to the back hoping they will miss something. It's true, you can look it up.

My initial observation focused on a guy sitting at the main table in front of the room with a gavel in hand. Behind him on the wall are two huge banners with the words Twelve Steps and Twelve Traditions plastered across the top of each. Hell, he looks like a judge ready to bring down judgment on someone.

I sit next to this Harley Dude who looks like shit, while I am in my appropriate business attire. He extends his hand, "Hey, I'm John."

I extend my hand and say, "Hey, I'm George, and I think I'm an alcoholic."

He says, "No shit, sit down and listen."

I then turn my head from side to side and am somewhat amazed. These people are chatting amiably to one another, and some of them were even laughing.

What is that about? Who admits they are alcoholics and then laughs? What is so fucking happy and joyous about being in an AA meeting? These folks are more screwed up than I thought. Maybe I really don't belong here. I thought this was serious business; no laughter allowed.

So the head alky slams the gavel down on the table one time and the room goes silent. Well, at least they have some discipline. He begins, "Welcome to the Serenity Group of Alcoholics Anonymous; my name is Tom, and I'm an alcoholic." The group in unison says, "Hi, Tom."

Well, at least these schmucks got some manners, eh? I listen as best as I can, but it ain't easy. I got shit going through my head at Mach-1. He announces something which I really don't hear, and then everyone in the room is looking at me. What the hell did I do? And then Tom repeats the announcement while looking right at me.

"Is there anybody here tonight new to AA, and would you like to introduce yourself by your first name?" Now I get it. I told you I was pretty smart.

I raise my hand. Tom smiles and says, "Yes?"

And I say, "Hi, I'm George" In unison the group says, "Hi, George." Now I'm thinking I'm in some kind of retard school where everyone is brainwashed and mimicking one another. But then a couple of people say things like, "Welcome, glad you're here." And what would later become my favorite, "Keep coming back."

The meeting begins. It's an AA literature meeting, meaning the people at this meeting will go around the room reading a paragraph at a time from whatever AA book was chosen for that night. Tonight's book is called, "Living Sober." Now my first thought was, "That's the biggest fucking oxymoron I had ever heard." How does one live sober when one is an alcoholic? The reading begins and once in a while I hear someone mumble the word, "pass," meaning they did not want to read. My turn came and I, too, mumble "pass." No way was I going to read out loud when I was desperately trying not to succumb to the diarrhea that was attempting to escape from the depths of my bowels.

At about 6:30 p.m., Tom stops the reading and says there will be a five-minute break, so grab some coffee or go outside to smoke or whatever. Half the room flies out the door. I initially followed them thinking maybe a fight or something was going to break out. But they were just all reefer addicts, toking on their Camels or Kools or Winstons or Marlboros.

I had stopped smoking in 1986, so I just stood there with my dick in my hand not knowing what to do. Then I hear this voice from over my shoulder saying, "Hey George, it's me, Seamus the guy who answered the phone." I smiled and shook his hand and immediately judged him.

He did not look too well. He had bloodshot eyes. He spoke with a quiver. When he lit his cigarette, his hand shook so much I thought he was going to light his fucking eyebrows on fire. But he was smiling and I was not. He felt at home in this meeting, and I did not. He was sober, and I was not. Yeah, I hadn't had a drink in 12 days, but I was far, far, far from sober.

We chatted for a minute or two. I couldn't tell you what he said; and before I knew it, we were all schlepping back into the meeting. Tom slammed the gavel again, all was brought to order and he said, "Ok, the meeting is yours." This is commonly known as the "sharing" part of the meeting. Each AA member introduces him-or-herself by name followed by, "...and I'm an alcoholic." I just sat on my hands hoping I would not launch myself toward the fucking door and freedom.

The second person to share was a woman named Pat. She was an attractive woman, possibly in her 50s, dressed in business attire. After saying she was an alcoholic, she looks right at me and says, "George, you are the most important person here tonight."

Now that is more like it! That's what I'm talking about! I'm thinking that Seamus, the dude who answered the phone, must have told her I was someone special, and these people were waiting for me. Maybe she saw me at the break with my eight piece business suit on and could see I was not just an ordinary, run of the mill alcoholic. Again, to contemplate that all of these people were here for me! But then it was over. She just shared about the reading and what it meant to her. A minute or two later she was done. Tom called on someone else. What just happened?

As you can surmise, it took a while for me to get over myself. Humility was not a trait in my arsenal of personal characteristics. As time slowly moved on day by day, the great "I am" learned a few things. The reason Pat said that I was the most important person in the room was not about me, personally. It was acknowledging that the "newcomer," that man or woman, who just walked into their first meeting, was the real reason that Alcoholics Anonymous existed. If people stopped coming to the rooms, there would be no AA. Here I thought Pat might have been attracted to me in some weird way at my first meeting. Not so; she cared about me, glad I was there and came in, but that was the extent of it. She was there for her sobriety, not mine!

The meeting ended at 7:00 p.m. with another gavel slam from Tom. I was ready to dash for the door, but Tom said, "I hope some of you can stay afterward and help clean up, and we have a nice way of closing."

Then 50 alcoholics quietly and reverently form a circle around this room, bow their heads and begin to say "The Lord's Prayer."

"Our Father who art in heaven, hallowed be thy name…" I was shocked and stunned, but I obviously knew the words—me, who could have been Pope.

After the "Amen" everyone said, "Keep coming back, it works if you work it" whatever the hell that meant.

Then, Seamus and a couple of other alkies came over before I could leave and asked where I was going for a meeting tomorrow night? Tomorrow night? Tomorrow night? I just made it through my first AA meeting feeling like Jesus did on his walk to Calvary, and these whack jobs wanted to know where I was going for my next meeting?

How the fuck was I supposed to know? This was the only meeting I had been to and didn't know where there were other meetings. They must have seen the angst in my eyes. Seamus kindly said, "Why don't you just come back here tomorrow night, and we'll see you then. Just don't drink today. Can you do that?"

Ok, I could do that.

And that was the end of my journey in darkness and the beginning of my journey into the light.

I had so many complex feelings that night as I left that first meeting. Parts of me wanted to sing the Hallelujah chorus from Handel's "Messiah." I had entered the rooms of Alcoholics Anonymous; and for the first time in 29 years, I felt welcomed by people I did not even know. People, who society had labeled losers, but who I soon discovered were anything but.

Other parts wanted me to put the car in drive and keep going until I hit Montana and Little Bighorn National Park where I could commiserate with the ghost of General George Armstrong Custer, one of the biggest losers of them all.

But I held on to Seamus' last question as I departed, "Could I not drink just for today?" Yes, I knew I could do that. Not sure how I knew, but until tomorrow I would not take a drink. And without knowing it, I started living one day at a time.

CHAPTER 26

Travelin' Man

This is a fitting prelude for Part II of this chef-d'oeuvre. As I write these words today, I am sitting in the boarding area of an airport in Trenton, New Jersey. Last night we had an ice and sleet storm in and around Philly. Tonight, ten inches of snow are due with temperatures dipping near zero degrees.

Hopefully, we are getting the hell out of Dodge! We're heading to Florida to visit friends. There are no USAir Clubs or fancy restaurants or Boutique Shoppes here in south central Jersey. This is America moving people like cattle. If you were to put up different signage in a foreign language, we could be sitting in Kenya or Bangladesh or Bogota, Columbia. All we need are a couple of live chickens and a couple of wild dogs chasing a pig around with the unattended kids yelling and screaming… you get the picture.

I used to travel for about 20 years of my business life. Flying was a way of life. Whenever I would have to fly, I would get my travel agent or secretary to make sure I had an aisle seat. That way when the "go cart" with the drinks passed by, I'd have first dibs. Through the late 1960s and until April 15, 1986 I smoked cigarettes. In those glorious days of travel they had a smoking section in each plane. I am sure you Green People of the present day are just shaking your heads in amazement. If there were 28 rows of seats in a Boeing 737, somewhere around row 18 began the smoking section. The poor son of a bitch who was in row 17, 16, or 15 was just shit out of luck. I wonder how many of those poor souls died of second-hand smoke.

Meanwhile, we reefer addicts were puffing away on Marlboro Reds, Kools, Lucky Strikes, Larks, Winstons, and Camels, sucking on some suds at a buck a beer and hitting on the bee-u-tiful stewardesses. For those of us who loved to drink heavily, the longer the flight the better. One-hour flights from Philly to Boston did nothing for my disposition. It was those flights from Philly or New York to Dallas or Denver or LA or Vegas, they were joy rides… standing up in the rear galley, smoking a Camel, sucking on a Bud or ten, taking a leak at 33,000 feet in a closet, bullshitting with peers or the flight attendant; now that was sheer untainted heaven.

Today, in this third-world Jersey airport I know for a fact that I am an alky. Why? Well, first thing I noticed in the small bar-eating area are the prices of beers and alcoholic beverages that are posted on a chalkboard. I cannot imagine paying $6.00 for a draft beer. In 1970 we were paying $4.00 for a case of quarts of beer from the oldest brewery in America. Now the beer in those days was not a lager.

Hell, it tasted downright awful, usually, given the nomenclature: Panther Piss. But come on, we alcoholics knew our intake of booze was strictly based on volume, never on quality. Now for you non-alcoholics that is $4 for

374 ounces of beer vs. $6 for an eight ounce draft today (if you are truly an alcoholic, you had that figured out before you got to the end of this sentence!). Many of us old timers in recovery readily confess we could never afford to be an alky in today's world at today's prices. We all would have been low-bottom drunks.

Our plane was delayed an hour. More time to kill. The second thing I noticed was a group of young guys in their 20s or 30s woofin' down those $6 beers. My wife, on the other hand, who is not an alcoholic, never paid them any attention.

This is one of those "wiring" things I talked about earlier. We are just wired wrong. I have not had a drink in 18 years, yet I'm still watching people getting toasted. I can tell the alky from the non-alky in a few minutes. They get that glow in their eyes. You can see their world just lighting up, smiling, laughing, having a good time and getting louder. What I will miss is them pissing their pants at 2 o'clock in the morning or hugging the porcelain god as they vomit all they ingested this glorious day. I will not see them waking up with the Irish Flu. Best of all, I won't be waking up with that same malady.

The neat thing about traveling in sobriety is that there are AA meetings everywhere. During this trip I once again got to a couple meetings at an AA clubhouse. The primary difference between AA meetings in Florida and those in Pennsylvania in early March, the natives do not resemble an albino, as do I. No sun for this Irish kid and my skin tone resembles a white ceramic chicken.

Toward the end of one of these meetings, a young guy raised his hand. He wore a nice golf shirt, pair of shorts and sandals—a clean-cut kid. I think we were all waiting to hear him share something about his good life in sobriety and then he opened his mouth. In a soft and somber voice he described how just the week before he was sitting on the porch of this AA Club House, sick as a dog, with a serious case of the DT's, alcoholic shakes. He had awakened that morning on the floor of his kitchen lying in his vomit. He had a slight recollection of his wife telling him she was leaving and taking the kids. All of us nodded our heads; we had heard this before. But then he added this kicker, which tells you the mind of a true alcoholic, he said, "Although I knew my wife had taken the kids and left, that's not what I was upset about. My first thought was how much booze was left in the bottle of Jack that was out in the garage. Was there enough to get me through this day?"

Now, THAT IS HOW ALCOHOL TALKS TO US ALCOHOLICS. Can it get any lower than that? Sadly, the answer to that question is yes. This young guy cared more about the bottle of Jack than what he had inflicted on his wife and children.

You could have heard a pin drop. Every alcoholic in that meeting had their heads bowed in deep thought. We call this "keeping it green" in the rooms of sobriety regardless if you have one day, 18 years or 50 years sober. It had only been a week since that day, but he shared that he called the guy who had given him his phone number when he was on the porch with DT's. He'd been going to two meetings a day since then. Then he said something that again struck home with all of us.

Let him tell it, "Gotta be honest, I've been here before, desperate and in an AA meeting. I always did it so my wife wouldn't leave me or for my parents so they would pay my college tuition. This time I'm here for me and I told my wife that the moment I saw her last week upon her return." Does this guy have a shot at sobriety? Sure. Is it guaranteed? Nope, nothing is guaranteed when we are dealing with alcohol or drugs. The only guarantee that I, with 18 years sober, and this guy with one week sober has, is that if we do not pick up a drink today it will be physically impossible to get drunk. That is the only guarantee.

I will now tell you a true story of what happened to me when I was three-weeks sober. I had just asked Chuck to be my sponsor. I still had my big-bucks job, still traveling and had to go to a sales convention in Las Vegas. I was terrified, scared shitless. Three weeks without a drink may not seem like a long time to you, but to me it was an eternity. The guys in my AA home group gave me a list of meetings that were in Vegas. Some of them gave me their phone numbers as did my new sponsor, Chuck. They told me to call them if I got jammed up. Shit, I hadn't even taken off and I was already jammed up.

I arrived at Philly's airport, boarded the plane and took the aisle seat that the travel agent booked for me four weeks in advance.

Yep, four weeks ago I was still drinking. Now the guys in my AA group gave me a copy of the book ***Alcoholics Anonymous***. It's pretty thick.

I pull it out and in huge gold lettering on the spine of the book it says, "A-L-C-O-H-O-L-I-C-S A-N-O-N-Y-M-O-U-S. Real subtle, eh? On top of that...I am afraid. I am afraid of the go cart that will be coming by shortly, I am afraid of taking a drink, I am afraid of being alone, I am afraid of what will happen when I get to Vegas.

I bury my head and eyes into the Big Book to avoid all contact with my fellow passengers. Fortunately I love to read, so I accomplished this task without much consternation. The pilot makes his first broadcast as we level off and begin cruising at 33,000 feet. Suddenly, the guy across the aisle from me taps me on shoulder. I jump out of my skin. He apologizes for the intrusion. He nods to this monstrosity of a book I have in my lap and asks, "Are you a friend of Bill Wilson's?" I reply in a not so subtle voice, "Who the fuck is Bill Wilson? Is he from Philly?"

"No," he replies, "I think he is from Vermont." When I share this in the rooms of sobriety this usually brings down the house. Why? Bill Wilson is the co-founder of Alcoholics Anonymous along with another boozer named Dr. Bob Smith. They began AA in 1935. And I had no friggin' idea at three weeks sober who the hell he was.

This guy sitting across from me was sober 21 years. Without trying to sound blasphemous, he turned out to be my bloody guardian angel. Of course he did not shut up for the five or six hour flight. He told me the history of AA, its founders, the groups he belonged to in the Philly area, and the meetings he attended around the country. He told me he still remembers when he was three-weeks sober, which I believed was complete horse shit. Told me he still remembered his last drunk. In AA terminology, this angel "twelve stepped" me across the country. He was helping another alcoholic and practicing these principles in all his affairs. He was taking care of his sobriety.

The go cart must have gone up and down that aisle six times. I never saw it. Before I knew it we were descending into Sin City, but I was no longer afraid. Do I think for a moment that it was a coincidence that this man, this drunk in recovery, was sitting across the aisle from me? Hell no! When it comes to my faith and sobriety, there are no coincidences.

We parted ways at the baggage claim, and I never saw him again. This God, whom I did not believe cared one iota for me, had sent me a gift in the guise of another drunk in recovery. I am sure Bill Wilson probably broke into a smile, too. They kept telling me in the rooms that more would be revealed. This was the first inkling of that. I am sure this Good Samaritan told me his name, but it is gone from my memory banks. Maybe that is why they call it Anonymous.

This was my second trip ever to Sin City. Got off at my gate, started walking through the terminal, and I hear the sounds of the "one armed bandit," the slot machine.

Are you kidding me? They want your money before you even take a leak. I head to baggage claim, retrieve what's mine, head outside and grab a cab. Within minutes, I arrive at the famous MGM Grand Hotel where I will be lodged for the next five nights.

Now the guys back at Serenity Group instructed me to call Chuck after I got settled in Vegas. As an active alcoholic I was never good at "taking direction." During those first couple of weeks, Seamus, Albert, Ned, Tom and the rest of the group kept telling me that if I wouldn't follow directions or the suggestions of those in the rooms who knew how to stay sober, I would probably drink again.

So, I looked at my watch, it was 10:00 p.m., call Chuck. This barely audible scratchy voice answers the phone and says, "Who the hell is calling at this ungodly hour?"

"Chuck, it's me George." Now Chuck is a former cop and immediately his voice goes to high alert status. "Are you ok? Where are you? Do you need help?"

I casually say, "No, I'm fine. The guys told me to call you once I got settled into Las Vegas, so I'm just following their directions."

"Well numbnuts" says Chuck, "it's fucking 1:00 a.m. in the morning and I have to wake up in three hours."

"Holy crap I'm not on Eastern Time but on Pacific Coast Time," I say. "I am so sorry." Then, I hear him softly laugh and tell me not to worry. Yeah, he was a little pissed that I woke him, but he was glad I was safe and even happier that I had actually followed direction.

The rest of the week went pretty well. My boys back home told me to stay out of the casino and avoid temptation. That was not a problem. I was never a gambler. However, to get to the convention floor in the MGM, you had to walk through the casino, so I saw it all anyway. I heard the noise of the slots, the bantering of the card dealers, and the rolling of the craps and saw the scantily and brightly clad, lovely barmaids floating around with their trays filled with complimentary drinks, mysteriously appearing at the side of the next gambler and the next. Music seemed to play incessantly in the casino 24/7 and strobe lights were everywhere. An alcoholic could surely "romance" the drink in these surrounds.

Chuck gave me the name of an AA meeting in Vegas. It was at a Club House, just like Serenity Group was back home. AA Club Houses have lots of meetings throughout the day. I called the number I had and this deep, baritone, husky voice answers, "H-e-l-l-o."

Oh no, are we doing the "hooked on phonics" routine again? Did my buddy Seamus back home tell this dude to answer this way? So I say, "Hi, I'm George, an alcoholic from Philly and I need a meeting." This guy says, and I kid you not, "Hi, I am Running Badger. Where are you staying?" I tell him the MGM. He tells me that he and another guy will pick me up in an hour for the 6:30 p.m. meeting. I hang up. "Running Badger." What kind of a fucking name is that?

At 6:30 p.m. sharp the Badger and his buddy pull up in a beat up, rusted out, looking like a piece of shit Ford

Explorer and tell me to get in. Like I've said before, I am a street kid from Philly. My instincts are to run like hell in the opposite direction. But when I look at these two guys through the passenger side window, they are smiling and appear harmless. I bow my head, say a quick prayer like, "God don't let these bastards kill me" and get in. To my utter surprise the inside of this piece of shit is immaculate. No kidding, you could eat off the dashboard.

I soon discover that these two recovering alcoholics are Native Americans, Navajos. Running Badger reintroduces himself to me and then his buddy extends his hand and says his name is Bear. That's it. Not Running Bear, Prancing Bear, Drinking Bear…just Bear.

I shake his hand. They call me Georgie. I do not correct them. They are much bigger than I am.

The meeting is great. I can still remember it. I have been to thousands of meetings in 18-years of sobriety, but those in the very beginning had the greatest impact on me and are most memorable.

This was a speaker meeting. The man who spoke had been seven-years sober. He looked to me like a normal guy in a golf shirt, khaki pants, and wearing a pair of Docksiders. He then related how the year before he got sober; he had lost everything because of booze. His wife left him with the kids, his house went into foreclosure and he had to file for bankruptcy. He found an old-burned-out VW Beetle and this became his home until he walked into the rooms of sobriety. He carried all his life possessions around in green trash bags. He had nothing.

He then described to us his life today, how he possessed all he ever desired. Not things, but everything he ever truly wanted. He met a woman in the rooms whom he married. They had a child together. He has the children from his first marriage back in his life.

Yes, he had a good job, but you could hear and see that he felt most grateful because he was truly "loved." He felt loved by his real family and loved by his AA family.

Shit, I never thought about it that way, but he was right. I now had two families to lean on, and as far as I could tell, the more the merrier.

Running Badger and Bear picked me up every night for the meeting. On the last night, someone made a cake for the group, so we hung around afterward and relaxed on homemade chocolate cake and AA coffee.

I never visited Las Vegas again. I may never. However, I will always remember the gifts of sobriety that were freely given me by Running Badger and Bear in the desert of Las Vegas, and if I do visit Sin City again, I will knock on that AA Club House door and know that a hand will be extended in welcome, offering me a chair, a cup of coffee, and if I am lucky, some chocolate cake.

CHAPTER 27

"Only the Lord Saves More"

From 1973 to 1976 the Philadelphia Flyers Hockey Club of the NHL were known as the "Broad Street Bullies." Everyone, I mean everyone, outside of Philly hated, loathed, detested and prayed that these bullies in orange and black would never win a game. The saying, "I went to a boxing match last night, and a hockey game broke out" can be attributed to my Flyers.

On that both famous and infamous team was a goaltender by the name of Bernie Parent (sounds like Pair-aun). Bernie is a French Canadian and is a member of Hockey's Hall of Fame. He was so good during these years that the Flyers went to three Stanley Cup Finals in a row and won two of them. Gene Hart, the television and radio announcer for the club dubbed him great with the following saying, "Only the Lord saves more than Bernie Parent." I love Bernie. He still is one of my favorite athletes of all time. He, too, has talked about his battles with alcohol.

In Alcoholic Anonymous, we have what are called sponsors. We can steal Gene Hart's line and say, "Only the Lord saves more alcoholics than sponsors." If you are still reading this book and are possibly convinced that you or a loved one are one of us and do come into the rooms, you will eventually need a sponsor.

I mentioned briefly in an earlier chapter that Chuck was my sponsor. The guys in the AA Club House where I got sober, night after night in the beginning, kept telling me I had to get a sponsor if I wanted to stay sober. Hell, they did not just keep telling me this, they downright harassed the shit out of me to get one. They told me I could try to sponsor myself but then my sponsor would be an asshole and I would probably drink again. Not a good plan.

Here is what it says in one of AA's pamphlets titled, "Questions and Answers on Sponsors:" In A.A., sponsor and sponsored meet as equals, just as Bill W. and Dr. Bob did. Essentially, the process of sponsorship is this: An alcoholic who has made some progress in the recovery program shares that experience on a continual, individual basis with another alcoholic who is attempting to attain or maintain sobriety through A.A."xv

Let's clarify the players here. In the last chapter in this magnum opus I mentioned Bill W. on my trip to Vegas at three-weeks sober as one of the co-founders of AA. The other is Dr. Bob Smith. It is a given documented fact that AA would not exist if these two gentlemen did not do what they were led by the Spirit to do. Briefly explained, Bill W. in 1935 was getting sober on his own. He did not have a drink for few months, when he had to leave his home in New York and travel on business to Akron, Ohio. Alcoholics Anonymous did not exist. He was sober, but very alone. At the end of his first workday in Akron he checked into his hotel. The hotel had a bar.

Toward dinner, he wandered the lobby and heard the

noise in the bar, and it was calling to him. He began romanticizing the drink. The clink of the ice cubes in the tumbler of scotch and the atmospheric pop of a champagne bottle. He began, as we say in the rooms, to white knuckle it. He was being tempted and he knew it. He wanted to drink.

Also in close proximity of the bar were a couple of pay phones. (If you are under 40 years of age, google it.) Bill had an inspirational thought. He jumped into one of the phone booths, got the yellow pages and started calling churches in the area. No, he was not looking for God or his Higher Power. He was looking for another alcoholic. He was positive a priest or pastor could tell him of at least one of their flock who was a drunk and needed help. He struck out on the first few calls. Finally he called a Protestant church and the pastor did indeed know an alcoholic who was a great man, helped a lot of people, but could not stay sober; meet Dr. Bob Smith.

Bill visited Dr. Bob in his home. Dr. Bob was both an alky and a pill popper. His story is in the Big Book of AA. Three or four hours and a couple pots of coffee later and the birth of AA occurred. By themselves, they both realized they would drink again. But helping each other, talking things through before picking up that first drink, they could stay sober a day at a time.

So, yes AA has a program of recovery based on the Twelve Step program, but it is one drunk helping another drunk that makes it work.

Bill eventually went home to New York and found

other drunks, while Dr. Bob stayed in Akron and did the same. Pretty cool, eh? So, Bill was Dr. Bob's sponsor and Dr. Bob, Bill's.

Today, AA has about two million members. Those who come into the rooms and get a sponsor and follow directions, usually but not always, stay sober.

One of my buddies in the AA Club House was Greg. He was about 15-months sober when I got there. We were only a few years apart in age, but he looked much older. He still had red eyes, his hands shook but he was sober and working the program. I asked him if I could have a woman as a sponsor. He said, "No knucklehead, men with men, women with women." Shit.

The reason I wanted a woman had nothing to do with sex. I was and am happily married. However, I knew that I would have to talk about myself. I find it extremely easy talking to women. I could tell a woman anything. It may be all bullshit, but I can trust a woman. To find some dude whom I eventually have to trust, work the steps and talk to him on a regular basis, no bloody way. I said this to Greg. He handed me a five dollar bill and told me to go to the corner bar and start drinking now, because without a sponsor that's where I'll end up. No subtle message there from my buddy, Greg, eh?

Obviously, I trusted no man because I had no relationships with any man. There were none in my life. Sure I had a couple of male friends. Two of my best, whose names are Reggie and Tim, I trust with my life. But they are not alkies.

Three weeks sober, I said a prayer before entering an evening meeting. This may be the first prayer I ever said where I was not "bargaining" with God. I was not praying, "I'll do this, if you do that." This time I prayed, "Lord, I do not want to drink. Lead me to a man whom I can trust to be my sponsor. Amen." During this meeting, Chuck raised his hand and said, "Hi, I'm Chuck, and I'm an alcoholic and today I am pissed off. I am sober a long time (18 years at that time to be exact) and my stepson is driving me fucking nuts." He expounded on this theme for about three minutes. He spoke of his second wife, his other kids and step-kids and how even though he was sober a long time, he thought about taking a drink. He did not drink, but he thought about it.

I knew that God put Chuck at that meeting for me. I also have two step-kids and a second wife and three kids of my own and an ex-wife. I drank a lot over the crap that sometimes happens to step-parents and step-children, second wives and ex-wives and shit going on with my own kids. After the meeting, I think I did the bravest thing I'd ever done to that point in my life, I asked a man, Chuck, to be my sponsor. He said he would and would be honored to be my sponsor. I thought he was a little nuts to say it would be an honor but I thanked him anyway.

At this brief introduction, we discovered that we grew up in the same neighborhood in Olney, attended the same grammar school, drank in some of the same bars, and knew some of the same drunks from the old hood. Chuck is two years older than me. We both now lived in Bucks

County and were both alcoholics in recovery. Chuck had 18 years sober, and I had two and half weeks.

Once I had chosen Chuck as my sponsor, I actually thought "well that's over with, let's move on with life." He always told me not to put him on a pedestal, that he was a drunk just like me. He had one day, today, not to drink. Although he had 18 years of sobriety, he knew the fall from any pedestal would be catastrophic. He gave me his phone number and told me to call him as often as I wanted. That phone number was like an anchor in my wallet. The first few weeks I did not call him at all. I saw him at the same meetings in the Club House, but I did not want to bother him with my shit. That was part truth and part lie. The truth was that I began to realize that prior to sobriety, it was always about me. I was sick of talking about me. The lie part, well, I just did not want to call him at all. I didn't know what I'd say, and if I did say something, maybe he'd tell me to get laid, buzz off or plain out reject me (like the other men in my life).

Finally, Chuck knew what I was going through. That is the beauty of sobriety in AA.

Even though Chuck had 18 years sober, he also had two-and-a-half weeks at one time. So he told me to call him even if it was to say hello and tell him that the Philadelphia Eagles suck, meaning just talk about life. It took a while, but the phone calls started happening. Chuck soon became not only my sponsor but my friend. Sometimes it doesn't happen that way. Sometimes the sponsor is just a sponsor. He/she helps the alcoholic through the twelve steps and it's more of a business relationship. I am not built that way. I'm a sensitive guy; if you help me in any way, I will always consider you a friend.

I do not like throwing any old statement around when it comes to sobriety so I say this with all sincerity, at 53-days sober, Chuck saved my life. Now he will always tell you that God saved my life; he just used Chuck as an instrument. After many years, I have sponsored other guys and I tell them the same. However, as this story unfolds, the God of my understanding didn't appear to have a cell phone.

I was attending a huge software convention in Phoenix, Arizona. It was October 1997. Most companies hold a corporate gathering in a suite prior to heading over to the convention hall, sort of a kick-off. Well for 12 of us in a small division of this company; it was a kick-out. We all got laid off. Are you kidding me? These schmucks flew us across the country to tell us they cut the division…might as well have cut our throats. And me, 53-days sober, what the hell was I going to do, now?

One of the engineers had a brilliant idea. There was Hooters about half a mile from the convention center and this dude says, "Road trip!" So we headed off to Hooters. Now I knew these guys were going to tie one on, and they wanted me to join them. My buddy Greg back at home in AA always told me to stay away from people, places and things that could jam me up about taking a drink. I'm pretty sure he was talking about Hooters. I did go in and sit with the boys and ordered a Coke. I never touched it. Yes, the scantily clad women waiting on tables had nice hooters, but I had to get out of Dodge. I had my travel bag with me, so I said my goodbyes knowing I'd never see any of these people again and bolted out of Hooters. Problem was, I had four hours to kill before my flight home.

Then, another God moment occurred. It was blazing hot in Phoenix, temperature about 110 degrees even though it was October. Now people out there will tell you, "Yeah, but it's a dry 110 degrees." Yeah, well, put a pizza in a dry heated oven and it will cook the hell out of it. I had to get off the street and hide out for a few hours from booze. I vividly remember dropping my head and saying a prayer, "Lord, I don't want to drink, help me." Not real original, but hell, I was in sheer panic mode.

When I raised my eyes, tucked away on a side street about a block and a half from Hooters, I see a church steeple with a crucifix on its peak (not a cross but a crucifix).

This is what tells a person that it's a Catholic Church. (For you non-religious types, the crucifix has the crucified body of Christ replicated on its surface). Amen. I don't remember my feet hitting the surface of the street. Within a minute or two I was sitting in a pew in a Catholic Church. There was no one in sight and I did not care in the least. I knew for a fact that the God of my understanding was there in that Tabernacle. I sat way in the back. I sat in silence. I was alone again.

And then it really hit me. I was not alone at all.

Yes, God was with me, and Christ himself was in the tabernacle, but all my buddies back at home in AA were there, too. Chuck was there, as was Greg, Penn State Timmy, Five-minute Andy, Finn, Cryin' Brian and all the rest. I had my Big Book with me so, just as I did on that first trip to Vegas, I pulled it out and started to read. An hour went by, and I had not thought of a drink at all. However, I still had to get to the airport where there were bars, a lay-over in Pittsburgh where there were more bars, and then home to Philly.

Feeling a bit better, I headed to the airport in Phoenix. I checked my bag and went right to a phone booth and called Chuck. "Please, God, let him answer." And he did. I told him what happened. He could hear the angst in my voice. He listened to me ramble and curse those fother muckers who ruined my life. He just listened. I must have dumped on him for eight monotonous minutes, and he said nothing. When I stopped talking all I heard was silence. "Chuck, are you there?"

"Yeah," he said, "I'm here." Then he asked me only one question, "Did you pick up a drink today?" I almost shouted into the phone, "FUCK NO!" Then he said, "Dude, you are a winner." What the frig' does that mean? I told him I just lost a six figure job; I have a wife and five kids and a dog back home that depend on me, and he's telling me I am a winner. I thought, I gotta get me a new friggin' sponsor.

Then Chuck said, "George, did you just listen to yourself?" Huh? "You said you have a wife, five kids and a dog that depend on you...you...not your fucking six figure job. So get your head out of your ass, and when you hang up the phone, thank God for that wife, five kids and that dog and the fact that you did not drink. They are His gifts to you, not your fucking six figure salary. Got it?"

Damn, right between the eyes. I meekly said, "Got it." He told me to call him again when I got to Pittsburgh, and I did. I was much calmer this time and thanked him for the shot across my bow. He said no problem. That's what sponsors are for.

Well to end this tale, I got home safely. I was home before my wife got in from work, and the kids were not home. Only our yellow lab, Goldie, was home. She bounded toward me full of joy and almost knocked me on my ass. I hugged her as hard as I could hug any creature that God created. I began to cry, not tears of sorrow or fear, but tears of joy. This four-legged creature that God had blessed us with loved me unreservedly and I needed to hold on to her for dear life at least for a minute or two.

My wife came home. I calmly told her what had happened, told her not to worry that I would get another job. I had some severance from the shit company that laid us off, and I would get unemployment compensation until a new job appeared. The next night I went to the Club house, saw Chuck and hugged him, too. I thanked him and told him that he saved my butt.

"Nah, God saved your ass," he said, he was just a drunk like me trying to stay sober. Helping another alcoholic is how you do that. Bill W. and Dr. Bob, Chuck and me...this sponsor thing works.

Yet, my sponsors in AA meant and mean so much more. I have had three. Chuck was my sponsor for the first four years of my sobriety. Whenever I share in an AA meeting, I usually quote from something Chuck taught me. I recall he told me that the difference between me and God was that God did not wake up this morning thinking he was George. He also taught me that I would hear of three programs in Alcoholic Anonymous; my program, your program and the AA program and two out of the three suck! He told me to always extend my hand to the newcomer, the guy or gal with a day sober.

To counteract my ego he told me two things: first, that when I'm at a meeting, pretend everyone in the room is a newcomer, then when I do share, I might say something that is actually worthwhile for that new person to hear rather than some esoteric bullshit that I might want to share. The second thing he told me kind of hurt and I can still remember the day he said it.

Let me explain. A cool thing occurs in AA. I call it one of the perks. Trust me; there are hundreds of perks in the rooms of sobriety. However, one usually happens at the end of every month in AA. We celebrate anniversaries. They may seem a useless exercise to some, especially the newcomer; but take it from this alcoholic, the psychology behind it works. In 99% of the AA meetings I have ever attended in my own area and all over the country, each group celebrates anniversaries by giving the celebrant a coin. The following are the usual celebrations: you get a coin for 30 days, 60 days, 90 days, six months, nine months, your first-year anniversary and then annual coins for continuous sobriety.

Well, it was September 30, 1997. The guy running the meeting during the pre-meeting announcements asked was anyone celebrating an anniversary, and then he went through the litany starting with 30 days. I raised my hand. At this moment, you are supposed to stand up, say your name, "Hi, I'm George; and I'm an alcoholic; and today I have 30 days." I did this and the cheers in the room were deafening. You would've thought Babe Ruth just crushed one out of Yankee Stadium or it was the end of the 12th round of the *Thrilla in Manila* between Ali and Frazier.

I was embarrassed and sat down. A couple other people also celebrated anniversaries and received the same reception. I really thought all of this was a bit juvenile.

At the break, Chuck meets me outside where the reefer dudes are lighting up their cancer sticks and hands me this coin. I look at it and on the front it says ONE MONTH sober. I could tell this moment meant a lot to Chuck. He then said, "Thirty days is a long time to be without a drink. Congratulations."

But I said, "Yeah, easy for you to say who has 18 years." You see, I couldn't even take a compliment when it was offered. I told him I didn't feel all that sober. Yeah, I hadn't drunk or drugged in 30 days but I still felt shitty. And then I started to analyze the shit of my first 30 days.

Then Chuck taught me this lesson—and it hurt. As I was ready to continue with my speech, he cut me off at the knees and said, "George, stop thinking about you. Getting the 30-day coin isn't about you. It's to show the guy with one day or ten days sober that it can be done. Get it? And, George, you're probably smart enough NOT to get this program." Then he turned and walked back into the meeting once again, leaving me with my dick in my hand.

Ouch! What a screw up I was in early sobriety. But neither Chuck, nor Finn, nor Greg, nor Ned, nor Tommy, nor anyone ever told me not to come back. Sometimes in the middle of me sharing something totally ridiculous and off the wall, someone would wait until I was done, smile and then say, "Keep coming back." Meaning, keep coming back and yes, even you will one day figure some of this shit out.

I stayed long enough to get my 60-day coin, 90 days, 6 months and all the rest. I carry my yearly coin in my pocket everywhere I go. The one in my pocket today reads XVIII years, Roman numerals for 18. Prayerfully, one day at a time, I will continue receiving these coins, reminding me that getting one is not about me. It's about that man or woman who has one day or ten days sober, knowing that they, too, if they stay around long enough, will see the miracle happen.

CHAPTER 28

24

No, do not look for a description of some Jack Bauer episode. The 24 here refers to the number of hours in one calendar day, the time it takes the earth to make one complete turn on its axis, taking us from day to night back to day. I believe I mentioned this earlier. If you are at a party, at the mall, walking down Main Street, in a Starbucks, at a bowling alley, in a restaurant, at a church social or at the beach and you hear someone say, "Well, we only have today" or "Listen, just take it one day at a time," you may be in the presence of a friend of Bill W's.

The first time I remember hearing this saying, I was still actively drinking. For a few years our seminary class, both the guys who got ordained priests in 1978 and the "quitters" as we called ourselves, got together at one of the quitters aunt's home. They had a huge back yard and swimming pool. Many of us quitters had kids and the pool was a great treat.

Mickey and Tinker came to these events along with some others, and Mrs. Tinker and Mr. Tinker came, too. Not many other parents of the priests or quitters came; the Tinkers were always there.

In the early 1990s, Mr. Tinker died. He was an ok guy, but always had an edge about him. He had been ill a very long time. Mrs. Tinker took care of him until the very end.

The following year, I can still see her sitting in the living room alone, hands clasped, head bowed as if in prayer. I happened to walk by, looked in and she looked up with mist in her eyes. I knew why. I gave her a hug and simply asked her how she did it, how she got through the last couple of years with the love of her life so ill. I can see her face still. She meekly smiled and said, "George, a lot of one days at a time."

I'm sure my face said, "What?" She continued, "My life with my husband wasn't always easy. For many years, he had a problem with the drink." Where did I hear that from later in my life? "There is an organization out there that taught me to live, "one day at a time, to just take today and not worry about tomorrow." I never asked her or Tinker if his dad was an alcoholic or whether the organization was AA or Al-Anon. I knew my buddy Tinker had some issues with depression and booze at the end of his life. As we have discovered, it is hereditary.

Besides taking one day at a time, early on in sobriety we are taught to live in the moment and not project. For at least the third or fourth time, we alcoholics are wired differently. Let me proceed once more. One of the shorted circuits that attempt to run the gray matter between our ears on a continual basis, even when it is broken, is our projection machine. Now even non-alcoholics have projection machines. They just usually have a different way of dealing with it…of fixing it.

Now, this device in the brain of an alcoholic is extremely dangerous. Why you may ask? It constantly has us living in tomorrow. For normal drinkers that may be fine; but for a drunk in recovery, that is a country to avoid at all costs. The other device in our brain that leads us to bad places is our instant replay machine. This apparatus has the alcoholic reliving what happened yesterday.

Tomorrow and yesterday—can you see how this can lead to utter disaster for the alcoholic and addict? Tomorrow is filled with dread and fear of what might never happen. Yesterday is filled with guilt, shame and remorse of that which is in the past, gone forever. There is not a thing you can do about it.

There is a piece of literature in AA called the Green Card.

Let's hear what it says about these two days:

> "There are two days in every week about which we should not worry, two days which should be kept free from fear and apprehension.
>
> "One of these days is YESTERDAY with its mistakes and cares, its faults and blunders, its aches and pains. YESTERDAY has passed forever beyond our control.
>
> All the money in the world cannot bring back YESTERDAY. We cannot undo a single act we performed; we cannot erase a single word we said... YESTERDAY is gone.
>
> "The other day we should not worry about is TOMORROW with its possible adversaries, its burdens, its large promise and poor performance. TOMORROW is also beyond our immediate control. TOMORROW'S sun will rise, either in splendor or behind a mask of clouds, but it will rise. Until it does, we have no stake in TOMORROW for it is as yet unborn.

"This leaves only one day...TODAY. Any man can fight the battle of just one day. It is only when you and I add the burdens of these two awful eternities...YESTERDAY AND TOMORROW that we break down. It is not the experience of TODAY that drives men mad—it is remorse or bitterness for something which happened YESTERDAY and the dread of what TOMORROW may bring.

"LET US, THEREFORE, LIVE BUT ONE DAY AT A TIME!!"xvi

You have already read one of my examples of this malady of living in either yesterday or tomorrow in a different context. Remember when I discovered I had testicular cancer in 1988? Well, all the other bullshit aside, as soon as that urologist told me I had a malignant tumor, I was already writing my eulogy.

The family was already planting me six feet under, the wife was looking for a new husband, the kids for a new Dad, my mom—nah even she wouldn't want another me—and that is why I really drank.

This thing in my skull was telling me I was dead; and the saddest thing of all, I believed it. A rational person might have a similar experience concerning their plight of getting cancer and been totally afraid and dreaded the prospect of dying. Yet, only an alcoholic would have himself planted in the ground before surgery, and then drink every day before surgery, after surgery and during 30 radiation treatments. Think about it.

When I took that turn toward the light, toward sobriety, I thought I'll never go there ever again. I will live in today and only in today. Yeah, right.

Putting down the drink I discovered and continue to discover that if I'm anything in sobriety, it is the fact that I am still human, filled with human defects of character, flaws, personality quirks, other shortcomings and still possess a projection machine.

Living one day at a time is the answer, but it ain't easy.

CHAPTER 29

Relationships

I made a statement earlier in this opus of mine that alcoholics, me in particular, suck at relationships. Now I'm not talking about just getting along with people. I get along with just about everyone I meet. Most alcoholics and addicts in recovery readily admit they were people pleasers when they were out there. I am a likeable guy. I believe those who know me would say that. What I am talking about is me in a real relationship with you, where we know each other, maybe not intimately, but enough that we know strengths, weaknesses, likes and dislikes. Know what makes us tick, what makes us happy, sad, angry, frustrated and joyful.

The first real relationships I cared about were my first girlfriend and then subsequent girlfriends until I entered the seminary. Yeah, I cared about guy relationships, the guys who hung on the corner, but I would never let my guard down around one of those dudes. The less they really knew about me the better. (Do you think fear had anything to do with that?)

Looking back through the lenses of time, early on, I must honestly state that alcohol played a role in these relationships from the beginning.

My first girlfriend's name was Shari. We kissed in her parlor in September 1968, my junior year in high school.

It was a warm night and she asked me to walk her home. I said sure. I remember her grabbing my hand and how soft the texture of her skin felt against mine. I don't think I had been touched tenderly by anyone since the day we planted my Dad in Beverly National Cemetery those many years ago.

Shari was a year younger than me. We both kind of hung around the same locality, near the Dundee house, near our old grammar school. You all should know that before alcohol, that kiss was the biggest BAM! in my life. I was not expecting to be kissed, but it was the greatest surprise, Pearl Harbor kiss ever! That sneak attack buckled my knees and curled my toes. I fell head over heels in love. For the next couple of weeks all was good, but I went and screwed it up.

Our first official date was to be a Cardinal Dougherty High School football game. The short version of the story: I stood her up. My Uncle Jim, the pre-Archie Bunker dude that didn't really like me, gave me two tickets to a Philadelphia Eagles football game because he had the guilts and the Eagles sucked. If those Eagles were any good, I'd never have seen those babies. My buddy, Al Dundee, was supposed to take Shari's sister, Debbie. I told him about the Eagles tickets and he said, "Listen, we're late anyway, so the girls are probably pissed. I'd rather not get yelled at. Let's boogie. To the Eagles we go!" I remember knowing this was not the right thing to do, but I did it anyway. So within weeks of the first kiss and my first love, it was over.

I remember trying to make it up to Shari, but she would have none of it; and I could not blame her. We still hung out in the same hood, but she got a new beau, and I discovered booze which killed all the bad feelings I was having. A few months passed and another girl whose name was Mary crossed my path. It was April 1969.

For a couple of months we dated. I actually showed up for Mary. She was one of 12 kids. On the first date all 11 siblings plus Mom and Dad where there to inspect me. They lived in a row home like I did. We had three people living in it, they had 14! Yes, they were all skinny except for one brother who was a tub. I'm guessing he ate all the shit no one else wanted for dinner.

It sounded like they called Mr. Hanson "Da" so I knew he was Irish. He told me to have her home by 11 p.m. or he would send the IRA after me. He kind of laughed and made the gesture with his right hand like he was pointing a gun at me. Shit, I had Mary home at 10:50 p.m. which kind of ticked her off; but you don't fuck with the IRA even when they're kidding.

Mary was the first girl with whom I shared an "our song." You know, you date someone and sooner or later you both love the same song for dancing or singing or just for listening. Ours was "Bad Moon Rising" by Credence Clearwater Revival (CCR). Part of the chorus' lyrics went, "… there's a bad moon on the rise."

We changed those words as did lots of kids in the 60s and shouted, "…and there's a bathroom on the right." Corny, I know, but it was groovy back then. Mary also had a great laugh. I mean it started at her toenails; and when she exploded in laughter, it was genuinely infectious. She had beautiful eyes that were penetrating. When I spoke to her, her attention was undivided. It kind of scared me a little. She had a great bullshit filter and would call me on it when I was shoveling it. Later in life, Mary became a successful lawyer defending the poor and underprivileged in the city of Philadelphia. I am sure these attributes, these God-given talents, aided her immensely.

In June of '69, the neighborhood had a "we're done school" party at another Irish family's household, the McNally's. Of course, there were no parents around. There was a lot of beer and someone stooped low enough to buy a case of Boone's Farm Apple Wine. This was the shit that you drank where you had a severe hangover the next day and a case of the zits. That is how sweet it was.

Well, I started the party with Mary, but she had to leave early. I'm guessing the IRA had a search party out for her. (Only kidding) The rest of the hood was there.

Everyone was getting trashed. I was drunk and before the night was over, I was outside making out with Shari. So in one evening I actually had two girlfriends. Mary found out about it and dumped me. Shari was just drunk and really didn't want to get back together.

We were an item for a month or two and then it was over for good. And what did I do? I drank more, got drunk and killed that pain of rejection that had rented space in my head.

I had one other girlfriend in high school, Ellie. She was the coolest and "funnest" (I know it's not a word) girl I ever have dated. I can honestly say I truly loved Ellie. She made me laugh. I made her laugh. To boot, I don't really remember ever being really drunk around her. We hung out, loved music, held hands, kissed; damn did we kiss! Our song was by the Temptations, "I Can't Get Next to You."

We had dance moves for every part of the song. For two white kids, we did Motown pretty well. Unlike the first two relationships, the only reason this one ended was my decision to enter the seminary to study for the priesthood. I still remember the night I told her. I couldn't look her in the eye, so I called her on the phone. She cried. I cried. She hung up. I got drunk. I saw Ellie years later in 1985 when I was single again. She lived in Montgomery County, Pennsylvania, in a lovely home. She still had the same twinkle in her eye. Ellie was a class act.

I still remember thinking what a loser I had become. Shari had married, became a nurse, had children of her own and lived happily in Florida. Mary was the successful lawyer, and Ellie married a fantastic fella, had kids, and was extremely content with life. At this moment in my life in 1985, my wife and children had left me in Florida, our beautiful home near Clearwater beach with the bar and pool was now a mausoleum, and I was emotionally and spiritually spent. There was nothing left in either of those accounts. Again, I was alone.

That night, after I met with Ellie and her husband and

kids, I connected with Stretch at the Wheel Pump, a pub near Chestnut Hill, and the both of us got wasted. I told him about seeing Ellie and how desolate I felt. He just shrugged and said, "Move on, dude. Have another Guinness. And I did, and another after that, and another until the pain went away.

I tell you about these three relationships because they came at the end of my teen years. Adulthood was on the horizon. The effect of them and how I handled them haunted me until August 30, 1997, my sobriety date. Remember me saying that people in the rooms made statements that when they picked up their first drink they were 16 years of age; twenty nine years later, when they arrived in the rooms of sobriety, they were still 16? Think about it. Are you still handling the relationships in your life the way you did years ago? And if you're still drinking, do you think there is a connection? Can you identify?

The tide did not improve in my adult life. Between marriages, I had what I would call two serious relationships. The first was a long-distance one; doomed to fail. I met a terrific lass named Paula. She was as Irish as they come, red hair, freckles and a bubbly personality. We met at a bar in Clearwater. A couple of nights later my phone rang. Honestly, did not expect to ever hear from her again. Paula wanted to know if she could drop by and chat. If I would order pizza, she would bring the wine.

And chat we did. Were we both completely honest with each other that first night together? Who knows? She did tell me she had a little girl from a previous marriage who lived with her. No problem here. I had three kids of my own. In a few hours we were drunk, naked in the shower, then in my bed and that is how our relationship began. Funny thing, the next morning when these types of episodes normally happen, one, if not both parties, wish they were somewhere else. No so with Paula. I made breakfast for the two of us, we drove to her home. She ran in and came out a few minutes later with bathing suit in tow, a beach towel and sunscreen; and off to Clearwater beach we went.

When we hooked up on that fateful night, I was now living in Pennsylvania, coming to Florida for meetings and taking care of the home I still owned. My boss had moved me back to Philly so I could live near my children who now resided with my soon to be ex-wife and her boyfriend. We had sales meetings in Florida about every six weeks. After this first weekend together, Paula and I began that long-distance relationship.

We called each other during the work week and on weekends. I recall the conversations being somewhat shallow. I would talk about my kids and then ask her about her little girl. She would hesitate, say something nondescript, and the dialogue would move on.

The next couple of trips down South were passionate and filled with great sex, but not what I would call a lot of love. I know that sounds weird coming from an alcoholic who knew so little of love, but I got the feeling Paula wanted this relationship on her terms. Through the few months that we dated, I never met her daughter. I was never invited into her home. Call me paranoid, but I just sensed something missing.

On our last weekend together we journeyed to Disney World with a work buddy and his wife. We stayed at a nice hotel in the Disney Village. At this stage, Paula was into a bubble-bath phase and wanted me to join her all the time in bubble baths. Now don't get me wrong, taking a bubble bath with a woman is very sexy. But night after night? It got old quick. Making love and gargling a gallon of fucking bubble bath was not my idea of a good time. The last night was a disaster. The drive home was worse. We parted, and I never saw Paula again.

I do not blame her for anything. She was a great gal. Her secret ways bothered me, and I never did find out what was up with her daughter. Hell, we met in a bar and alcohol was the catalyst of our sex life. Put those together and eventually one of us will start thinking that something's wrong with this relationship. There has to be more to this, if it's meant to last, than booze, sex and bubble baths. Thus ended that brief chapter.

Back in Pennsylvania, I had eventually moved to a more permanent apartment in Bucks County, my old stomping grounds. I rediscovered my old watering hole, made new friends and tried to move on with life. One night while bowling with some friends, I met Linda. She was a joyful person. She also hung at our watering hole, so we started to hook up after work. The first night she asked me to take her home. I knew what was coming, but I really looked forward to it. This, for me, was not just about sex. I actually liked this woman and wanted to take the relationship further. Our exchanges were awesome. We were only a couple of years apart in age and had similar backgrounds. I met her son who was around 20, and he and I hit it off.

I actually felt I had found the woman for me.

I still traveled a lot, so I was not home every night. But I faithfully called Linda and stayed true blue to her. I stopped seeing any other woman. Linda was for me. Then, in the blink of an eye, it was over.

One weekend, the folks at the watering hole wanted to plan a 60s Rock 'n' Roll party. Gary, the bartender, asked me to DJ the party, and I was thrilled. We were to dress in Woodstock regalia. What could be better? A few days before the party Linda and I had a great night at her home, and I dropped the "L" word, told her I loved her. She gazed at me and smiled. I guess I took her smile as some type of assent that she, too, loved me.

The night of the party, Linda came dressed as a high school cheerleader. Being the DJ hindered some of our time together, but I put a couple of long, slow dancing tunes on and walked her to the dance floor. As soon as I took her in my arms I knew trouble was brewing. I had not seen her cry in the months we had been together. Tears were in her eyes. I asked her what was wrong, and she just shook her head. At some point that night, she left the party without saying goodbye. Two days later I discovered through a friend at the hole that she had been dating a guy named Chad the entire time I was seeing her. It appears he gave her an ultimatum to choose him or me. She chose him.

I took this rejection extremely hard. I had opened my heart to another woman and in the end, my heart wasn't enough. I would see Linda again at our watering hole, but I would just nod hello and keep my distance. Chad and she were now being seen as a couple. And there I was once more with my dick in my hand and alone. I did what I did best and drank.

This then led to many one-night stands with some of the women who drank at the hole. They didn't want a relationship and neither did I. Booze and sex. Sex and booze. Since I sucked at relationships, I promised to avoid them at all costs. I kept this promise until I met my wife in August of 1986.

Yet, I still had many years of active alcoholism that got in the way of the most important relationship I could imagine, with the woman I loved and called my wife.

Today, living a clean and sober life, my relationships with others are quite different. First of all, I no longer have the option of running and hiding and killing pain using booze or drugs. Of course, if I want to die, then yes it is still an option. In the beginning of this book I quoted page 66 of the Big Book where it reads, "...and with us, to drink is to die." I'll restate what I said before. The author is not only talking about a physical death, but also a mental, spiritual, and emotional death.

Another major difference today I also learned in the

rooms of AA. That lesson: do not place expectations on anyone. I have learned that the higher my expectations are of someone, the greater disappointments I incur and any serenity I might have had with that person or with life in general is now in the shitter.

Hell, I had high expectations of all in my life. I thought the old man would be kinder and gentler. I thought my mom would stick up for me. I thought that someone would at least show up for my 8th grade graduation. I thought my first wife would understand that in order to provide the lifestyle we had, I had to travel. It was not my choice but the company's. I always thought that my boss should appreciate everything that I brought to the table so the team would be successful, ad nauseam. It took a few years in sobriety to get it; high expectations equal huge disappointments; no expectations equal serenity. I choose the latter today.

This topic of expectations and serenity actually comes at the end of one of the stories in the book ***Alcoholics Anonymous***. However, in the middle of the same story which carries the title "Doctor, Alcoholic, Addict," there is actually, in my humble opinion, the most important line in the entire book. In the third edition, this line appears on page 449. In the present fourth edition, it appears on page 417. It reads, "And acceptance is the answer to all my problems today."xvii

Chuck had me memorize this line in early sobriety. He then told me to get used to the fact that when I either called or saw him at a meeting and belly ached to him about my life, about my job, about my boss, about my wife, kids, brother-in-law, sister-in-law, my own sister, the Pope, the Magisterium of the Church, someone in AA who tends to piss me off, the Blessed Virgin, Jesus and the all the saints, that his instructions would be to me, "read page 449 and then read it again." (In 1997, the Big Book was still in its third edition)

To you the reader, whether you are the loved one of an alcoholic, someone who thinks they might be an alcoholic, or you just happened to purchase this book because you love memoirs, I am now going to quote the rest of the paragraph that follows this extremely important line. "...When I am disturbed, it is because I find some person, place, thing, or situation—some fact of my life—unacceptable to me, and I can find no serenity until I accept that person, place, thing, or situation as being exactly the way it is supposed to be at this moment. Nothing, absolutely nothing, happens in God's world by mistake. Until I could accept my alcoholism, I could not stay sober; unless I accept life completely on life's terms, I cannot be happy. I need to concentrate not so much on what needs to be changed in the world as on what needs to be changed in me and in my attitudes."xviii

Before proceeding, I am going to ask you to read that again. Got it? Ok, let's talk about it. Hopefully, you see that the wisdom given here not only pertains to alcoholics, but can be utilized by every human being on our small planet. Every so often in an AA meeting someone will say something to the effect, "I wish all the members of my family had a 12-Step Program." Or "I would like to give this book as a gift to all of my non-alcoholic friends, but it may send the wrong message." Why? Because although much of the Big Book is obviously geared toward those who have problems with booze, it also has much wisdom in it geared toward those who have problems with life…thus, everyone. Maybe someday I'll write a book and call it something like "12 Steps for the Rest of the World." I know acceptance would be one of those steps.

I confess, however, I did not "get it" right away. I mean why should I accept my in-laws who tend to piss me off at every opportunity they get? Why should I accept the fact that I believe I have other family members who belong in the rooms of sobriety, but just don't get it? Why should I be the one who is the first to compromise in relationships with family and friends? Why should I even listen to some horse's ass who is early in sobriety, spouting bullshit at a meeting when I know what they are saying is completely untrue? Why? Why? Why?

This kind of ties into another, don't-get-pissed-at-me, great saying in the rooms, "I'd rather be happy than right!" Notice in the above paragraph from page 449, the word serenity is italicized. In black and white, "…I can find no serenity until I accept that person, place, thing, or situation as being exactly the way it is supposed to be at this moment."xix

As an active alcoholic I had the propensity to accept very little in my life. From the time I was a kid until I got in the rooms of sobriety, my life never appeared calm or in good order. I flew by the seat of my pants day after day. Life to me was exhausting. From dawn to dusk, I felt like the hamster in the cage running on the wheel that proceeded to nowhere. I have never experienced the reality of this, but life was like running through a mine field. I knew that sooner or later some bad shit was going to happen. Serenity? What the hell was that?

I obviously could never accept that my Dad checked out when I was only eight years of age. I could not accept that no one came to my graduation. I could not accept that I was forced to go to a high school where I know I did not belong and could never fit in. I could not accept that my first marriage ended in disaster. I could not accept that when I was ready to commit to another woman that she had someone in mind and it wasn't me. I could not accept that sometimes at work my boss was just having a bad day and it wasn't about me, but I took it personally. I could not accept that maybe, just maybe, I had some issues that needed to be addressed and addressing them with booze was not the proper solution.

I have also had individuals in my life that I just did not accept for what they are or what they were. Family members, friends, peers in the workplace, the police officer who pulled me over for speeding, the doctor who gave me bad news about my health, the professor in college who did not like my writing style or my subjective answer in an objective exam, and the list goes on and on. I hope you can identify with me here, regardless if you're an alcoholic or not.

Surveying my life from 30,000 feet and 18 plus years into sobriety, I have to ultimately look at the man in the mirror. This really was not about other people, places and things. It was about me. Sure, we all meet the proverbial asshole once in a while. But not everyone is an asshole. Most people are pretty decent human beings. Because we see the world through different lenses, does not make them wrong and me right.

If I want any type of serenity in my life, then I must accept this fact about them and about me.

Sadly, through roughly 29 years of my 63 years on this earth, almost half, I drank when I did not accept what was happening around me. I am not God. God did not wake up this morning thinking He was George. If I can remember that, I just might have a serene day and the relationships I have with other people might bear good fruit.

Maybe today I will meet someone whom I can accept for who and what they are, and my life will change for the better. Maybe they are the next suffering alcoholic I encounter, and their life will change for the better, too.

CHAPTER 30

Vacations: With & Without Booze

As the lyrics said in the early 1960s tune by heartthrob, Rick Nelson, "I'm a travelin' man." It is while I've been on some glorious vacations, having witnessed God's creation and been filled with awe, that I realize how fortunate I am. I still remember my first trip in an airplane. Heck my grandkids at age three have already been in a plane. I, on the other hand, was 23 years of age in 1975 when I stepped from planet Earth and ventured into the stratosphere for the first time.

The place of departure was Philadelphia International Airport. The airline, the now defunct Eastern Airlines. The destination, Disney World in Orlando, Florida.

In my mind's eye, once again, I can see this Boeing 737 resting on the tarmac at our departing gate. When they called our row, damn, that was exciting. I think handing the flight attendant at the gate my airline ticket for that first flight and taking those steps down the passenger way leading to the plane, to that point, had to be the bravest thing I ever did. Shit, why would I leave planet Earth and trust my life at 33,000 feet to some dude I did not know? But you know, I did it and was not really afraid! Climbing through the sky, shooting through those puffy cumulus clouds that I read about as a kid was mind bending.

Other vacations had me standing in places that at one

time in my life I could only fathom. My wife and I have the great fortune to have several wonderful friends who live in Florida. In 1989, two of them moved to the United Kingdom because of work and lived there for three glorious years. They had only been there a few months when I picked up the phone and said, "Yo, Murph, you want some company?" Ok, I was more discreet than that. They said to come on over the Pond and visit. Murph and wife, Brenda, welcomed us with love and open arms.

We landed at Heathrow Airport, London and once again, when my feet touched the earth in this land of Henry VIII, Thomas More, Cromwell and Dickens, I felt at home. My mom's Dad was a Brit, actually an Irishman whose family moved to England during the years of the great famine in the 19th century. I was hoping for a warm welcome from our British ancestors who had tried to keep us Americans in bondage two plus centuries ago, and I was not disappointed.

We rode a train to a small Hamlet called Watlington in Oxfordshire where Murph and Brenda took up residence. As the train meandered through the English countryside, I half expected Frodo Baggins to pop out of the forest on a pony with Gandalf the Gray in tow and wave as we trekked through Britain. In this area of the United Kingdom we visited Blenheim Palace, the home of Sir Winston Churchill. We feasted on succulent Steak, Kidney and Guinness pie for lunch at a restaurant called Brown's near Oxford University.

Although it was 1989 and I was still drinking, there was

not a night that I got trashed...buzzed a few times, but I took it all in.

We met friends of Murph who lived in a 700 year-old thatched-roof cottage with wood beams taken from sunken ships that supported the structure. I remember sitting in front of a fireplace, drinking whiskey from a goblet and puffing on an atrocious English cigarette and loving every minute of it.

The second half of our trip found us leaving our friends and returning to London. We stayed in a hotel at Knightsbridge, took the tube to Piccadilly Circus, ventured down to the Thames and ate lunch at the Dickens Inn.

We then crossed the Tower Bridge and went to the Green where they wacked off poor old Anne Boleyn's head. In the Tower, I sat in a cell where the great St. Thomas More had been imprisoned by Henry VIII for not signing the document that stated that Henry's first marriage was null and void and that his present wife, Anne, was his wife and true Queen. Henry broke from the Catholic Church on this issue and formed the Church of England. He tried to break Thomas More but could not. St. Thomas was beheaded. History states that when he met his executioner, that he blessed the man and forgave him. He died a martyr's death, unafraid with his God, his Higher Power.

I have literally bent over backwards and kissed the Blarney Stone in Ireland on another vacation with my wife and our good friends, Tim and Kathy.

We spent 11 glorious days and nights in Erin, the land

of my ancestors, well, at least three of them. My Dad's father was born in France.

To discuss this vacation in detail would take another book, so let's give the short version. It was October 1, 1999 when we landed in Shannon on the west coast of Ireland. We procured our rental car, with the steering wheel on the opposite side, and drove out to explore this land of the Druids, Patrick, the Four Green Fields and the home of Danny Boy.

Our first stop was in Knock, then up the coast to the Connemara Peninsula and back down to Galway. Knock happens to be the scene of another Marian apparition that occurred in the 19th Century. Since my first pilgrimage in 1993 to Lourdes and Fatima I had prayed that someday my wife would join me on such a voyage. Although we were not on a pilgrimage, I have a picture of the two of us kneeling in the Basilica at Knock in prayer. God is good.

From Galway we drove south and then took a ferry and journeyed to the famous Cliffs of Moher in the town of Liscannor in County Clare. These cliffs rise hundreds of feet above the Atlantic. Standing there inhaling the salt air, closing my eyes and listening to the pounding surf below as a shroud of mist pelted my face, I felt at home with my God, and I was unafraid.

Our trip ended with three days in Dublin City visiting Trinity College, taking bus tours hither and yon and listening to a guide speak of the infamous Molly Malone. Notice I did not say "Dooblin" for on this journey I was sober. Me, the Irish Mick from Olney, who drank with the best of them, had finally arrived at the very home of where they brew my brew, Guinness Stout, and I was sober. Ain't life fucking grand? And it is.

We boarded our flight home in Dublin. Before entering the terminal, I bent down and kissed the Irish ground where I stood. The four of us who had come so far from America were leaving with tears in our eyes but with great joy in our hearts. Memories would be held within these hearts for years to come.

In 2003 and then again in 2013 with Tim and Kathy by our sides we ventured to the Tiber, to the City of Romulus and Remus, Julius Caesar, Peter and Paul—to Rome. Two words come to mind when I think of these trips, sensory overload. In 2003 our journey lasted ten days; in 2013, eight days. Trust me, eighteen days is not enough. We visited three cities during these ventures Rome, Florence and Assisi and fell in love with Italy.

The trip in 2003 was special for one prayer that had been answered. For ten years I had been praying that the wife would go on pilgrimage with me, as noted above. This was a spiritual, musical pilgrimage initiated by our parish choir in Bucks County, Pennsylvania. A few of the choir members attempted to recruit me for this pilgrimage, to sing in the choir.

I actually went to one practice, stood in the dark recesses of the church, watched and listened. Gotta admit, fear won over on this one. I just did not see myself good enough to praise God in song with this talented group of singers and musicians.

However, a woman named Irene told me that parishioners were also invited to join the group. The cost was affordable. One night in early September of 2003, I approached my wife, again thinking negatively that she would say no, and told her about the trip. To my utter amazement she answered in the affirmative! We would be pilgrims together.

The first several days were spent in the Eternal City. My first memory is of watching my spouse walk through the doors of St. Peter's Basilica. I followed on her heels and almost crashed into her. She had stopped suddenly and was looking right. She beheld Michelangelo's famous Pieta and tears freely flowed from her eyes. I asked what was wrong. She just pointed and said, "Look how Mary is holding her dead Son." That is how life-like the Pieta is. In writing these words, tears formed in my eyes again.

Since we're talking about alcoholism, let's talk about Francis of Assisi, the 13th century young man who eventually gave up everything, even the very clothes on his back, to pursue spiritual perfection. Do not get your bowels in an uproar, I'm not implying that Francis was an alky, although as a wealthy youth he was quite the ladies' man and party animal. No, I bring his name up because he is actually mentioned in the book, ***Twelve Steps and Twelve Traditions of Alcoholics Anonymous***, specifically in Step 11.

Step 11 reads the longest of all the steps. It says; "Sought through prayer and meditation to improve our conscious contact with God, as we understand Him, praying only for knowledge of His will for us and the power to carry that out."

Now I am not going to bore you with my personal philosophy about prayer and meditation. There are enough books you can purchase that will do that. And I'm positive there are others that are worthwhile and can keep you on the edge of your seat. I'm talking about Francis.

In the Twelve and Twelve (as we call this book in the rooms), the Step 11 prayer attributed to Francis of Assisi is noted in its entirety. It begins, "Lord, Make me a channel of your peace." In the middle, Francis states, "…O Divine Master, Grant that I may not so much seek to be consoled, as to console; To be understood, as to understand; To be loved as to love."

Now when you think of all the prayers in the entire world that have been said and formulated from the time of Abraham, I think it's pretty cool that the founders of Alcoholic Anonymous chose this prayer from a poor saint who lived in a hillside town in northern Italy.

To get a picture of Francis, we had to travel to Assisi, and we did on both of these pilgrimages. Other than the occasional SmartCar or other compact vehicle, Assisi is pretty much as it looked in the 13th century. Yes there is electricity and other modern amenities, but the town itself, nestled on a hill overlooking a magnificent plain and valley, remains untouched. It is like Francis, simple. This prayer, therefore, is simple, too.

He asked God, his Higher Power, to make him a channel of peace. Think about it. If I could just hold on to that thought every day, my days might be serene. Channeling peace to all, now that is a great goal.

Yet, it's the middle of the prayer that has always swayed me. That I would seek to console others rather than be consoled myself. That I would try to understand others rather than to be understood myself. That I may not so much seek to be loved, as to love. In AA there is a saying, "If I give it away, I'll keep it forever." If I console others, I will discover consolation. If I understand someone else, I being understood will appear less significant. If I love others, love will come back to me a hundred fold, and I might even realize it. I'm glad Francis is part of my life in sobriety, even if he was not alcoholic. Think about it, an Irish kid from Philly learning one of life's greatest lessons from an Italian. Miracles do happen.

During these sojourns across the Pond, especially being sober, I have been able to appreciate so much about other people. When do you and I really get to know someone? I think it is when we break bread together. Have a meal with an acquaintance, and that acquaintance can become a friend. Have a meal with a business associate, and that associate becomes a peer. So while we were traipsing around Italy, whether it be in Rome, Florence or Assisi, I truly became closer to my wife, our friends and the choir members from our parish.

On our 2013 journey, eight of us from our parish group broke away from the main group after visiting the Vatican Museum. All of us were a bit whipped. Our days had been filled with some touristy affairs, and our evenings were tied up with preparing for Church liturgy and the music we were to sing the following day. On this occasion, the eight of us said, "Enough!" (Ever hear that word before?)

So we crossed the Tiber River and ended up in, I know this is hard to believe, an Italian Restaurant. It had your basic fare, pizza, pasta, beer, wine, water and soft drinks. But it was the ambiance that we needed. As we entered, this establishment reeked of garlic! The next sense attacked was our hearing; it was loud with the clientele chatting in foreign languages. Italian music was waffling from speaker to speaker. The colors of the Italian flag pleasantly blinded us. Waiters and waitresses were running hither and yon from table to table shouting drink orders to the bartender as they passed. God, it was exhilarating!

Now, of these other seven individuals, only my wife knew I was sober and an alcoholic in recovery. In years past, while sober, if I was in a group such as this, I usually told them up front about my sobriety, so they wouldn't be left wondering why I was the only schmuck not drinking alcohol.

Yet, this time, I felt no need to do this. I was among friends. No one was here to judge me.

The waitress took our drink order and yes, I was the only one who ordered a Coke. Within an hour, I ordered my second Coke and everyone else was either still nursing their first glass of wine or beer. Go figure.

These folks were not alcoholics. Remember me and my

five glasses of sake? We had a wonderful exchange. We talked of Rome and Assisi; we talked of possibly singing for the new Pope, Our Holy Father Francis. We talked about our kids and grandkids, about our jobs, about this pilgrimage, and then these amazing people just started talking about how they felt about each other, about each of us sitting at this table.

We soon discovered that we truly "loved" one another. I remember my wife and me walking back to our hotel holding hands in silence and me thinking, "If I hadn't stopped drinking would this have ever happened?" I knew the answer. I silently gazed toward the Tiber and smiled.

CHAPTER 31

What Makes Me Tick?

Damn, if I can answer this; this opus deserves the Pulitzer. Get ready to read the longest chapter of this book. However, I want you the reader to do me a favor, especially if you are still drinking and think you might be an alcoholic. Pour yourself your favorite drink. It could be Guinness, a glass of port wine, a tumbler of scotch, a Cosmopolitan, a bottle of Corona with a twist of lime. Whatever it is, go get it now. I'll wait.

Ok, got it? Now I'm going to ask you that for however long it takes to read this chapter, do not drink any of it. Not a sip, ok? I trust you.

Now, in telling you what makes me tick, do I really want to be this vulnerable? One of my good friends, a guy named Rob, told me to tell you what makes George tick. What makes me the funny guy I am? Why do I care to bring a smile to others? What makes me so sensitive to those around me? Why did the chameleon appear during my alcoholic days? Why are some days so light and others so dark while I was drinking, but even in sobriety? Why did I drink in victories and in defeats? How could I be so egotistical and loving at the same time when active in my alcoholism? How could I rationally blame my Dad for all that went wrong in my life until August 30, 1997? Did I realize that I was making those around me sick while in active alcoholism? If I had such great morals, values, character, why couldn't I just stop drinking? Where do I think I'd be if I hadn't stumbled upon a book, answered a few questions honestly and ended up in the rooms of sobriety? Who is it that really intervened and prevented my life from being a complete catastrophe?

How, Who, What, Where, Why? Hopefully, I have touched on some of these questions while conveying my journey to you. Prior to publication, I must have reread this manuscript twenty times or more, hoping that the message is clear, especially if you, the reader, are struggling with alcohol and the disease of alcoholism and addiction. If not, then I have failed miserably and the blame is on my shoulders, not my Dad, not God, not my mom, nor any family member, not anyone.

I think the very first question might be the most important and tale-telling. What makes me tick? Due to life's early circumstances I had no guiding light. I'm not saying that my mom didn't give it her best or even my pre-Archie Bunker uncle. They did, they tried. Other men and women, early on, also attempted to bring some semblance of order to a young boy's life. I just didn't or couldn't or wouldn't listen or follow. I was a street urchin.

A few years into our marriage, my present wife and I went to marriage counseling for a variety of reasons. When it was my turn on the "witness stand," I still remember telling the counselor that I honestly remember always being afraid as a boy: afraid my mom would not come home from work, afraid she would die, afraid my sister and I would end up in foster homes, afraid of other kids, afraid of monsters in my closet, afraid of my Dad's ghost showing up unannounced, afraid I would never be loved, afraid of the nuns who taught me, afraid that I would fail at everything I attempted…simply afraid.

The counselor looked at me with sympathy in her eyes and said, "George, do you realize that being afraid and carrying around all those red flares was normal for a 12-year-old boy, but not normal for a 42-year-old man? I sat in stunned silence. I honestly did not know how to answer her. I knew the answer she wanted to hear, and I know for certain it was the right answer; but I was incapable of answering it. Why? Shit, I was still afraid! Three years later I'd find myself in the rooms of Alcoholics Anonymous and would be forced over the next 18 plus years to address these fears.

Ok, so I was afraid, but I still functioned pretty well in society as the years flew by. Yet, I knew inside there was something missing. Although I never remembered anyone telling me that they loved me, I knew that my mom did. She never said those words, but I knew. In the chapter, "I Am Unlovable" I hopefully conveyed how I felt, and why I felt that way.

Ok, what makes me tick? Sunrises make me tick. I've noted more than once that I love the beach. There is something purifying about the ocean, salt air, the sandy beach, seashells, jellyfish and waves. But waking up at 5:30 a.m., grabbing a cup of coffee, a windbreaker, my rosary beads, a beach towel or chair, sand between my toes, and sitting in the dark awaiting the sun, now that is a visual that has always proven there was someone greater than I. Prior to the rising sun, as described by the author of the book of Genesis, the ocean appears a huge void. You can smell and hear it, but you cannot see it. Then as our Earth spins on its axis, a tiny slither of light appears. Clouds, that were invisible on the horizon a few seconds earlier are now visible, puffy white with a tinge of orange.

The gull gliding in the night sky was invisible, but now appears in majestic flight, cooing to let the world know it is now time to awake. Waves pounding the surf impossible to see in darkness now appear as whitecaps in their beauty, grace and power. I find myself in awe as I gaze toward this rising light that we call the sun. It moves me, and I am unafraid.

Music makes me tick. In my mind's eye, I can still visualize an image of me on a Christmas Eve in 1970. This was the first Christmas while I was studying to be a priest. I left our home before Mom and Sis as I had to help prepare the liturgy with the Bishop, priests and other seminarians in our parish. It was snowing a fine, gentle snow, barely perceptible. But the small flakes touched my face and I looked skyward trying to think of what this night was really about. As I approached the back door of our parish Church, I turned and looked outward over my neighborhood.

Somewhere in the distance I heard carolers singing. The words touched me and to this day it is my favorite Christmas hymn, "God rest ye merry gentlemen, let nothing you dismay. Remember Christ Our Savior was born on Christmas Day. To save us all from Satan's powers when we have gone astray. O tidings of Comfort and Joy, comfort and joy. O tidings of Comfort and of Joy."xx

Little did I know then, that my life would go astray on many, many occasions. Fortunately this Christ, the God of my understanding, never turned His back on me. Music was the connection. It moved me and I was unafraid.

My mother-in-law from my first marriage became one of my best friends and remained so until her death. Her name was Bridget, but we all called her Bridie or Bid. She was born in Dublin, Ireland. She had maybe the equivalent of a fifth grade education. She came to America through Canada in 1949.

She was the greatest American I ever encountered. Her husband, my father-in-law, was an alcoholic. He too came from Ireland. Sadly, he was the stereotypical Irish alcoholic; yet when sober he was a funny guy and a good man, truly.

Well, Bridie loved music, all kinds of music. Yes, she loved to hear ballads from Erin like "Danny Boy" or "Four Green Fields" but she liked everything American, too. Whenever the family would gather, and it was a large Irish family, eventually it would be time to sing.

Sometime during this music fest she would turn to me and ask me to sing, "Amen," the song made famous by Academy Award winner Sidney Poitier in the motion picture, "The Lilies of the Field." Everyone knows and sings the "Amen" chorus of this tune, but I knew all the lyrics of each verse. The beginning of this song is joyous, "See the little baby, wrapped in the manger, on Christmas morning. See Him in the Temple talking to the Elders. See Him at the seaside, talking with the fishermen and making them disciples."

Then the tone changes, in a very hushed quiet voice I would sing, "See Him in the garden, praying to His Father, in weeping sorrow. Amen, Amen, Amen." And then the tone becomes so hushed it's almost inaudible, "Before Pilate, then they crucified Him," then a crescendo, "BUT HE ROSE ON EASTER, AMEN, AMEN, AMEN. ALLELUIA." Just to see Bid's eyes light up at the end meant all to me.

Through my years of drinking, music may have been the one steadying influence. You already know I love the Beatles. Certain songs by them and other groups meant a lot. Years ago, when working for a major HVAC corporation, we had a sales meeting in Baltimore. The hotel had a huge piano bar area with a stage area for a band. The band that night asked if anyone in the audience wanted to sing. I had a few brews in me, the courage was up so I ventured up and asked them if they knew the melody and tune to Rocky Raccoon. They did and I sang it. There must have been 150 people in the audience. Sober, I would not have gone up. Buzzed, I grabbed the microphone and gave one of the best performances of my life. I received a standing "O" at the end. The band wanted more, but I knew to quit when I was ahead. Always leave the stage to applause!

In 1990, I took my wife, two oldest girls, ages 14 and 15 and oldest boy age 12, to see Paul McCartney and the remnants of his Wings band at Veterans Stadium in South Philly. That night made me tick. The night was electric. The sun was setting and the weather cooperative. As we got to our seats and settled in, some old Harley dudes lined the row in front of us. Of course, they were passing a doobie up and down the row. The head dude turned and offered me a hit.

Honestly, if my family members were not there, I would have joined them. Fortunately, I said no. Then our two teenage girls in unison shouted, "Say no to drugs, Dad!" The quote came from an anti-drug campaign begun in the 1980s by Nancy Reagan, the President's wife. Little did they know.

The concert began with McCartney playing some old Beatles tunes and some Wings hits. It was a three-hour concert. At the hour-and-a-half point the band left the stage. We all assumed an intermission. Not so. Paul never left the stage. He said his old friend, John, loved Philadelphia; and, therefore, he felt obligated to sing some of his tunes.

John was my favorite Beatle. Paul sat at his piano/organ and banged out "Help," and then he played and sang "A Day in the Life of a Boy." It was the song Stretch and I played from Sgt. Peppers the night I first got drunk. The people were on their feet. Then Paul played the greatest sing-a-long tune that John created on his own, the song New Yorkers sang the night he was killed outside his apartment complex, "Give Peace A Chance."

During the entire soliloquy, the entire stadium, 55,000 strong, flipped their Bic lighters, struck matches, lit candles, swayed to the music and sang with tears in their eyes unashamed. I'm sure all of us Boomers there were remembering that night in December of 1980 watching the news and seeing those native New Yorkers chorusing the same, "All we are saying is give peace a chance." At the last "give peace a chance" thunder reigned down and tears poured in South Philly. I had never felt so vulnerable around my wife and kids than I did that night. And you know what, it did not matter. That night they saw a side of me they probably and possibly would never see again. And…I was not afraid.

Music does make me tick. Even in my darkest hours, when I felt deserted and alone. When the world offered me no solace, music did. "And in the END, the love you take is equal to the love you make." Even in the dark, music was a light; and I was unafraid.

Laughter makes me tick. I do love to laugh. But the greater high comes when I make others laugh. The late Robin Williams, himself an alcoholic and drug addict compared this rush of making others laugh with the BAM that alcohol gave him. When he made this statement, I understood. It is such a gift to lift people up. Life ain't easy. The old adage, laughter being the best medicine is quite true.

I am a great story teller. My jokes can last several minutes. In the chapter, "The Chameleon" you met Sean, that Irish lad, that was me being afraid to be me. Yet, this talent of nationality accents plays well when entertaining. Here is one of my favorite jokes: Sean walks into an Irish Pub in Center City Philly. It is Friday night. A day ago he left Ireland to make his way in America. He pulls up to the bar, introduces himself, "Aye, I'm Sean from Dooblin. Can I have three Guinness'?"

The bartender, himself Irish, gladly pours them. Sean downs them quickly, leaves a generous tip and departs. Well, this occurs each Friday night for the next month. Sean orders his three pints of Guinness, downs them and leaves. Now the people in the Pub have gotten curious, yet they are respectful when Sean does his thing. Around the fifth week, the barkeep asks, "Sean, why the three pints of Guinness?" Sean replies, "When I left Erin five weeks ago, I departed from me brothers, Seamus and Patrick. We told our Da and Ma that wherever we were each Friday night at an appointed time we would salute each other, the three pints for three brothers. Seamus is in Australia and Patrick remains in Dooblin' "

Now the people in the Pub were in awe of this telling, and they grew to love Sean as he came in each Friday night. Then, one Friday night in early March, Sean came in at the appointed time; with head bowed he came up to the bar as the people gathered around and said to the bartender, "Can I have two Guinness'? Two? Two, says Sean. He slowly lifts the first and downs it, but not with the usual vigor he had when drinking three, and then the second even more slowly and reverently. The crowd can't stand the suspense and in unison you hear the question, "Sean, Sean who died? Was it Seamus or Patrick? Oh God!" Sean, turns toward the multitude, lifts his head and says, "Christmas, no body feckin' died. I gave up drinkin' for Lent."

Isn't that feckin' great? What a hoot.

Being that street urchin from North Philly living with all nationalities and races, I can pretty much imitate anyone. And you know what, it makes people laugh. For a few moments they smile and life does not seem so heavy, so dull, and so monotonous. However, there was a time that I could not imagine ever being funny again without alcohol…ever. The thought of standing in a crowd of family and friends telling my repertoire of stories without a pint in my hand was unfathomable. Here is the kicker; I think I'm even funnier sober. And, an added bonus, I even remember what I say when the night is through. I used to use my sense of humor, as I did alcohol, to keep you at arm's length. Today, I use my sense of humor to draw you into an armful of love.

Battlefields make me tick. I have discovered that all the freedoms I have are actually not my rights, but have been purchased at great cost. Go to Washington D.C. If you can't go there, find the National Cemetery near your home. Even if you must travel a hundred miles or more, drive there. Just do it once. Walk and look at the headstones. See that PFC John Smith died on May 2, 1863 at the Battle of Chancellorsville. See that pilot Rupert Jones died in the fight for Midway Island in 1942. See that Charlotte

Higgins died in Afghanistan in November 2001. They are the reason I and all of you have our freedoms. Please do not forget this or allow your children and grandchildren to forget. As a nation I pray we must never forget, but I do fear it a possibility.

My first encounter with a field of battle was more a field of misery due to many battles.

I have pictures of me, Sis, my mom and my Dad at Valley Forge National Park standing beneath huge black cannon, and then again next to one of the replica cabins that housed these misfit soldiers who had no idea how to fight the bloody Red Coats but still won us a country. Since the Battle of Trenton on December 26, 1776 Washington had waged and lost almost every battle. Lesser men would have surrendered. Almost a year to the day, December 19, 1777 Washington and his rag tag army of 12,000 retreated to Valley Forge. The Continental Congress had fled Philadelphia and was now in York, Pennsylvania.

This starving Continental Army was all that stood between the Red Coats and the hangman. Fortunately, the British still fought by gentlemen's rules and did not attack in the winter. By spring 1778, 25 percent of these heroic boys were dead from starvation, dysentery, fever, the rot and infection. They were living in conditions not fit for any human being, while the British warmed themselves in colonial homes in Philadelphia 20 miles away. This was our beginning.

I have walked the fields of Gettysburg and climbed the

cupola of the Lutheran Theological Seminary on Seminary Ridge where Gen. John Buford watched Gen. Harry Heath and 10,000 rebels converge on his 2,500 cavalry men in blue marching down the Chambersburg Pike. Within minutes a shot would ring out and the bloodiest three-day battle ever fought on this continent would begin. I then strode into the woods behind Little Round Top on Cemetery Ridge in Pennsylvania. Here a professor from Bowdoin College named Chamberlain, with his troops depleted of ammunition, fixed bayonets and made the greatest downhill charge, in the history of warfare.

This protected the Union flank from collapsing and being overrun by the Confederates who were led by Robert E. Lee and James Longstreet. From July 1 to 3, 1863, 51,000 boys dressed in Blue and Gray turned into casualties. Only the eight years of the War in Vietnam can compare to these numbers that occurred in these three, hot humid days in that summer midway through this conflict we called Civil.

I have stood in Antietam Creek in Sharpsburg, Virginia, where on September 17, 1862 the Army of the Potomac led by George C. McClellan matched Robert E. Lee bullet for bullet, shell for shell and maneuver for maneuver, until the creek they called Antietam turned red in blood. Both sides suffered approximately 23,000 casualties, the costliest one day battle in the history of warfare. This marginal victory allowed Abraham Lincoln to issue his Emancipation Proclamation that became law on January 1, 1863.

Then, in February of 2007, my wife and I celebrated our

20th wedding anniversary by going to Paris. Through all my travel for work I had accumulated a mess of frequent flier mileage and hotel award points. When our plane landed at Charles de Gaulle Airport and we put our feet on French soil, there was part of me that sensed this, too, was home. My Dad's family is from the Northeastern corner of this beautiful country. We were in Paris for a week, but mid-week, I planned a surprise trip. We traveled with friends of ours, Debbie and Phil, great people. This side trip was taking us to Normandy, in particular, to Omaha Beach.

The day was overcast as we left Paris; a drizzling rain pounded our car. My mood for some reason matched the dreariness of the French countryside as we departed the City of Lights. Our French guide, a woman named Celine, told us not to worry. The Norman forecast was better. Now, I have heard interviews by more than one Veteran of the Second World War that in the movie "Saving Private Ryan" what was depicted on the big screen was the most realistic visage of any portrayal of that day.

Celine kept her promise. As we saw signage pointing the way to this beach named Omaha, my heart began to flutter; and I became extremely nervous. I would soon be walking where boys from that Greatest Generation gave the ultimate sacrifice so that I could be here this day, in freedom. On the 6th of June 1944, approximately 35,000 troops landed on this swath of sand that fateful day on the Norman coast. The invasion began at dawn. By nightfall, 10,000 U.S. soldiers were considered casualties; that is killed, wounded and missing in action, 2,500 of those believed dead littered the beach. Omaha Beach proved costly real estate.

We parked our car a few hundred yards before the dunes, so we had to actually walk up and over dunes to get to the beach. As we crested a hill and our eyes beheld the English Channel, my feet became like lead anchors, my toes like claws gripping the earth and my feet were immobile. My wife, along with Debbie and Phil, proceeded before me with our guide. I stood still staring out. To this day, I am not sure why I am so affected by battlefields and what occurred there. I am no hero.

Finally, Celine waved me forward and we made our way to the German pill-boxes that housed Rommel's troops of the famed Atlantic Wall. I entered one by myself, and I could sense the tension, smelt the salt air, and heard the pounding of the surf being stirred up from the Channel. As I looked west, in my mind's eye, I could see those landing craft approaching the beachhead, the doors opening downward and the slaughter of those young boys commence. A mist formed around the inner edges of my eyes. I held the tears back.

I departed the pill-box and met Phil beneath the long-range cannon the Germans had pointed toward the beach and the Channel. We took some photo ops, but I had another goal in mind.

I turned to my companions and asked if they wanted to venture down onto the beach. Selfishly, I was hoping they would not, but I knew this was wrong. They had as much right to walk upon this hallowed ground as I. To my surprise, they declined. Celine sensed what this meant to me.

I slowly plodded toward the water's edge. Within a moment or two, the sun broke through a cloud bank and enveloped me in its garment. I looked back and could not see my wife or friends. The combination of white sand and sunlight encased me in an aquamarine-like tomb. I turned left and right, all was white. Finally, a small wave flowed over my left foot. I had removed my shoes before descending to the beach and the frigid February water of the Channel pierced the whiteness that had surrounded me. I was once more among the living. What had I just experienced? I dare not say, for you might think me a bit mad. But to me, it was gift. For one brief moment, I was alone with those 10,000 brave souls who paid the ultimate price.

And I cried, not sobbing tears of sorrow, but gentle tears of love and compassion. I looked west toward England. I then gazed left toward Pointe du Hoc and Utah Beach, then right toward Juno, Gold and Sword Beaches and inhaled this scene. I then began one final trek on this journey to the Cemetery above the sand.

The United States National Cemetery is located on a bluff overlooking Omaha Beach and the English Channel. It covers 172 acres and contains the remains of 9,387 American military dead, most of who were killed during the invasion of Normandy and ensuing military operations in World War II. Included are graves of Army Air Corps crews shot down over France as early as 1942 and three American women.xxi I remember standing in the midst of these graves, holding my wife's hand and thinking of my Dad. He, who had fought in the same War, some 9,450 plus miles from Omaha Beach in the Solomon Islands in the South Pacific, had something in common with these boys laid to rest on the bluff of this cliff. They had all stared down the barrel of an enemy rifle knowing death could occur within seconds and did not flinch. Were they fearful? Absolutely. Were they fear-filled, I would venture a resounding, no. So, in the end, I had stood on Omaha with my wife, my friends, a French woman named Celine in freedom and maybe for the first time in my life, I was truly unafraid.

My family makes me tick. It started out so small or at least that is how it appeared to me. After my Dad died, it was just Mom, Sis and me. My mom's family was somewhat disjointed and not close at all. My Dad's family deserted us the moment he was planted at Beverly National Cemetery. Thus, we were three and remained that way until my first marriage. As noted, I have three beautiful children from that marriage. In my second marriage, I inherited two other wonderful kids and of course, married my beautiful wife. The seven of us survived through some very tough times, through alcoholic times and times in sobriety.

Today, those five children are all married and have blessed my wife and me with ten grandkids. Ten! As of this writing I am a youthful 63 years of age and I know I am way too young to have ten grandkids!

Unlike our children, these ten blessings have never seen Pop pick up a drink. Simply put, they have never seen me drunk. I have been able to tell all of them that I love them and that I am here for them. Some live closer than others, but I pray as their lives go on, that they know they can depend on me. I want to be there to dry their tears and kiss their cuts and scrapes. I want to listen to them rant about how unfair their parents are! (Paybacks are hell!) I want to hear about their victories and share in their glory and listen, also, about their defeats and let them know that the sun will indeed shine again on the morrow.

My wife has turned out to be way more than a wife, she is my best friend. Like all friendships they are filled with good and not so good times. But like all great friendships they withstand that test of time, bearing all, good and bad. She has an extremely difficult time understanding why I feel at times, even in sobriety, so unlovable and yet still loves me. She gives me her heart every day. I take it and give her mine. I try to remember each and every day to say those three important words, not from just my lips, but from my heart, "I love you."

Is love easy? Hell no. Love is tough. Life is tough. Getting up in the morning, sometimes, is really tough. But I, like many of you, have been blessed with three great gifts from my Higher Power; faith, hope and love, and yes, the greatest of these is love. There is no fear in love.

Lastly, sunsets make me tick. For me there are two types of sunsets. In the first, again, most have occurred on beaches or on cruise vessels sailing the Caribbean. For three years in the 1980s I owned a home in Clearwater, Florida, on the Gulf Coast. One of my first memorable sunsets occurred in December 1984. My first wife had told me at Christmas that she had a boyfriend and wanted a divorce. I will say up front, it takes two to tango. Years have passed and I have forgiven her. I pray she has forgiven me for anything I did to cause her heartache or pain. Today we are friends.

However, on this day in late December I truly felt friendless. I had only been in Clearwater since June. I traveled a lot with my job so any friends I had were work friends. As with any good alcoholic, I purchased a large bottle of wine, grabbed a beach towel and headed toward Clearwater beach, alone. Honestly, I had thought of calling a single, female co-worker trying to make this into something romantic, but I knew before the first sip of wine that that would be a huge mistake. I went alone.

The temperature was in the 70s with partly cloudy skies. I remember surveying my surroundings as I gazed out over the Gulf of Mexico. There was a young couple with a small child searching for shells walking toward me from the left.

I could only think about what had gone so terribly wrong. I honestly had no answers, so I drank. Within an hour the sun had set and I hadn't really noticed. One moment there was a shroud of light around me, the next I was enveloped in darkness. For not the first time, I grew afraid as the horseman approached. To scare him off I did the only think I could, and I drank some more.

Now you may say, this is a pretty messed up sunset that made me tick. But then again, you are not me. However, if you are an alcoholic you may empathize and understand. At that moment, I truly believed alcohol was my friend. If you are reading this and struggling with booze and agree, you may truly be one of us. Do not be afraid. Do not drink again. Never have a sunset like this. There is a solution, and it's called sobriety.

But it's the sunsets I've enjoyed with my wife, children and grandchildren through the years that are most memorable. To hold a loved one in your arms as the earth continues to spin on its axis, to watch the sun struggle to keep aloft on the horizon as those cumulus clouds shimmer with orange and yellow halos and finally drop from view, that is truly awesome. The darkness that arrives with these sunsets has no horseman on the approach. Awe and wonder fill my heart as I head back to our cottage or our cabin on a cruise ship. My cup is overflowing on nights like this with the love for my Creator and my family. In this darkness there is light, and I am unafraid.

The second type of sunset you may or may not have already guessed. This sunset is the one I am living today, the sunset of my life. As I bang away at the keyboard of my laptop while sitting in my kitchen in Montgomery County, Pennsylvania, I wonder where has the time gone? In the seminary while studying Virgil in Latin class the term "tempus fugit" was put forth by our professor.

Simply translated into English, "time flies." Funny how that is. In my teens, 20s, 30s and 40s time stood still. I could not wait to get to the next business trip, the next sales convention in New Orleans, the next vacation in the Bahamas, the next birthday and more important the next drink. When I reached my 50s the time fulcrum changed. I wanted time to slow down. I was now sober, and I wanted to savor each moment with my family.

I was 48 when our first daughter married. The next three children were married when I was 51 and 52 years of age. When I'm asked to speak at an AA meeting, which for me is always an honor, I usually say, "In sobriety, I have married off three daughters. My 401K instantly became a 101K, and I owe it money!" This usually draws a laugh from the crowd. Then on a serious note I continue, "But the great gift, was that all three of these beautiful women wanted me at their weddings. They want me with them and their children—my grandkids, who call me Pop and that melts my heart. Me, the former alcoholic, the unlovable drunk is now loved. Actually, I was always loved, but alcohol kept all that love at a great distance, in a far off country."

My lovely bride is now retired. I have been forced to shut down my career due to some disabilities. All is good. Actually, when I arrived at the doors of Alcoholics Anonymous I had many things. I've touched on some, the condo down the shore, a six-figure job, two cars in the driveway and trips around this great country and across the Pond into Europe. I also had a more intact body.

In sobriety I have had both knees replaced, had quadruple lumbar fusion surgery and triple cervical fusion surgery. I have titanium knees, 13 screws and three rods in my back and three titanium plates in my neck. I am a walking Home Depot. I need an extra hour just to get through security at an airport because of the hardware in my body. Financially, I find myself on disability income, working a part-time job just to make ends meet. And…life has never been so good.

Today, I awoke, thanked the good Lord for another day, asked him to keep me sober and tonight, God willing I will thank him as I crawl under the covers for one more day sober. I have not seen or thought about the horseman that haunted me for those 29 years in quite a while. It has taken years of sobriety to finally realize he was not real but a figment of my fear-filled imagination. Yet, under the lash of alcohol he was indeed real for me. If you are still out there drinking, I am positive he is real for you, too. But there is a solution, and it's a phone call away.

I know I asked you to pour yourself a drink. Why would someone who is writing a book that is supposed to help someone stop drinking tell them to pour a drink?

Because you and you alone can refuse that last drink. We alcoholics have always been convinced that we did not have a choice when it came to booze. That is the lie. We always had a choice.

Of course, falling down, blind drunk in a blackout there are no choices to make, that choice has already been made. Yet that can change now; but I will tell you, you cannot do this alone. The first step in Alcoholics Anonymous reads, "WE admitted we were powerless over alcohol and that our lives had become unmanageable."

This is a "we" program. I've shared many times "I got drunk, but it took a village for me to get sober." That same village is awaiting you. Do not be afraid, someone is actually there.

CHAPTER 32

Amends

This fellowship in sobriety is huge on a multitude of converging issues. Making amends to all we had harmed in our life, I believe is the toughest to fulfill. We are told to do this in the ninth step except when to do so would injure them or others. This means that we should not make an amends if the sole purpose is to make us feel better or look better in the eyes of others. It must also be noted, that by making amends to others does not mean that the person we are making the amends to need forgive us. Our job is to clean our side of the street. Admit our mistake, seek forgiveness and move on. If forgiveness is not given, we must accept that, hold no resentment and move forward with our lives.

Forgive me if I touched on this and am being redundant, but Chuck, my first sponsor, told me to make amends to my Dad. Huh? He was the one who left me fatherless. He was the one who did not care. He hit me when I was down, rather than pick me up and rather than dust me off and point me in the right direction, he hit me again. Why the fuck should I make amends to him? Chuck told me that if I did not do this he was convinced that I would drink again. That got my attention.

He explained that the resentments we keep within our hearts are like termites eating away at a cord of wood.

After several months, the cord of wood, externally, appears the same. Yet as you grab a few logs and feel their weight or you watch as they literally crumble within your hand, you understand. I understood.

Chuck told me that I must, at all costs, forgive my Dad, absolutely, no strings attached and then I must tell him that I love him. Damn; this was going to be hard. Then Chuck added the next requirement that I must do this in writing. Now he was pushing the envelope and he knew it. But his question to me was direct and simple, "Did I want to drink again?" No. So with pen and paper I sat down on our front porch, with my Labrador retriever, Goldie, at my feet and wrote a letter to my dead father.

Honestly, to you my reader, that first letter sucked. It was self-serving. It did not come from my heart. I wrote it because Chuck told me if I didn't, that I would drink again. I could not endure another shot at sobriety. I could not start this process all over again. So today right now, I'm writing my Dad another letter. I promise all of you that this will be from my heart. I also promise that I will print it out, sign it and take it to Beverly where my Dad today rests in peace and bury it next to his headstone. This is not looking into the past…this is real time.

Dear Dad:

I know you are alive and will receive this letter. Our God is the God of Abraham, Isaac and Jacob, the God of the living, not the dead. I have to be honest; I have hated you for many, many years. Heck, hatred might be too kind of a word. I detested you, how's that? Yet, today I find myself in a quandary. It has been suggested that I write this letter to you, telling you that I forgive you. The list is long, so bear with me. I forgive you for yelling at me when I was a little boy trying to piss in the men's room of a diner when I could just about reach the urinal. I forgive you for shaking me and then throwing me in your truck, verbally abusing me and taking me to the nun, my first grade teacher, for playing hooky two days in a row. I forgive you for being the intimidating presence in my life that I feared and was afraid to love. I forgive you for never having uttered those three important words, "I love you." I forgive you for ignoring me when you came home from work, exhausted from a day I cannot really imagine. I forgive you for not taking the time to teach me to throw a ball or ride a bike. I forgive you for the beating you gave me, six months before your death. Trust me, Dad, this ain't easy.

I wasn't told to do this Dad, but I'd like to say thanks to you and Mom for bringing me into this world. Thank you for putting a roof over our heads. Thank you for coming home to Mom alive after the War in the South Pacific. I am also sorry there was no one there for you to tell all that you had been through. I cannot comprehend spending one night under the canopy of a jungle with enemy soldiers yards away, let alone three years. I am sorry that you suffered from those malaria-induced blackouts for all those years subsequent to the war. I can still hear your screams. They scared the shit out of me, but now I know you had no control over that. I am so sorry that you died at such a young age. Hopefully, you know that Mom cried for you many a night through those first few years.

I heard those tears and felt hopeless to help her, and I hated you for that. And all you really did was die. So for all of this I forgive you, and I am sorry.

What I am most truly sorry for is that you never got to meet your wonderful grandchildren. Maybe you know this, maybe you don't, but I brought each of them over to see you in Beverly when they each became a teenager. All kids must have "the talk." You know, hormones are raging, teenage thinking is reigning supreme in their hearts, they want to be adults but don't know how, and they just want you to accept them for who they are at this moment in time. I missed all of that with you, and I blamed you. I had to learn life's lessons the hard way on the streets of Olney, and I blamed you for that. And all you really did was die. I am sorry for blaming you.

I am sorry you haven't met my wife, the love of my life, my best friend. Living with me has not been the easiest task assigned her in life, but she is still here and loves me. I know you would love her, too. She has a great laugh and sense of humor, just like you did.

Now here is something you did not know, I am an alcoholic; and yes, I blamed you for that, too. I am sorry for laying this blame at your feet, at your grave, in this letter. I understand that your Dad might have been an alcoholic, too. It seems to run in families. I am sorry for this, also. I drank pretty regularly for 28 plus years and finally I was just plain sick and tired of being sick and tired. By the grace of God and Alcoholic Anonymous and a sponsor named Chuck, I am now sober 18 years.

All five of our children, your five grandchildren and your ten great-grandchildren miss you. They call you Grandpop George. I think you would like the sound of that. The ten little ones call me Pop, and it melts my heart.

Lastly, I was told to write you this letter 18 years ago and I did a shitty, self-serving job, but today it is different. Today, I write this letter with love in my heart for the man who was instrumental in giving me life, and who passed on his love of music, laughter, history and love itself to his grateful son who shares the same name. And, oh by the way, you could have at least given me a cooler name than George Albert, but that is all forgiven, too! So I end this letter with three words, Dad, "I love you."

George

Holy shit, I never saw that coming. You, my unknown audience, just witnessed me bare my soul to the man I once hated. I had to leave my laptop, the tears were that blinding. Thank you for listening. I know this book may or may never see the light of day, but for what just occurred, it has been worth the toil.

Prior to writing that letter, I was thinking of discussing with you how to make amends to your loved ones. I have had some practice with that in AA. I was then going to talk about the one woman whom you've met but don't really know, my mom.

Her name was Bernadine Gillespie Walder DeFrehn and you could call her Bern or Bernadine, but never were you to call her Bernie. There would be hell to pay for calling her Bernie. She was 35 when she gave birth to me. For two and a half days at the end of February 1952 she was in labor at the old Philadelphia General Hospital also known as Metropolitan Hospital. She told me I just wouldn't come out. Well, I finally arrived on February 29, 1952, Leap Day! The joke in the family early on and even today remains one, that my wacked personality is directly related to being born on February 29.

I can tell you it toughened me in the streets of Olney. On my 12th birthday, a kid named Jim Long started the rumor that I was really only three years old, having had only three actual birthdays. We dusted each other for about 20 minutes in a schoolyard brawl near our local recreation center. Bloodied and battered, I was still standing. Jim gave it the first "no mas" in the history of

Olney, way before Sugar Ray Leonard defeated Roberto Duran on November 25, 1980. After that we kind of became friends. No one from that point on gave me shit about my birthday. But it wasn't the last time my mom heard about it!

Sixty years later she stroked in the midst of suffering from Alzheimer's. It was on a Monday. She just wouldn't die. Five days later, she finally went home. It took me almost 3 days to enter into this world and five for my mom to leave it. Like Mother, like son, eh?

My memories of her reach back to age four or five. Thus, I think I knew Mom for about 55 years. She was all of four feet, ten inches tall. Her max weight in her life about 104 lbs., minimum weight, about 102 lbs. I kid you not. She lived on tuna fish, salads, soup, fried shrimp (her favorite) and had a sweet tooth for crumb cake and cheese cake. She would start and end each day with a cup of tea. In between she drank water.

Bernadine was the worst cook I knew. God knows she tried. Her meat loaves were bricks. Her pasta tasted of rubber. Canned peas were a food group in our house growing up, served with everything from peanut butter to, you guessed it, tuna fish. In later years, when I would bring up her deficiencies in the kitchen, she would tell me that when Dad was alive she was indeed a good cook. My response was, with tongue in cheek, "Well, then Dad did die entirely too young." That usually got me the evil eye. Every Mom has that look that freezes their kids, and Bern had one of the best.

Yet, that description of my mom touches not the person she was. Primarily she was my first teacher. I mentioned early in the book that when my dad was fighting in the jungles of the South Pacific, his sister, Cindy, was writing letters to him telling him that Bern was a whore, cheating on him at every chance she got. Fortunately, one of these letters ended up in the hands of Dad's mother and that was the end of that. However, the harm caused was deep. This act by his sister cut my Dad to his core. When my mom spoke to me about this, she said that George never once doubted her fidelity. He knew his sister. He knew she hated Bernadine for her faith, being a Roman Catholic. Cindy had refused to come to their wedding, the only family member not to attend. Thus, when he received a letter from his Mom, telling him that Bern loved him more than life and just wanted him home safe, he put the episode behind him and went after the Japanese.

Upon his return to the States after VJ-Day, the rift between brother and sister was deep and wide; and I believe it was never fully repaired. Amazingly, Bern forgave Cindy for the entire episode and all the hatred that Cindy could muster. Mom used to tell me, "Kill them with love, George, and they'll die and rise again." I've tried to follow that wisdom throughout my life. She taught me forgiveness.

I still remember Bern sitting in the kitchen at night with a copy book lined in red. In '62 I was a mere ten years of age and knew nothing of finance. Yet, when I saw the sadness and redness that surrounded my mom's beautiful blue eyes, I knew once and for all that we were poor. She would sometimes sigh when times got tough and exclaim, "Well, I've got to rob Peter to pay Paul." My saintly Mom committing grand larceny? This could not be true. I shared this worry with Tim's Mom—who through the years would be a surrogate Mom of sorts—this robbing of Peter to pay Paul. Mrs. C, as all of us so lovingly called her, told me not to worry. It was just an expression that adults used when shifting household money from one bill to another. Adults were weird people.

We lived pay check to pay check. Without knowing it, Bernadine was following one of the principle axioms of Alcoholic Anonymous. She was living one day at a time, for that is all she could afford, just for today. Through all of this financial hardship and poverty, she never once gave up. Oh, I heard her crying at night either in her bedroom or in the kitchen after Sis and I had retired to our bedrooms, imploring God Almighty and her dead husband to come to her aid. It was on these nights that I became most fearful. Yet, when I awoke the next day, she had a smile on her face and got us ready for the next school day.

She would not surrender. She taught me perseverance.

Bernadine was a saint, breathing, walking saint. Ok, she'll never be canonized in the Catholic Church, but I never met a more faith-filled person, woman or man. Some would say that people of her generation who lived through the Great Depression and World War II had, what some theologians would describe as, blind faith. If the

Church or the priest told you it was wrong and sinful, you accepted that it was wrong and sinful whatever "it" was. This was not my mother. Yes, she respected the clergy and followed and believed the dogmas of the Holy Mother Church, but she was a questioner. She was the one adult who wanted to know why. Faith, she would tell me is a gift from God. Like all gifts I should cherish it.

Long before she died and while I was sober I made amends to her, asking her for forgiveness for all the heartache I may have caused through my childhood years up to the present. She did not understand what I was talking about. You see, my mom never kept a scorecard. She knew I was human and was flawed, but I was her son. She stood by me in good times and in bad. Her love was absolute. If you don't mind, since the letter to my dad worked for me, I'd like to write this letter to Bern and tell her what is in my heart.

Dear Mom:

It's been almost three years since you departed this earth of ours. I know that I told you many times that I loved you, but never really got to tell you why. I miss you, Mom. How do I say thank you for your company and friendship for 60 years while you walked this earth? One of my first memories after Dad had died was of you, in the spring of 1961, taking a little nine-year old boy to his first Phillies baseball game at Connie Mack Stadium. You, who did not know an inning in baseball from a quarter in football, grabbed me by the hand and led me to a place where I fell in love with guys named Ashburn, Allen, Bunning, Short and Culp, Bowa, Carlton, the Bull, Maddox and Schmitty, the Wild Thing, Dutch, Utley, Rollins, Hamels, Howard and Lidge. Thanks Mom for giving me the love of the game. I love you for that.

Thanks for praying for me every day when I left the house and every night when I returned safely. I know I was not an easy kid to love, but you loved me anyway. You were always like the Prodigal Father in the Bible, my Prodigal Mom, awaiting my return at the door as her wayward son came home from a far off country. You were always waiting, your door always open. Thanks for waiting, Mom. I love you for that.

Thanks for keeping the three of us together. I am in awe as I write this letter thinking of how lonely you must have felt, how much hurt you carried within your heart, knowing that you were now alone raising two kids without a father. You could have run away. You could have just given up, but you did not. Thanks Mom, for not giving up on yourself and on us, your children. Thanks to you, I think we turned out all right. I love you for all of that, Mom.

I can still see you and me watching the television as JFK was being buried after the assassination on November 22, 1963. I can still see you and me watching as Lee Harvey Oswald was killed by Jack Ruby in Dallas the following Sunday morning after we returned home from Mass. I can still see you and me watching Jim Bunning throw a perfect game for the Phillies on Father's Day of 1964 vs. the New York Mets. I can still visualize us watching the television on July 20, 1969 as Neil Armstrong walked on the Moon. I can see us watching the Andy Griffith Show and both of us howling with laughter at the antics of Barney Fife, Gomer and Goober Pyle and Otis the town drunk. Thank you, Mom for sitting with me through all of that history, good times and bad. I love you for all of that, too, Mom.

Thanks for being the best Nan, our five kids could have had. They still marvel how you would take all five of them to the mountains in Pennsylvania for a week's vacation. I know you did this for them, but I also knew you did it for me and my bride, so we could have a week to be together by ourselves to renew our marriage and strengthen our relationship. You were such a selfless woman; where did that come from? When God created Bernadine, He created the most giving person I have ever known. For all of that, Mom thanks and I love you.

Thanks for taking me on pilgrimage with you to Fatima, Lourdes and Paris in 1993. I can still see the two of us saying the rosary at the Grotto of Massabielle in Lourdes, the place where Our Lady appeared to a peasant girl, Bernadette Soubirous, with tears streaming down our faces in joy.

Thank you for all the cups of tea we shared and all the loaves of bread we broke together; for the Catholic faith you imparted to me; for dragging me to Church Sunday after Sunday, and laying the foundation of my faith that would one day save my life. For all of this, Mom, I love you.

Toward the end of your life, you were suffering from dementia and ultimately your life was claimed by Alzheimer's disease. For fourteen months you lived with us before we could no longer take care of you. I must tell you that it was an honor to take care of you. I know you were embarrassed at times to have your son bathe you and carry you to your bed. But for me it was a privilege to do all of that. You who changed my diapers, cleansed my wounds, picked me up when life had kicked me down; you who were always there to listen when I needed a sounding board, you who never gave unwanted advice, you who were silent when you may have wanted to shout. Thank you, Mom. Thank you.

When I gave your eulogy, toward the end of Mass, I made a statement that now I knew you were once again extremely happy to be with your George, your husband, the love of your life and, of course, with Our Dear Lord, Jesus. I also said that you no longer suffered and that you truly knew that you were loved by so many that were in Church that day.

I just wrote a similar letter to Dad. You both must think me a bit loony, but I think you knew that anyway. I have been sober now for 18 years, and this has been the most honest I believe I have ever been. Thanks again for listening, Mom. I will come over to see you in Beverly soon to visit the gravesites of both you and Dad. I know you are not there, but it is the last tangible thing that connects me to you both. I, also, know that you will be waiting for me, as you did all those nights in Ol-a-ney long ago, when I am called home by Our Lord, the God of my understanding from this far off country.

I love you, Mom, and always will.

George.

On a lighter note, and Bern would have loved this, I have mentioned that 1961 brought us to the streets of Olney. Now, I have not actually mentioned this one special peculiarity for those of us who grew up there. We never pronounced it "OLNEY." When asked where we lived, it was always, "Ol-a-ney."

We carried the dialect further. We did not shop at the Acme, but at the Ac-a-me. Trees were not beautiful, but bee-u-ti-ful. We would never swim in a polluted creek, but we would swim in the polluted crick. It's the way we "tawked."

Years living away from Philly has seen me lose this dialect, but put me in a class or neighborhood reunion with boys and girls from the hood, and once more someone eventually will say, "Yeah, I grew up in Olaney and lived down by the Acame near the bee-u-ti-ful crick." Does it get any better than that?

Thanks again, Mom, for choosing Ol-a-ney.

CHAPTER 33

The Hurricane

His name was Rubin Carter, professional boxer, nicknamed the Hurricane due to the ferocity of the punches that he threw. He was a man on the rise in the sport of boxing in the 1960s. Many believed him to be the next middle-weight champion of the World. Then, in Paterson, New Jersey shots rang out one night in a local bar. The year was 1966. Three patrons were killed. Carter was seen in the area with a friend, another black man. Police were told and before he knew it, Rubin "Hurricane" Carter was wrongfully accused and behind bars.

In May of '67 he and the other man were formally sentenced to three life prison terms and Carter would spend nearly 20 years of his life incarcerated. While in prison, he would write his autobiography aptly named, "The Sixteenth Round," his journey from his rough and tumble youth in New Jersey through his first stint in solitary confinement in Trenton State Prison.

In 1999, film director Norman Jewison brought the story of Carter to the big screen. Carter was played by Denzel Washington. During the first half of this flick, a young black youth by the name of Lesra Martin from Brooklyn, a foster kid living in Toronto, is seen in a bookstore, rummaging through some old used books. It's what he can afford.

He picks one up, discards it and picks up another. He does this a few times then his eyes behold the title, "The Sixteenth Round." He picks it up in earnest, reads a brief description on the back cover, smiles and purchases a book that will change his life forever. Sound familiar?

The remainder of the movie concerns Lesra's quest to free Rubin from the shackles of injustice. Carter initially balks after receiving a letter from Lesra stating his intentions of wanting to help. He is a self-sufficient, stubborn man. Before and while in prison he accepted help from no man. His life story was written to let the world know that an innocent man was behind bars; that the justice system had failed. Celebrities intervened; two in particular were Muhammed Ali and Bob Dylan. Dylan even penned a song, "Hurricane" co-written with song-writer Jacques Levy. For a brief moment, the quest to free the Hurricane is headline news, but as with all things in our culture, within months, the name Rubin "Hurricane" Carter slips from the front page, to page 6 to the middle of the paper and then gone. He is a memory.

Fortunately for Carter, he ran head-on with a young kid who proved just as stubborn. Lesra convinced the people who ran his communal foster home, one of which had some legal experience, to join in this plight to free the Hurricane. In his next communiqué with Carter, he writes that he would like to visit him at Rahway State Prison in central Jersey where Rubin was housed. Carter hesitates but then acquiesces to Lesra's request; they meet and a friendship is cemented that will eventually lead to Carter's freedom in November of 1985.

Toward the end of the movie, The Hurricane, at one of their meetings, asks Lesra about the day he discovered his autobiography while rummaging through old, used books in that bookstore back in Canada. To somewhat paraphrase, Carter asks Lesra, "…so do you think you discovered my book or did my book discover you?"

When I began writing this epic, which you hold in your hands, I initially had chosen this as my central theme. The afore-written paragraphs are a shortened version of that "Preface." So, why did I change it? After all, it was a book that I discovered, like Lesra, in a bookstore that changed my life. So why?

Honestly, I began thinking that it was too self-serving to believe that a book that I would write could also one day change someone's life. I had spent a lifetime wanting to believe that I was someone special. Remember that saying, "an egomaniac with an inferiority complex?" God, how I was sick of feeling that way. Yes, time in sobriety reminds me on a continual basis that I, George, as a recovering alcoholic, am nothing more than "another bozo on the bus and that I am not terminally unique."

That may sound to your ears as sort of demeaning, but if you are in the rooms of sobriety, you are smiling because you know what I mean.

Did the book discover me? Today I know it was more than that. Books are inanimate objects. They have no life; they have no soul. So was it a mere coincidence that I discovered Caroline Knapp's memoir on that fateful weekend in August of 1997? No, I do not believe in coincidences when it comes to my faith and my sobriety. You may be an atheist or agnostic and have no faith in a Higher Power and that is perfectly ok. I, on the other hand, cannot deny the facts of what happened to me. Mere happenchance and fate connote a world in flux, in chaos with no beginning and no end. If that were the case, for me, why would I even bother with sobriety? Why not believe as the ancient world Epicureans did who held the philosophy, "Eat, drink and be merry for tomorrow we die." In our culture today, we in America have a similar saying, but actually even a little more morbid and depressing, "Life sucks and then you die." Shit, at least the Epicureans ate and drank, eh?

No, I unashamedly profess a belief that the God of my understanding led me step by step to that bookstore on that night in August of 1997, at the Jersey shore, to that book rack of NY Times Best Sellers. I will always believe this, always.

Throughout the course of writing this, I forgot to mention a previous episode that hopefully helps proves this point. It was New Year's Eve, December 31, 1997. The day before, on the thirtieth, I had celebrated four-months sober. We had made dinner plans with old friends at an exclusive Inn. Talk about romanticizing the drink? Christmas was the most important stretch of time during my drinking career, year after year. I could not wait for the pubs and restaurants to be decked out in Yuletide regalia. Trees decorated, lit and placed cleverly, tinsel outlining the mirrors behind the bar, waitresses wearing red stockings, patrons wearing a little bit more of a smile on some of their miserable faces. Yep, 'twas a grand time to drink.

Well, it was a frigid night with the smell of snow in the air. We arrive a few minutes before our friends. Four months prior, I would have led my wife to the bar and ordered us a couple of drinks.

Of course, I would have already started getting tuned at home with a Guinness and at least a tumbler of scotch, maybe two. Tonight the Inn is appropriately dressed for the holidays and its decorations are faultless.

I sense my wife is a bit uncomfortable standing out in the foyer, but that was just my head talking shit. She was fine. She looked beautiful. I, on the other hand, must appear as if a boll weevil is nesting in my pocket. I breathe deeply, trying to remain calm. The door opens and a blast of air penetrates the lobby followed by our friends, Ned and Jane. Thank God.

Another five minutes and they might have had to peel me off the ceiling.

They sat us right away. As I slid into my dining room chair I kept my eyes fixed downward. I am afraid. I'm afraid I might drink. I'm afraid someone might recognize me and offer me a New Year's drink. How do I say no to that? "Can't have one, Bobby, I'm an alky"...WTF. Of course, our waitress soon follows and wants to take our drink order. Ned and Jane do not know I'm sober. My wife and our friends order beer and wine. My turn, I look at our waitress and ask, "Do you have any root beer?"

"Sure" she replies and says that she'll be right back. My first thought was that she probably went over to the bar and said to the bartender, "Give me two wines and beer and one root beer for the fucking alky." No shit. That is what I thought. It never occurred to me that most people in today's world really don't give a rat's ass what you drink. Actually, with the health kick at full tilt in our society, everyone seems to ask for water! As an alcoholic I could never understand that one.

We begin our conversation, and Ned makes a crack about me ordering a root beer. No offense taken, he does not know. My wife looks at me with a nod to let me know that now is as good a time as any to spring the, "Hey, I'm an alcoholic, been sober four months, taking it a day a time" on our friends.

Got it out. They were cool. I mean what the hell are they supposed to say to that one? In my head it was as if I had said, "Hey Ned and Jane, I have fuckin' leprosy, let's order dinner!"

Yet, they are good people and friends, and as the minutes rolled by our banter turned to our kids, our jobs, anything but alcohol. At this point I excused myself and said I had to hit the loo. The British are so refined when it comes to bodily functions. They visit the loo or the water closet to urinate. Americans, especially those drinking, will say, "Be right back, gotta piss." No wonder the world hates us. As I get toward the lobby, I make a beeline for the front door. Need some air. Spend a few minutes breathing in the chilled night air. It's purifying and calms me down.

I reenter the Inn, turn toward the back stairs where the restrooms are located, when a voice comes from a corner table near the side window. "Yo, George, how are you doing and Happy New Year." I recognize the face and voice but can't place it. My mind is racing. Who the frig is this dude? He must have known I was in a panic. "It's me…Bill…from the rooms. Are you ok?" Now it hits me that I recognize this guy from our local AA meetings. How the hell did he know I was going to be here?

And that is how screwed up I was on that first New Year's Eve night in sobriety. I actually thought that someone had sent the local AA police (inside AA joke) to the inn making sure I didn't drink. How bizarre is that thinking? I sometimes tell that story when I am asked to speak at an AA meeting, especially if it's during the holiday time. Eighteen years later, Bill and I still laugh at this episode of my sobriety. Yet, again, for me this was no coincidence that someone from AA was in that inn that night when God knows I wanted to drink. I remember getting back to my seat in the dining room, and it was as if a cross had been lifted from my shoulders. A guardian angel, in the form of Bill, had been there when I needed it and least expected it…and that is how sobriety works.

And that brings us full circle. Not sure about you, but I'm exhausted, but in a good way. I haven't cried "in forever," and in writing this book I got to do that and that is a good thing. I've spent most of my life starting things and never finishing; I have finished this and that is a good thing, too.

I still think of John Adams every now and then pacing the floors of Independence Hall by himself, a forlorn figure in history, whose only friend at times appeared to be his bride, Abigail Adams. To her he wrote many letters speaking of his frustrations, his anger, his depression, his sorrow and his love. This book has been like those letters that I have written for you. I used to concern myself with Mr. Adams' first two questions when all appeared lost. "Is anybody there? Does anybody care?" But it is the last question that he asked, which I should have been paying attention to, "Does anybody see what I see?"

So…did you discover this book or did the book discover you? What will your answer be?

CHAPTER 34

Is Anybody There?

As the movie, "Saving Private Ryan" draws to a close, we find Captain John Miller (Tom Hanks) saying some final words to Private James Francis Ryan. Prior to this, everything around them has been blown to hell. Bullets, mortars, fragments of falling rock buzz from one side of the river to the other.

All is chaotic as Miller yells, "Alamo, Alamo" which is the signal for every G.I. to get across the bridge to the other side of the river. An explosion occurs. Miller appears stunned. He has one goal, to blow the bridge before the Nazis can cross. He sees the detonator, but it's lying in a direct field of fire. Yet, he is determined and crawls to the detonator which is out in the open. There is no cover. As Miller reaches it, he is hit several times.

An explosion does occur, but it's the planes of the Army Air Force strafing the bridge with bullets and bombs.

The Germans are defeated.

The next scene has Miller apparently dying. Ryan has been a mess during this last battle at the bridge, at times looking heroic, at other times he is shown scared out of his mind, afraid to move, afraid to live and afraid to die. Miller then mouths words that Ryan cannot hear.

He shouts to Miller, "What did you say?" Miller grabs Ryan and pulls him close, looking eye to eye, and says to

Ryan, "Earn this." He repeats it one last time, "Earn this." Miller dies, and Ryan is left alone on that bridge.

The next scene has Ryan as an old man walking through that cemetery I described on the cliff overlooking Omaha Beach. He finds Miller's grave, his body shudders, tears form in his eyes, the weight of his body gives way and he falls to one knee. Ryan then rises somewhat unsteadily, looks at Miller's grave and proceeds to tell him that he still remembers that day on the bridge, and he has tried to live a good life and hopes that he has "earned it." We surmise that the "it" is the freedom and the life we all find ourselves possessing, even today some 71 years later, after those fateful days in June of 1944.

But the movie is not over yet. He gazes at Miller's headstone and looks over his shoulder. He tells the dead Captain that his wife and family have come with him, and he hopes that that is ok. Finally, his wife comes to his side and Ryan asks a very poignant question. "Have I been a good man?" She hesitates and asks, "What?" And he now states, "Tell me that I've been a good man." His wife then looks at the headstone and back to her husband and says, "Yes, of course you have." The movie ends with Ryan saluting Captain John Miller and looking a bit steadier than he had a few minutes earlier. We then see Old Glory flying in the breeze over Omaha Beach and the screen fades to dark.

Now you may be asking, what is this alcoholic dude writing about? Bullets flying, Miller dying, the bridge blown to bits, "Alamo, Alamo, " planes flying overhead,

Ryan heroic, Ryan afraid, "earn it," "Am I a good man?" Well, these words may mean absolutely nothing to you, but if you're an alcoholic like me, they may mean everything in the world.

That last scene at the bridge in this epic movie looks a lot like my life at the end of my drinking days. Morally, spiritually, emotionally and even physically, my life was blown to bits. My entire life from age 16 to 45 was one big Alamo. I knew every once in a while that someone, somehow, someway was trying to reach me, to help me climb out of the darkness I inhabited, like those planes flying overhead stopping the German advance.

However, it seemed that every day the bullets and fragments of life were buzzing and cluttering my thought process. All appeared chaotic. I saw lips moving trying to tell me something, but I was deaf to it all. Through the booze, I could hear only John Barleycorn telling me more lies.

When I see the last two characters on that bridge, as an alcoholic, I could be casted to play either one, the one who dies or the one who lives. Many alcoholics will tell you that by the time they got into the rooms of AA, death was looking pretty good. For some, suicide looked like a positive thing. That is what alcohol and drugs can do to any human being. I can, also, decide to choose to live; but life is not easy. Life is earned through toil, hard work, sweat, victory and defeat, wins and losses, good times and bad. The problem for the alcoholic is that in their lives, when life did get tough and there was pain or consequences on the horizon, they drank. They drank to kill the pain. I drank to kill the pain.

Yet, life is also a gift from my Higher Power whom I choose to call God. When a gift is given, we teach our children to say "thank you." We alcoholics deep down don't believe we deserve gifts. I, as an active alky, did not believe. As my life continued from youth through adolescence to adulthood, what I perceived as rejections kept piling up one on top of another. And that's the kicker. I lived in a world of perception. I felt horrible about myself, a loser. How sad is that? I have children and grandchildren and all of them are precious gifts. If someone, within ear shot, were to call any of them losers, there would be hell to pay. Yet, I did not think twice at labeling myself a loser.

"Cunning, baffling and powerful," that is how the Big Book describes alcohol.xxii Take it from someone who is an alcoholic, this is a true statement. If you are allergic to wasps and get stung, you will have an allergic reaction, possibly hives, a rash, swelling of the skin near the bite, constriction of the throat, trouble breathing and if left untreated, possible death. This person who is allergic to wasps, I guarantee, will take all precautions to never get bit again.

In AA's literature, it talks about the alcoholic as having an allergy toward alcohol. The biggest difference from the wasp sting or other allergies is that when the alcoholic gets drunk, crashes his car, vomits all over himself, craps and pisses his pants, falls down and ends up in handcuffs sitting in jail, he or she may not even remember what they did that got them in the jail cell. But it gets worse. The person getting stung by the wasp never wants to see another wasp again. The drunk gets out of jail, and the first thing they usually do to celebrate their freedom, you guessed it, is pick up the next drink and then once again, they are off to the races. As it says, alcohol is "cunning, baffling and powerful."

Okay, I am in somewhat of a quandary. How do I end this magnum opus, this epic masterpiece? I started with John Adams and ended with Private Ryan. I did not actually intend to do that, but there is some symmetry there. Their wars and times in history are 168 years apart from one another. Private Ryan is a fictional character, but actually based on the true story of Sergeant Fritz Niland. But I'll stay with Adams and Ryan.

In Adam's letters to his wife Abigail, he openly talks of his fear that the Congress will disband without a resolution for Independence. He also feared that Jefferson, initially, would not be up to the task of writing the Declaration. One of his other primary fears was that Washington would not have the troops or arms he needed to mount a war against British Red Coat regulars.

But Adams was a visionary. Through all his foibles, if Adams was anything, he was a true patriot who believed that America desired, needed, and ultimately would gain its Independence from Great Britain and King George III. He truly could see what everyone else could not.

The fictional James Francis Ryan, played by Matt

Damon, at first appears a pretty courageous fellow. When Miller and his platoon finally find him and tell him they came to take him home, he balks. He makes the team player's statement summarizing, "If my brothers here cannot go home, I'm not leaving them." Don't know about you, but if I'm at D-Day plus 3 and someone says I can go home, "Adios amigos!" So Ryan has courage.

That scene at the bridge, however, when the world is literally caving in on the G.I.s in this small village in France, bombs and bullets flying, shows another side of Ryan, sitting in a fetal position crying and screaming for help. He is human after all.

And that's part of what alcoholics forget. It's as if someone or something snatched the alcoholic's ability to reason and just be human. I remember a woman named Ruth in a meeting making a statement that, "I didn't really know that it was okay to fail. That it was okay to feel like crap and have a bad day. That it was okay to just say, 'I don't feel like visiting my kids today.'" She said her parents were good people, not the kind who demanded straight A's, just do your best.

But she perceived that B's and C's were really failures. She continues, "If I felt like crap both emotionally and physically and my parent asked how I was doing or my husband would say that I looked a little pale or out of sorts, I would just say that all was okay, afraid to tell them the truth. I cannot remember a time in my entire life before sobriety telling someone, 'You know what, I feel like shit,' never."

Another alcoholic named Loud Jake once shared that he had kids that lived in North Jersey, about a 90-minute to two-hour ride on the Jersey Turnpike and Garden State Parkway from his home in Pennsylvania. He was in his late 50s, not old by any means, but after working all week he was beat. His daughter would call him on Saturday morning and say, "Come on up, Dad, for dinner. We all would love to see you." Now four hours of windshield time, up and back, was not Jake's idea of a good time, but he never wanted to hurt his daughter's feelings. He even said that he was afraid to give her "No" for an answer, fearful that she wouldn't ask him again. So, he would make up some lame excuse or just outright lie and tell her he had other plans, the proverbial white lie. He never thought that he could just be honest and tell his daughter that he was beat, thank her for the invite, and that he would take a rain check and maybe next week they could look at calendars. We are indeed wired differently.

Notice with Adams, Ryan, Ruth and Jake that the word fear permeates throughout. My God, it has echoed throughout this memoir. Fear dwells in the mind, body, soul and heart of every alcoholic and it is all-embracing and paralyzing. And it would be great if just by putting down the drink that fear would vanish. I would have loved it if on August 31, 1997, the day after I got sober, that all of sudden fear was gone and poof, like a cumulus cloud caught in a stiff wind, gone. There one moment and gone the next. I could say, sadly, that is not the case. But fuck sadly! That is nothing more than playing the self-pity game once again. Guess how many alcoholics have relapsed with the sad, self-pity party going on…hundreds, thousands, maybe tens-of-thousands.

If you come into the rooms of Alcoholics Anonymous and hang around long enough, you will learn how to deal with fear. As it says in the AA Promises on page 84, "You will intuitively know how to handle situations that used to baffle us!"xxiii Doesn't that sound great! Is it true? After 18 years sober I can truthfully say, "YES."

Now, will fear go away? Hell, no. Fear will finally go away when you and I are planted on the other side of the daisies. Until then, like anything else in life, you have to deal with it head-on. On page 58 in the Big Book it reads, "…half measures availed us nothing."xxiv We alcoholics are notoriously famous for being passive when in our doldrums. We could watch the entire world flush itself down a toilet, and our only real concern would be, "Shit, I hope there's some booze when we get to the bottom of that."

AA is a spiritual program. Based on that statement I will tell you that true fear comes from the Evil One. You may call him Satan, the devil, Lucifer, the Angel of Darkness or whatever. You may not even believe in him and that is where he really gets you. Disbelief in a Higher Power plus disbelief in evil equals jails, institutions and eventually death for the alcoholic. You may see commercials for the "magic" pill that will cure you of alcoholism, but trust me, none exist. Why, because you can't put the God of your understanding into a pill.

Early in this memoir I paraphrased another line that appears in AA literature. It reads, "...one day you discover that the only thing between you and the next drink is your Higher Power." Talk to any alky in recovery who has relapsed. I guarantee that more than 50 percent of them went out and picked up a drink or drug because they did not get the spiritual part of the Twelve Step Program in AA.

Fear, true fear, will never come from this loving God—never. We learned as children that we were made in his image and likeness. We are His children, His gifts to humanity. He loves us. In all my years of active alcoholism I knew in my heart that it was I who turned away from God, not the other way around. He has always been the Prodigal Father awaiting my return from that far off, distant country.

Well, you may ask, "What does He want from me? I'm a bum. I'm an alcoholic. I have lost it all or I am about to lose it all. No one loves me. All have rejected me. I'm sitting in a jail cell. Will He reject me, too?" That last question is the question regarding fear. I, probably in my sick, alcoholic thinking, could handle everyone in the world deserting me, hell; I perceived most of them had already. But to truly believe that God would desert me...then it's time to commit the sin of Judas Iscariot, total despair. I have my final excuse to pick up the next drink and say "Fuck the world and all that is in it."

Yet, today, I know and believe the truth about my Higher Power, the God of my understanding. The apostle

John wrote many centuries ago that "God is Love."xxv

My problem, I was looking for love in all the wrong places. He was right in front of me. He was right beside me. He has always been calling me by name. Today, I see Him in my beautiful wife, my wonderful children and my "melt my heart" grandchildren.

I see Him in the Downs Syndrome adults who visit the fitness center where I work out. I see Him in the woman at the Wawa convenience store who makes coffee and works as a cashier. I see Him in the homeless old man who sits with his green plastic bag filled with his life possessions under the bridge near the Interstate. I see Him in the beauty of that sunrise and sunset and also in the winds of a hurricane like Katrina. And I always see Him in the next suffering alcoholic who walks through the door of sobriety, despondent and loveless, not knowing what to do, what to say, who to believe or where to go.

If that last sentence describes you, please know that you are loved. You just need to hang around long enough for the miracle. Sobriety is hard work. Yet, most alcoholics are hardworking people. If we put the amount of effort into our sobriety that we did into our drinking, hell, no one would ever relapse. So, please walk through the doors of sobriety and know that you never really have to feel the way you feel right now, again…never.

That image of me sitting on that cold, iron plated bench across the street from Mr. Adams' Old North Church is a distant memory. I would love to tell you that today after being sober for many years that I'm no longer haunted by his words, "Is anybody there? Does anybody care? Does anybody see what I see?" But that would be a lie because I am still an alcoholic. I will always be an alcoholic. Yet, I'm an alcoholic in recovery. We are told early on there is no graduation from Alcoholics Anonymous, but that living one day at a time, I can have a hell of a life and I do!

So...Is anybody there? Yes, people like Chuck, Jay, Pat, Seamus, Tom, Finn, Running Badger, Bear, Bill, Ned, Ruth, Loud Jake, Caroline, George, Upstate Stan, Greg, Gandhi and many others, along with God, as you understand Him. Knock on the door, open and enter; they're waiting. I think what you'll discover is that there really is somebody there!

Acknowledgements

My editor has been a colleague in the business world and a friend on my path of life since we met in the year 2002. Without knowing it, she, too, has inspired me. She is also an author, but that just touches the surface of the depth of ***Marie Murphy Duess***. I believe I told her I was going to write a book approximately five years ago and every year since. She never lost faith that I could do this and kept telling me that once I truly began to write that I would not want to stop. She was correct. Her husband, Deacon Ed Duess is my "salt of the earth" Catholic deacon. Deacon Ed spreads the Good News from his hip and is loved for that by all who know him. During our time at St. Mary, Marie introduced me to her sister-in-law, Chrissy Duess. Chrissy had stage-four terminal cancer. She thought that possibly I could help a little bit being a cancer survivor myself. Marie, Chrissy helped me more than I helped her. Thank you, Marie, for sharing your talents, friendship, your family, and your faith with this rookie author. You keep leading, I'll keep following!

To my copy-editor Kathleen Pisauro: this being my first book, I needed a copy-editor.

I wanted someone who would add credibility to this project and also someone who would be brutally honest in discerning if this memoir could pass "muster" in the publishing world. I found both in Kathleen. Little did I know that we shared that Catholic connection being we were both taught by nuns, lessons to this day we have not forgotten. Thank you, Kathleen! It has been an honor to meet you, work with you and here's hoping we have many more adventures together! And thanks for sharing Sister Paulette with me. I'm sure she is smiling wherever she is!

In 1996, while I was on a pilgrimage to the town of Medjugorje in Bosnia-Herzegovina, a woman by the name of Jane Walker told me, while we were walking up Cross Mountain, that someday I would write a book. Unbeknown to both Jane and me was that within a year I would be walking into the rooms of sobriety. It is now almost 19 years since she planted that seed. I have discovered that God's trees and plants grow and develop in His own good time, not ours. Thank you, Jane.

To my "beta-readers" I say thank you, thank you and thank you. To you who took days and weeks out of your life to read rough draft after rough draft and "shoot from the hip" with your comments, I cannot thank you enough. Your comments made me both a better writer and a better listener. You made me reach deeper into the depths of my soul. I was about two-thirds through my writing when I came to a dead end. I received an email from Rob Zingaro, a friend and fellow tenor with St. Andrew's Choir in Newtown, Pennsylvania. Rob told me, "Please tell me and all your readers what 'makes you tick.'" The chapter with that title is because of Rob. Thank you, brother, for your words of wisdom.

To Rosalia Milone, another woman and friend who I met in Medjugorje. As I sent out the first truly rough draft online to a few readers, she was the first to print it out, read it and was commenting on it within a couple of days. In the early days of writing she became my cheerleader. She has a laugh that is contagious! Thanks Rosalia for your cheers, your prayers, and especially for your friendship.

To George Regan, friend, neighbor and the best elementary mathematics school teacher that the State of New Jersey has ever produced. As a neighbor, in some of my darkest days after multiple surgeries, George would stop over at our house carrying a freshly made dinner of pasta or homemade soup, being the Good Samaritan that no one knew about. He exudes humility. His comments made me feel that I was indeed getting the message across that I wanted. Thank you, George. I treasure your friendship.

To Eileen McLaughlin, friend and fellow choir member at St. Andrew's. She also was the head of the bereavement program at Holy Redeemer Hospital in Meadowbrook, Pennsylvania that treated my dear mother, Bernadine, during the last days of her life. She told me that she could "feel" me in some of the scenes of my life depicted in this book. She told me I made her laugh and cry. With "tongue and cheek" I've been told I have had that effect on people for a long time.

Thank you, Eileen, for your cherished friendship and for all your team did for Bern.

To my sister-in-law, Judy Smith, who told me to just keep writing, I give huge thanks. I sent her the first couple of extremely rough and not so well written drafts. Thanks for your encouragement and friendship through the years. When I was five years sober she came to a meeting with me to celebrate that fifth anniversary! It meant a lot. Thanks Judy for being the forthright and loving person I have known since the moment I met you.

To Karen Crowell, compatriot and friend at Rider University. Karen is the most positive person I may have encountered on this planet of ours. The glass is "always" more than half full. I knew that her comments about this journey of mine would not only be heartfelt, but true to the core. If it stunk, she would tell me. If the message was muddled she would let me know. Thank you, Karen for being the positive force you have always been for others and for me.

To Tony Pisa, psychologist and friend. I chose Tony as a reader because in his practice he has counselled many who either are suffering or directly affected by the disease of alcoholism. He is also a great audience. He has a hearty laugh that starts deep within his being. Thanks for your encouragement, Tony and taking the time to read this, my first book. I know you enjoyed many of the characters especially Running Badger and Bear. I also knew that if this book did not connect to the reader, Tony would be honest and tell me so. Thanks for your comments and encouragement for future books!

To Judy Walmsley, wonderful woman and friend.

Thanks, Judy, for all of your feedback. Judy has seen the direct effect of alcohol in her own family. She has expressed to me how helpless the non-alcoholic can feel when alcoholism infiltrates close family members and friends, in particular that "functional" alcoholic. Her encouragement throughout my writing was always timely and heartfelt and for that I most grateful. Thanks Judy! I cherish your friendship.

To Susan Hudak, friend, neighbor and fellow parishioner of St. Andrew in Newtown for many years. Susan kept expressing how difficult it was reading much of the book, because she has only known me in sobriety. This is a comment many of us get in the rooms of AA. It truly is hard to imagine that the person sitting next to you was at one time a full-blown, active alcoholic. Susan, I am fortunate that you are in my life and yes, I am glad you did not know the "other" George. Keep hugging those grandkids!

To Catherine Ard, possibly the most musically gifted singer I have ever met. She joined our choir on our journey to Rome & Assisi and what a "find" she was for the entire choir. Thanks for your feedback and encouragement, Catherine, and for your friendship.

To Jeff Olseth, my one-time boss and dear friend, who will never realize the profound effect he had on me in my business career. We shared good times and bad, but at the end of the day we could always say that we gave it our best shot. Jeff has known me before and after sobriety and still calls me his friend and for that I am grateful.

Many thanks, brother, for everything. Maybe Father O'Malley will make it in my next book! Peace.

To Jane Higgins, co-worker and friend, who is one of the most selfless people I've encountered in life. Thanks for your encouragement, Jane, and yes, I will keep writing!

To Vicki McCann, proofreader extraordinaire! We met Vicki and her husband Jim at our local YMCA and a great friendship has ensued. When we met in 2014, writing this book was not on my radar screen. Vicki is a retired teacher. When I reached out and asked her to proofread this work, she immediately said, "Yes." This kind and patient woman spent ten days reading and proofing this text from beginning to end. The product you hold in your possession has a great deal to do with her. Thank you, Vicki.

To Caroline Knapp, the author I never met, of the book that saved my life. If you have not read her book, I recommend it highly. Like me, Caroline was college educated. She was a successful journalist in the Boston area. When I read her story I knew it was my story, too. She died of lung cancer in June of 2002 at age 42. She died sober. I know she can hear me, "Thank you, Caroline. We never met but I consider you my good friend."

Always first, never last, to my best friend and wife, Chris. Thank you, honey, for being so patient as I sat at my laptop night after night after night. Thank you for reading this book in depth. While reading it, I saw you smile and cry on different occasions. It's one of the best parts of you...your honest emotion in all parts of your life. God blessed me when He brought you into my life. We both know that alcohol could have destroyed all that we have together. Thank God we stopped at that bookstore these many years ago and that I was led to purchasing, ***Drinking: A Love Story***, by Caroline Knapp.

Thanks for never stopping to love me even at times when I feel so unlovable. So far it's been a great run. Here's hoping we have many more years together and even more beaches to visit together! Love you!!

To my children who have loved me while I was drinking and still love me today in sobriety. You are my precious gifts: Katie, Sean, Colleen, Amy, Brian along with your wonderful spouses. And of course to my ten grandkids, who call me Pop, and have never seen me with a drink in hand, I love you all. It is all of you who have blessed my life. You all continue to melt my heart!

---

[i] Alcoholics Anonymous World Services, Inc., Alcoholics Anonymous page 58. 1976 edition

[ii] Ibid, page 66

[iii] 2 June 2015: http://www.mayoclinic.org/diseases-conditions/alcoholism/basics/definition/con-20020866

[iv] 2 June 2015: https://ncadd.org/for-parents-overview/family-history-and-genetics/226-family-history-and-genetics

[v] Caroline Knapp, Drinking: A Love Story (1996) page 145

[vi] 2 June 2015: https://ncadd.org/learn-about-alcohol/alcohol-abuse-self-test

[vii] Dictionary .com http://dictionary.reference.com/browse/epiphany?s=ts

[viii] 2 June 2015: http://www.niaaa.nih.gov/alcohol-health/overview-alcohol-consumption/alcohol-facts-and-statistics

[ix] Ibid

[x] 2 June 2015: https://ncadd.org/learn-about-alcohol/alcohol-and-crime

[xi] Ibid

[xii] Caroline Knapp, Drinking a Love Story, (1996) pages 110–111

[xiii] 2 June 2015: http://ncadd.org/learn-about-alcohol/alcohol-abuse-self-test

[xiv] Alcoholics Anonymous World Services, Inc., Alcoholic Anonymous, page 31. 1976 edition

[xv] http://www.aa.org/assets/en_US/p-15_Q&AonSpon.pdf

[xvi] Alcoholics Anonymous Worldwide Services, The Green Card, General Services of AA, New York, NY

[xvii] Alcoholics Anonymous World Services, Inc., Alcoholics Anonymous, page 449. 1976 edition

[xviii] Ibid. page 449

[xix] Ibid. page 449

[xx] Hymn, "God Rest Ye Merry Gentlemen." 15th century Author Unknown

[xxi] http://en.wikipedia.org/wiki/Normandy_American_Cemetery_and_Memorial

[xxii] Alcoholics Anonymous Worldwide Serviced, Inc., Alcoholics Anonymous, page 58. 1976 edition

[xxiii] Ibid. page 84

[xxiv] Ibid. page 58

[xxv] Gospel of John, http://biblehub.com/1_john/4–8.htm